Holt Science & Technology

Animals

D0123933

ANNOTATED TEACHER'S EDITION

HOLT, RINEHART AND WINSTON

A Harcourt Classroom Education Company

Austin • New York • Orlando • Atlanta • San Francisco • Boston • Dallas • Toronto • London

Staff Credits

Editorial

Robert W. Todd, Executive Editor

Robert V. Tucek, Leigh Ann Garcia, Senior Editors

Clay Walton, Jim Ratcliffe, Editors

ANCILLARIES

Jennifer Childers, Senior Editor

Chris Colby, Molly Frohlich, Shari Husain, Kristen McCardel, Sabelyn Pussman, Erin Roberson

COPYEDITING

Dawn Spinozza, Copyediting Supervisor

EDITORIAL SUPPORT STAFF

Jeanne Graham, Mary Helbling, Tanu'e White, Doug Rutley

EDITORIAL PERMISSIONS

Cathy Paré, Permissions Manager

Jan Harrington, Permissions Editor

Art, Design, and Photo

BOOK DESIGN

Richard Metzger, Design Director

Marc Cooper, Senior Designer

José Garza, Designer

Alicia Sullivan, Designer (ATE), **Cristina Bowerman**, Design Associate (ATE), **Eric Rupprath**, Designer (Ancillaries), **Holly Whittaker**, Traffic Coordinator

IMAGE ACQUISITIONS

Joe London, Director

Elaine Tate, Art Buyer Supervisor

Jeannie Taylor, Photo Research Supervisor

Andy Christiansen, Photo Researcher

Jackie Berger, Assistant Photo Researcher

PHOTO STUDIO

Sam Dudgeon, Senior Staff Photographer

Victoria Smith, Photo Specialist

Lauren Eischen, Photo Coordinator

DESIGN NEW MEDIA

Susan Michael, Design Director

Production

Mimi Stockdell, Senior Production Manager

Beth Sample, Senior Production Coordinator

Suzanne Brooks, Sara Carroll-Downs

Media Production

Kim A. Scott, Senior Production Manager

Adriana Bardin-Prestwood, Senior Production Coordinator

New Media

Armin Gutzmer, Director

Jim Bruno, Senior Project Manager

Lydia Doty, Senior Project Manager

Jessica Bega, Project Manager

Cathy Kuhles, Nina Degollado, Technical Assistants

Design Implementation and Production

The Quarasan Group, Inc.

Acknowledgments

Chapter Writers

Katy Z. Allen
Science Writer and Former Biology Teacher
Wayland, Massachusetts

Linda Ruth Berg, Ph.D.
Adjunct Professor–Natural Sciences
St. Petersburg Junior College
St. Petersburg, Florida

Jennie Dusheck
Science Writer
Santa Cruz, California

Mark F. Taylor, Ph.D.
Associate Professor of Biology
Baylor University
Waco, Texas

Lab Writers

Diana Scheidle Bartos
Science Consultant and Educator
Diana Scheidle Bartos, L.L.C.
Lakewood, Colorado

Carl Benson
General Science Teacher
Plains High School
Plains, Montana

Charlotte Blassingame
Technology Coordinator
White Station Middle School
Memphis, Tennessee

Marsha Carver
Science Teacher and Dept. Chair
McLean County High School
Calhoun, Kentucky

Kenneth E. Creese
Science Teacher
White Mountain Junior High School
Rock Springs, Wyoming

Linda Culp
Science Teacher and Dept. Chair
Thorndale High School
Thorndale, Texas

James Deaver
Science Teacher and Dept. Chair
West Point High School
West Point, Nebraska

Frank McKinney, Ph.D.
Professor of Geology
Appalachian State University
Boone, North Carolina

Alyson Mike
Science Teacher
East Valley Middle School
East Helena, Montana

C. Ford Morishita
Biology Teacher
Clackamas High School
Milwaukie, Oregon

Patricia D. Morrell, Ph.D.
Assistant Professor, School of Education
University of Portland
Portland, Oregon

Hilary C. Olson, Ph.D.
Research Associate
Institute for Geophysics
The University of Texas
Austin, Texas

James B. Pulley
Science Editor and Former Science Teacher
Liberty High School
Liberty, Missouri

Denice Lee Sandefur
Science Chairperson
Nucla High School
Nucla, Colorado

Patti Soderberg
Science Writer
The BioQUEST Curriculum Consortium
Beloit College
Beloit, Wisconsin

Phillip Vavala
Science Teacher and Dept. Chair
Salesianum School
Wilmington, Delaware

Albert C. Wartski
Biology Teacher
Chapel Hill High School
Chapel Hill, North Carolina

Lynn Marie Wartski
Science Writer and Former Science Teacher
Hillsborough, North Carolina

Ivora D. Washington
Science Teacher and Dept. Chair
Hyattsville Middle School
Washington, D.C.

Academic Reviewers

Renato J. Aguilera, Ph.D.
Associate Professor
Department of Molecular, Cell, and Developmental Biology
University of California
Los Angeles, California

David M. Armstrong, Ph.D.
Professor of Biology
Department of E.P.O. Biology
University of Colorado
Boulder, Colorado

Alissa Arp, Ph.D.
Director and Professor of Environmental Studies
Romberg Tiburon Center
San Francisco State University
Tiburon, California

Russell M. Brengelman
Professor of Physics
Morehead State University
Morehead, Kentucky

John A. Brockhaus, Ph.D.
Director of Mapping, Charting, and Geodesy Program
Department of Geography and Environmental Engineering
United States Military Academy
West Point, New York

Linda K. Butler, Ph.D.
Lecturer of Biological Sciences
The University of Texas
Austin, Texas

Barry Chernoff, Ph.D.
Associate Curator
Division of Fishes
The Field Museum of Natural History
Chicago, Illinois

Donna Greenwood Crenshaw, Ph.D.
Instructor
Department of Biology
Duke University
Durham, North Carolina

Hugh Crenshaw, Ph.D.
Assistant Professor of Zoology
Duke University
Durham, North Carolina

Joe W. Crim, Ph.D.
Professor of Biology
University of Georgia
Athens, Georgia

Peter Demmin, Ed.D.
Former Science Teacher and Chair
Amherst Central High School
Amherst, New York

Joseph L. Graves, Jr., Ph.D.
Associate Professor of Evolutionary Biology
Arizona State University West
Phoenix, Arizona

William B. Guggino, Ph.D.
Professor of Physiology and Pediatrics
The Johns Hopkins University School of Medicine
Baltimore, Maryland

David Haig, Ph.D.
Assistant Professor of Biology
Department of Organismic and Evolutionary Biology
Harvard University
Cambridge, Massachusetts

Roy W. Hann, Jr., Ph.D.
Professor of Civil Engineering
Texas A&M University
College Station, Texas

John E. Hoover, Ph.D.
Associate Professor of Biology
Millersville University
Millersville, Pennsylvania

Joan E. N. Hudson, Ph.D.
Associate Professor of Biological Sciences
Sam Houston State University
Huntsville, Texas

Laurie Jackson-Grusby, Ph.D.
Research Scientist and Doctoral Associate
Whitehead Institute for Biomedical Research
Massachusetts Institute of Technology
Cambridge, Massachusetts

George M. Langford, Ph.D.
Professor of Biological Sciences
Dartmouth College
Hanover, New Hampshire

Melanie C. Lewis, Ph.D.
Professor of Biology, Retired
Southwest Texas State University
San Marcos, Texas

V. Patteson Lombardi, Ph.D.
Research Assistant Professor of Biology
Department of Biology
University of Oregon
Eugene, Oregon

Glen Longley, Ph.D.
Professor of Biology and Director of the Edwards Aquifer Research Center
Southwest Texas State University
San Marcos, Texas

William F. McComas, Ph.D.
Director of the Center to Advance Science Education
University of Southern California
Los Angeles, California

LaMoine L. Motz, Ph.D.
Coordinator of Science Education
Oakland County Schools
Waterford, Michigan

Nancy Parker, Ph.D.
Associate Professor of Biology
Southern Illinois University
Edwardsville, Illinois

Barron S. Rector, Ph.D.
Associate Professor and Extension Range Specialist
Texas Agricultural Extension Service
Texas A&M University
College Station, Texas

Peter Sheridan, Ph.D.
Professor of Chemistry
Colgate University
Hamilton, New York

Miles R. Silman, Ph.D.
Assistant Professor of Biology
Wake Forest University
Winston-Salem, North Carolina

Neil Simister, Ph.D.
Associate Professor of Biology
Department of Life Sciences
Brandeis University
Waltham, Massachusetts

Lee Smith, Ph.D.
Curriculum Writer
MDL Information Systems, Inc.
San Leandro, California

Robert G. Steen, Ph.D.
Manager, Rat Genome Project
Whitehead Institute—Center for Genome Research
Massachusetts Institute of Technology
Cambridge, Massachusetts

Acknowledgments (cont.)

Martin VanDyke, Ph.D.
Professor of Chemistry, Emeritus
Front Range Community College
Westminister, Colorado

E. Peter Volpe, Ph.D.
Professor of Medical Genetics
Mercer University School of Medicine
Macon, Georgia

Harold K. Voris, Ph.D.
Curator and Head
Division of Amphibians and Reptiles
The Field Museum of Natural History
Chicago, Illinois

Mollie Walton
Biology Instructor
El Paso Community College
El Paso, Texas

Peter Wetherwax, Ph.D.
Professor of Biology
University of Oregon
Eugene, Oregon

Mary K. Wicksten, Ph.D.
Professor of Biology
Texas A&M University
College Station, Texas

R. Stimson Wilcox, Ph.D.
Associate Professor of Biology
Department of Biological Sciences
Binghamton University
Binghamton, New York

Conrad M. Zapanta, Ph.D.
Research Engineer
Sulzer Carbomedics, Inc.
Austin, Texas

Safety Reviewer

Jack Gerlovich, Ph.D.
Associate Professor
School of Education
Drake University
Des Moines, Iowa

Teacher Reviewers

Barry L. Bishop
Science Teacher and Dept. Chair
San Rafael Junior High School
Ferron, Utah

Carol A. Bornhorst
Science Teacher and Dept. Chair
Bonita Vista Middle School
Chula Vista, California

Paul Boyle
Science Teacher
Perry Heights Middle School
Evansville, Indiana

Yvonne Brannum
Science Teacher and Dept. Chair
Hine Junior High School
Washington, D.C.

Gladys Cherniak
Science Teacher
St. Paul's Episcopal School
Mobile, Alabama

James Chin
Science Teacher
Frank A. Day Middle School
Newtonville, Massachusetts

Kenneth Creese
Science Teacher
White Mountain Junior High School
Rock Springs, Wyoming

Linda A. Culp
Science Teacher and Dept. Chair
Thorndale High School
Thorndale, Texas

Georgiann Delgadillo
Science Teacher
East Valley Continuous Curriculum School
Spokane, Washington

Alonda Droege
Biology Teacher
Evergreen High School
Seattle, Washington

Michael J. DuPré
Curriculum Specialist
Rush Henrietta Junior-Senior High School
Henrietta, New York

Rebecca Ferguson
Science Teacher
North Ridge Middle School
North Richland Hills, Texas

Susan Gorman
Science Teacher
North Ridge Middle School
North Richland Hills, Texas

Gary Habeeb
Science Mentor
Sierra-Plumas Joint Unified School District
Downieville, California

Karma Houston-Hughes
Science Mentor
Kyrene Middle School
Tempe, Arizona

Roberta Jacobowitz
Science Teacher
C. W. Otto Middle School
Lansing, Michigan

Kerry A. Johnson
Science Teacher
Isbell Middle School
Santa Paula, California

M. R. Penny Kisiah
Science Teacher and Dept. Chair
Fairview Middle School
Tallahassee, Florida

Kathy LaRoe
Science Teacher
East Valley Middle School
East Helena, Montana

Jane M. Lemons
Science Teacher
Western Rockingham Middle School
Madison, North Carolina

Scott Mandel, Ph.D.
Director and Educational Consultant
Teachers Helping Teachers
Los Angeles, California

Thomas Manerchia
Former Biology and Life Science Teacher
Archmere Academy
Claymont, Delaware

Maurine O. Marchani
Science Teacher and Dept. Chair
Raymond Park Middle School
Indianapolis, Indiana

Jason P. Marsh
Biology Teacher
Montevideo High School and Montevideo Country School
Montevideo, Minnesota

Edith C. McAlanis
Science Teacher and Dept. Chair
Socorro Middle School
El Paso, Texas

Kevin McCurdy, Ph.D.
Science Teacher
Elmwood Junior High School
Rogers, Arkansas

Kathy McKee
Science Teacher
Hoyt Middle School
Des Moines, Iowa

Alyson Mike
Science Teacher
East Valley Middle School
East Helena, Montana

Donna Norwood
Science Teacher and Dept. Chair
Monroe Middle School
Charlotte, North Carolina

James B. Pulley
Former Science Teacher
Liberty High School
Liberty, Missouri

Terry J. Rakes
Science Teacher
Elmwood Junior High School
Rogers, Arkansas

Elizabeth Rustad
Science Teacher
Crane Middle School
Yuma, Arizona

Debra A. Sampson
Science Teacher
Booker T. Washington Middle School
Elgin, Texas

Charles Schindler
Curriculum Advisor
San Bernadino City Unified Schools
San Bernadino, California

Bert J. Sherwood
Science Teacher
Socorro Middle School
El Paso, Texas

Patricia McFarlane Soto
Science Teacher and Dept. Chair
G. W. Carver Middle School
Miami, Florida

David M. Sparks
Science Teacher
Redwater Junior High School
Redwater, Texas

Elizabeth Truax
Science Teacher
Lewiston-Porter Central School
Lewiston, New York

Ivora Washington
Science Teacher and Dept. Chair
Hyattsville Middle School
Washington, D.C.

Elsie N. Waynes
Science Teacher and Dept. Chair
R. H. Terrell Junior High School
Washington, D.C.

Nancy Wesorick
Science and Math Teacher
Sunset Middle School
Longmont, Colorado

Alexis S. Wright
Middle School Science Coordinator
Rye Country Day School
Rye, New York

John Zambo
Science Teacher
E. Ustach Middle School
Modesto, California

Gordon Zibelman
Science Teacher
Drexell Hill Middle School
Drexell Hill, Pennsylvania

Animals

Skills Development

Process Skills

QuickLabs

Chapter Labs

Research and Critical Thinking Skills

Apply

Feature Articles

Across the Sciences

Eye on the Environment

Weird Science

Connections

Environment Connection

Physics Connection

Mathematics

LabBook

Program Scope and Sequence

Selecting the right books for your course is easy. Just review the topics presented in each book to determine the best match to your district curriculum.

	A MICROORGANISMS, FUNGI, AND PLANTS	**B** ANIMALS
CHAPTER 1	**It's Alive!! Or, Is It?** ❑ Characteristics of living things ❑ Homeostasis ❑ Heredity and DNA ❑ Producers, consumers, and decomposers ❑ Biomolecules	**Animals and Behavior** ❑ Characteristics of animals ❑ Classification of animals ❑ Animal behavior ❑ Hibernation and estivation ❑ The biological clock ❑ Animal communication ❑ Living in groups
CHAPTER 2	**Bacteria and Viruses** ❑ Binary fission ❑ Characteristics of bacteria ❑ Nitrogen-fixing bacteria ❑ Antibiotics ❑ Pathogenic bacteria ❑ Characteristics of viruses ❑ Lytic cycle	**Invertebrates** ❑ General characteristics of invertebrates ❑ Types of symmetry ❑ Characteristics of sponges, cnidarians, arthropods, and echinoderms ❑ Flatworms versus roundworms ❑ Types of circulatory systems
CHAPTER 3	**Protists and Fungi** ❑ Characteristics of protists ❑ Types of algae ❑ Types of protozoa ❑ Protist reproduction ❑ Characteristics of fungi and lichens	**Fishes, Amphibians, and Reptiles** ❑ Characteristics of vertebrates ❑ Structure and kinds of fishes ❑ Development of lungs ❑ Structure and kinds of amphibians and reptiles ❑ Function of the amniotic egg
CHAPTER 4	**Introduction to Plants** ❑ Characteristics of plants and seeds ❑ Reproduction and classification ❑ Angiosperms versus gymnosperms ❑ Monocots versus dicots ❑ Structure and functions of roots, stems, leaves, and flowers	**Birds and Mammals** ❑ Structure and kinds of birds ❑ Types of feathers ❑ Adaptations for flight ❑ Structure and kinds of mammals ❑ Function of the placenta
CHAPTER 5	**Plant Processes** ❑ Pollination and fertilization ❑ Dormancy ❑ Photosynthesis ❑ Plant tropisms ❑ Seasonal responses of plants	
CHAPTER 6		
CHAPTER 7		

Life Science

C — CELLS, HEREDITY, & CLASSIFICATION

Cells: The Basic Units of Life
- ❏ Cells, tissues, and organs
- ❏ Populations, communities, and ecosystems
- ❏ Cell theory
- ❏ Surface-to-volume ratio
- ❏ Prokaryotic versus eukaryotic cells
- ❏ Cell organelles

The Cell in Action
- ❏ Diffusion and osmosis
- ❏ Passive versus active transport
- ❏ Endocytosis versus exocytosis
- ❏ Photosynthesis
- ❏ Cellular respiration and fermentation
- ❏ Cell cycle

Heredity
- ❏ Dominant versus recessive traits
- ❏ Genes and alleles
- ❏ Genotype, phenotype, the Punnett square and probability
- ❏ Meiosis
- ❏ Determination of sex

Genes and Gene Technology
- ❏ Structure of DNA
- ❏ Protein synthesis
- ❏ Mutations
- ❏ Heredity disorders and genetic counseling

The Evolution of Living Things
- ❏ Adaptations and species
- ❏ Evidence for evolution
- ❏ Darwin's work and natural selection
- ❏ Formation of new species

The History of Life on Earth
- ❏ Geologic time scale and extinctions
- ❏ Plate tectonics
- ❏ Human evolution

Classification
- ❏ Levels of classification
- ❏ Cladistic diagrams
- ❏ Dichotomous keys
- ❏ Characteristics of the six kingdoms

D — HUMAN BODY SYSTEMS & HEALTH

Body Organization and Structure
- ❏ Homeostasis
- ❏ Types of tissue
- ❏ Organ systems
- ❏ Structure and function of the skeletal system, muscular system, and integumentary system

Circulation and Respiration
- ❏ Structure and function of the cardiovascular system, lymphatic system, and respiratory system
- ❏ Respiratory disorders

The Digestive and Urinary Systems
- ❏ Structure and function of the digestive system
- ❏ Structure and function of the urinary system

Communication and Control
- ❏ Structure and function of the nervous system and endocrine system
- ❏ The senses
- ❏ Structure and function of the eye and ear

Reproduction and Development
- ❏ Asexual versus sexual reproduction
- ❏ Internal versus external fertilization
- ❏ Structure and function of the human male and female reproductive systems
- ❏ Fertilization, placental development, and embryo growth
- ❏ Stages of human life

Body Defenses and Disease
- ❏ Types of diseases
- ❏ Vaccines and immunity
- ❏ Structure and function of the immune system
- ❏ Autoimmune diseases, cancer, and AIDS

Staying Healthy
- ❏ Nutrition and reading food labels
- ❏ Alcohol and drug effects on the body
- ❏ Hygiene, exercise, and first aid

E — ENVIRONMENTAL SCIENCE

Interactions of Living Things
- ❏ Biotic versus abiotic parts of the environment
- ❏ Producers, consumers, and decomposers
- ❏ Food chains and food webs
- ❏ Factors limiting population growth
- ❏ Predator-prey relationships
- ❏ Symbiosis and coevolution

Cycles in Nature
- ❏ Water cycle
- ❏ Carbon cycle
- ❏ Nitrogen cycle
- ❏ Ecological succession

The Earth's Ecosystems
- ❏ Kinds of land and water biomes
- ❏ Marine ecosystems
- ❏ Freshwater ecosystems

Environmental Problems and Solutions
- ❏ Types of pollutants
- ❏ Types of resources
- ❏ Conservation practices
- ❏ Species protection

Energy Resources
- ❏ Types of resources
- ❏ Energy resources and pollution
- ❏ Alternative energy resources

Scope and Sequence (continued)

	F INSIDE THE RESTLESS EARTH	**G** EARTH'S CHANGING SURFACE
CHAPTER 1	**Minerals of the Earth's Crust** ❏ Mineral composition and structure ❏ Types of minerals ❏ Mineral identification ❏ Mineral formation and mining	**Maps as Models of the Earth** ❏ Structure of a map ❏ Cardinal directions ❏ Latitude, longitude, and the equator ❏ Magnetic declination and true north ❏ Types of projections ❏ Aerial photographs ❏ Remote sensing ❏ Topographic maps
CHAPTER 2	**Rocks: Mineral Mixtures** ❏ Rock cycle and types of rocks ❏ Rock classification ❏ Characteristics of igneous, sedimentary, and metamorphic rocks	**Weathering and Soil Formation** ❏ Types of weathering ❏ Factors affecting the rate of weathering ❏ Composition of soil ❏ Soil conservation and erosion prevention
CHAPTER 3	**The Rock and Fossil Record** ❏ Uniformitarianism versus catastrophism ❏ Superposition ❏ The geologic column and unconformities ❏ Absolute dating and radiometric dating ❏ Characteristics and types of fossils ❏ Geologic time scale	**Agents of Erosion and Deposition** ❏ Shoreline erosion and deposition ❏ Wind erosion and deposition ❏ Erosion and deposition by ice ❏ Gravity's effect on erosion and deposition
CHAPTER 4	**Plate Tectonics** ❏ Structure of the Earth ❏ Continental drifts and sea floor spreading ❏ Plate tectonics theory ❏ Types of boundaries ❏ Types of crust deformities	
CHAPTER 5	**Earthquakes** ❏ Seismology ❏ Features of earthquakes ❏ P and S waves ❏ Gap hypothesis ❏ Earthquake safety	
CHAPTER 6	**Volcanoes** ❏ Types of volcanoes and eruptions ❏ Types of lava and pyroclastic material ❏ Craters versus calderas ❏ Sites and conditions for volcano formation ❏ Predicting eruptions	

Earth Science

H WATER ON EARTH

The Flow of Fresh Water
❑ Water cycle
❑ River systems
❑ Stream erosion
❑ Life cycle of rivers
❑ Deposition
❑ Aquifers, springs, and wells
❑ Ground water
❑ Water treatment and pollution

Exploring the Oceans
❑ Properties and characteristics of the oceans
❑ Features of the ocean floor
❑ Ocean ecology
❑ Ocean resources and pollution

The Movement of Ocean Water
❑ Types of currents
❑ Characteristics of waves
❑ Types of ocean waves
❑ Tides

I WEATHER AND CLIMATE

The Atmosphere
❑ Structure of the atmosphere
❑ Air pressure
❑ Radiation, convection, and conduction
❑ Greenhouse effect and global warming
❑ Characteristics of winds
❑ Types of winds
❑ Air pollution

Understanding Weather
❑ Water cycle
❑ Humidity
❑ Types of clouds
❑ Types of precipitation
❑ Air masses and fronts
❑ Storms, tornadoes, and hurricanes
❑ Weather forecasting
❑ Weather maps

Climate
❑ Weather versus climate
❑ Seasons and latitude
❑ Prevailing winds
❑ Earth's biomes
❑ Earth's climate zones
❑ Ice ages
❑ Global warming
❑ Greenhouse effect

J ASTRONOMY

Observing the Sky
❑ Astronomy
❑ Keeping time
❑ Mapping the stars
❑ Scales of the universe
❑ Types of telescope
❑ Radioastronomy

Formation of the Solar System
❑ Birth of the solar system
❑ Planetary motion
❑ Newton's Law of Universal Gravitation
❑ Structure of the sun
❑ Fusion
❑ Earth's structure and atmosphere

A Family of Planets
❑ Properties and characteristics of the planets
❑ Properties and characteristics of moons
❑ Comets, asteroids, and meteoroids

The Universe Beyond
❑ Composition of stars
❑ Classification of stars
❑ Star brightness, distance, and motions
❑ H-R diagram
❑ Life cycle of stars
❑ Types of galaxies
❑ Theories on the formation of the universe

Exploring Space
❑ Rocketry and artificial satellites
❑ Types of Earth orbit
❑ Space probes and space exploration

Scope and Sequence *(continued)*

	K INTRODUCTION TO MATTER	**L** INTERACTIONS OF MATTER
CHAPTER 1	**The Properties of Matter** ❑ Definition of matter ❑ Mass and weight ❑ Physical and chemical properties ❑ Physical and chemical change ❑ Density	**Chemical Bonding** ❑ Types of chemical bonds ❑ Valence electrons ❑ Ions versus molecules ❑ Crystal lattice
CHAPTER 2	**States of Matter** ❑ States of matter and their properties ❑ Boyle's and Charles's laws ❑ Changes of state	**Chemical Reactions** ❑ Writing chemical formulas and equations ❑ Law of conservation of mass ❑ Types of reactions ❑ Endothermic versus exothermic reactions ❑ Law of conservation of energy ❑ Activation energy ❑ Catalysts and inhibitors
CHAPTER 3	**Elements, Compounds, and Mixtures** ❑ Elements and compounds ❑ Metals, nonmetals, and metalloids (semiconductors) ❑ Properties of mixtures ❑ Properties of solutions, suspensions, and colloids	**Chemical Compounds** ❑ Ionic versus covalent compounds ❑ Acids, bases, and salts ❑ pH ❑ Organic compounds ❑ Biomolecules
CHAPTER 4	**Introduction to Atoms** ❑ Atomic theory ❑ Atomic model and structure ❑ Isotopes ❑ Atomic mass and mass number	**Atomic Energy** ❑ Properties of radioactive substances ❑ Types of decay ❑ Half-life ❑ Fission, fusion, and chain reactions
CHAPTER 5	**The Periodic Table** ❑ Structure of the periodic table ❑ Periodic law ❑ Properties of alkali metals, alkaline-earth metals, halogens, and noble gases	
CHAPTER 6		

Physical Science

M — FORCES, MOTION, AND ENERGY

Matter in Motion
- Speed, velocity, and acceleration
- Measuring force
- Friction
- Mass versus weight

Forces in Motion
- Terminal velocity and free fall
- Projectile motion
- Inertia
- Momentum

Forces in Fluids
- Properties in fluids
- Atmospheric pressure
- Density
- Pascal's principle
- Buoyant force
- Archimedes' principle
- Bernoulli's principle

Work and Machines
- Measuring work
- Measuring power
- Types of machines
- Mechanical advantage
- Mechanical efficiency

Energy and Energy Resources
- Forms of energy
- Energy conversions
- Law of conservation of energy
- Energy resources

Heat and Heat Technology
- Heat versus temperature
- Thermal expansion
- Absolute zero
- Conduction, convection, radiation
- Conductors versus insulators
- Specific heat capacity
- Changes of state
- Heat engines
- Thermal pollution

N — ELECTRICITY AND MAGNETISM

Introduction to Electricity
- Law of electric charges
- Conduction versus induction
- Static electricity
- Potential difference
- Cells, batteries, and photocells
- Thermocouples
- Voltage, current, and resistance
- Electric power
- Types of circuits

Electromagnetism
- Properties of magnets
- Magnetic force
- Electromagnetism
- Solenoids and electric motors
- Electromagnetic induction
- Generators and transformers

Electronic Technology
- Properties of semiconductors
- Integrated circuits
- Diodes and transistors
- Analog versus digital signals
- Microprocessors
- Features of computers

O — SOUND AND LIGHT

The Energy of Waves
- Properties of waves
- Types of waves
- Reflection and refraction
- Diffraction and interference
- Standing waves and resonance

The Nature of Sound
- Properties of sound waves
- Structure of the human ear
- Pitch and the Doppler effect
- Infrasonic versus ultrasonic sound
- Sound reflection and echolocation
- Sound barrier
- Interference, resonance, diffraction, and standing waves
- Sound quality of instruments

The Nature of Light
- Electromagnetic waves
- Electromagnetic spectrum
- Law of reflection
- Absorption and scattering
- Reflection and refraction
- Diffraction and interference

Light and Our World
- Luminosity
- Types of lighting
- Types of mirrors and lenses
- Focal point
- Structure of the human eye
- Lasers and holograms

HOLT SCIENCE & TECHNOLOGY

Components Listing

Effective planning starts with all the resources you need in an easy-to-use package for each short course.

Directed Reading Worksheets Help students develop and practice fundamental reading comprehension skills and provide a comprehensive review tool for students to use when studying for an exam.

Study Guide Vocabulary & Notes Worksheets and Chapter Review Worksheets are reproductions of the Chapter Highlights and Chapter Review sections that follow each chapter in the textbook.

Science Puzzlers, Twisters & Teasers Use vocabulary and concepts from each chapter of the Pupil's Editions as elements of rebuses, anagrams, logic puzzles, daffy definitions, riddle poems, word jumbles, and other types of puzzles.

Reinforcement and Vocabulary Review Worksheets Approach a chapter topic from a different angle with an emphasis on different learning modalities to help students that are frustrated by traditional methods.

Critical Thinking & Problem Solving Worksheets Develop the following skills: distinguishing fact from opinion, predicting consequences, analyzing information, and drawing conclusions. Problem Solving Worksheets develop a step-by-step process of problem analysis including gathering information, asking critical questions, identifying alternatives, and making comparisons.

Math Skills for Science Worksheets Each activity gives a brief introduction to a relevant math skill, a step-by-step explanation of the math process, one or more example problems, and a variety of practice problems.

Science Skills Worksheets Help your students focus specifically on skills such as measuring, graphing, using logic, understanding statistics, organizing research papers, and critical thinking options.

LAB ACTIVITIES

Datasheets for Labs These worksheets are the labs found in the *Holt Science & Technology* textbook. Charts, tables, and graphs are included to make data collection and analysis easier, and space is provided to write observations and conclusions.

Whiz-Bang Demonstrations Discovery or Making Models experiences label each demo as one in which students discover an answer or use a scientific model.

Calculator-Based Labs Give students the opportunity to use graphing-calculator probes and sensors to collect data using a TI graphing calculator, Vernier sensors, and a TI CBL 2™ or Vernier Lab Pro interface.

EcoLabs and Field Activities Focus on educational outdoor projects, such as wildlife observation, nature surveys, or natural history.

Inquiry Labs Use the scientific method to help students find their own path in solving a real-world problem.

Long-Term Projects and Research Ideas Provide students with the opportunity to go beyond library and Internet resources to explore science topics.

ASSESSMENT

Chapter Tests Each four-page chapter test consists of a variety of item types including Multiple Choice, Using Vocabulary, Short Answer, Critical Thinking, Math in Science, Interpreting Graphics, and Concept Mapping.

Performance-Based Assessments Evaluate students' abilities to solve problems using the tools, equipment, and techniques of science. Rubrics included for each assessment make it easy to evaluate student performance.

TEACHER RESOURCES

Lesson Plans Integrate all of the great resources in the *Holt Science & Technology* program into your daily teaching. Each lesson plan includes a correlation of the lesson activities to the National Science Education Standards.

Teaching Transparencies Each transparency is correlated to a particular lesson in the Chapter Organizer.

Concept Mapping Transparencies, Worksheets, and Answer Key

Give students an opportunity to complete their own concept maps to study the concepts within each chapter and form logical connections. Student worksheets contain a blank concept map with linking phrases and a list of terms to be used by the student to complete the map.

TECHNOLOGY RESOURCES

One-Stop Planner CD-ROM

Finding the right resources is easy with the One-Stop Planner CD-ROM. You can view and print any resource with just the click of a mouse. Customize the suggested lesson plans to match your daily or weekly calendar and your district's requirements. Powerful test generator software allows you to create customized assessments using a databank of items.

The One-Stop Planner for each level includes the following:

- All materials from the Teaching Resources
- Bellringer Transparency Masters
- Block Scheduling Tools
- Standards Correlations
- Lab Inventory Checklist
- Safety Information
- Science Fair Guide
- Parent Involvement Tools
- Spanish Audio Scripts
- Spanish Glossary
- Assessment Item Listing
- Assessment Checklists and Rubrics
- Test Generator

sciLINKS

*sci*LINKS numbers throughout the text take you and your students to some of the best on-line resources available. Sites are constantly reviewed and updated by the National Science Teachers Association. Special "teacher only" sites are available to you once you register with the service.

go.hrw.com

To access Holt, Rinehart and Winston Web resources, use the home page codes for each level found on page 1 of the Pupil's Editions. The codes shown on the Chapter Organizers for each chapter in the Annotated Teacher's Edition take you to chapter-specific resources.

Smithsonian Institution

Find lesson plans, activities, interviews, virtual exhibits, and just general information on a wide variety of topics relevant to middle school science.

CNNfyi.com

Find the latest in late-breaking science news for students. Featured news stories are supported with lesson plans and activities.

CNN Presents Science in the News Video Library

Bring relevant science news stories into the classroom. Each video comes with a Teacher's Guide and set of Critical Thinking Worksheets that develop listening and media analysis skills. Tapes in the series include:

- Eye on the Environment
- Multicultural Connections
- Scientists in Action
- Science, Technology & Society

Guided Reading Audio CD Program

Students can listen to a direct read of each chapter and follow along in the text. Use the program as a content bridge for struggling readers and students for whom English is not their native language.

Interactive Explorations CD-ROM

Turn a computer into a virtual laboratory. Students act as lab assistants helping Dr. Crystal Labcoat solve real-world problems. Activities develop students' inquiry, analysis, and decision-making skills.

Interactive Science Encyclopedia CD-ROM

Give your students access to more than 3,000 cross-referenced scientific definitions, in-depth articles, science fair project ideas, activities, and more.

ADDITIONAL COMPONENTS

Holt Anthology of Science Fiction

Science Fiction features in the Pupil's Edition preview the stories found in the anthology. Each story begins with a Reading Prep guide and closes with Think About It questions.

Professional Reference for Teachers

Articles written by leading educators help you learn more about the National Science Education Standards, block scheduling, classroom management techniques, and more. A bibliography of professional references is included.

Holt Science Posters

Seven wall posters highlight interesting topics, such as the Physics of Sports, or useful reference material, such as the Scientific Method.

Holt Science Skills Workshop: Reading in the Content Area

Use a variety of in-depth skills exercises to help students learn to read science materials strategically.

Key

These materials are blackline masters.

All titles shown in green are found in the *Teaching Resources* booklets for each course.

Science & Math Skills Worksheets

The *Holt Science and Technology* program helps you meet the needs of a wide variety of students, regardless of their skill level. The following pages provide examples of the worksheets available to improve your students' science and math skills, whether they already have a strong science and math background or are weak in these areas. Samples of assessment checklists and rubrics are also provided.

In addition to the skills worksheets represented here, *Holt Science and Technology* provides a variety of worksheets that are correlated directly with each chapter of the program. Representations of these worksheets are found at the beginning of each chapter in this Annotated Teacher's Edition. Specific worksheets related to each chapter are listed in the Chapter Organizer. Worksheets and transparencies are found in the softcover *Teaching Resources* for each course.

Many worksheets are also available on the HRW Web site. The address is **go.hrw.com.**

Science Skills Worksheets: Thinking Skills

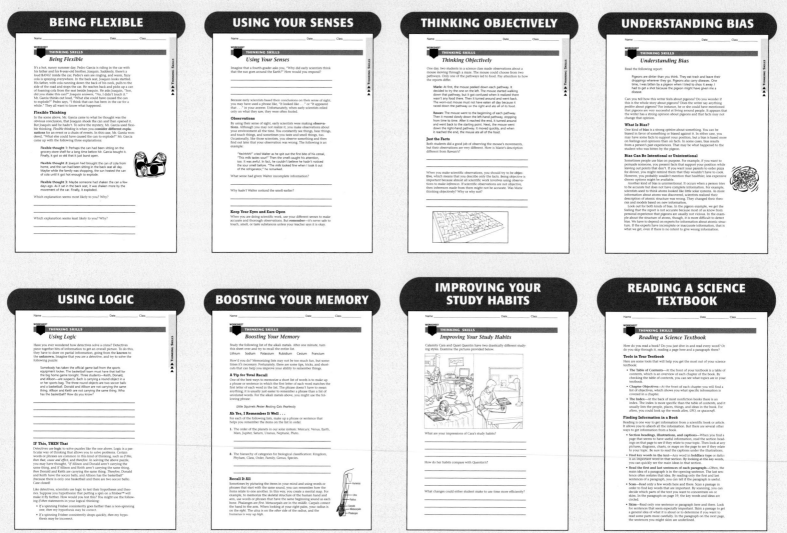

Science Skills Worksheets: Experimenting Skills

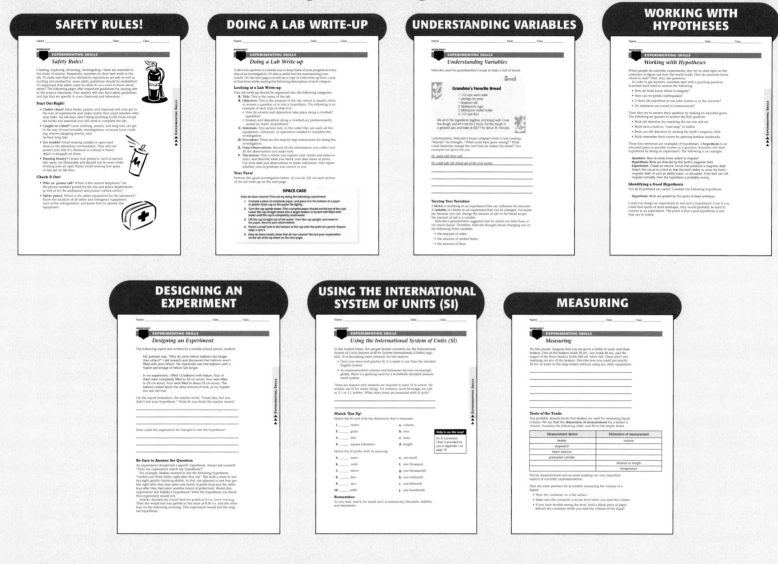

SAFETY RULES!

DOING A LAB WRITE-UP

UNDERSTANDING VARIABLES

WORKING WITH HYPOTHESES

DESIGNING AN EXPERIMENT

USING THE INTERNATIONAL SYSTEM OF UNITS (SI)

MEASURING

Science Skills Worksheets: Researching Skills

CHOOSING YOUR TOPIC

ORGANIZING YOUR RESEARCH

FINDING USEFUL SOURCES

RESEARCHING ON THE WEB

Science Skills Worksheets: Researching Skills (continued)

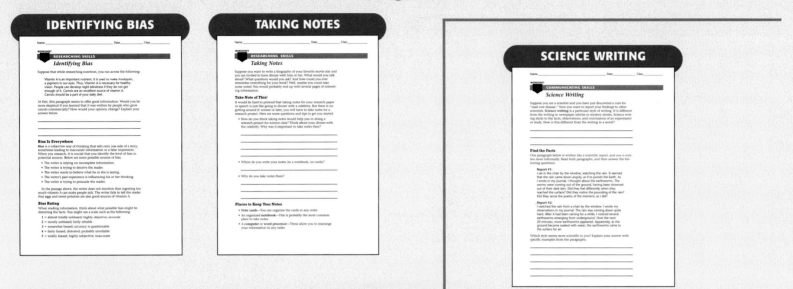

Science Skills Worksheets: Communicating Skills

Math Skills for Science

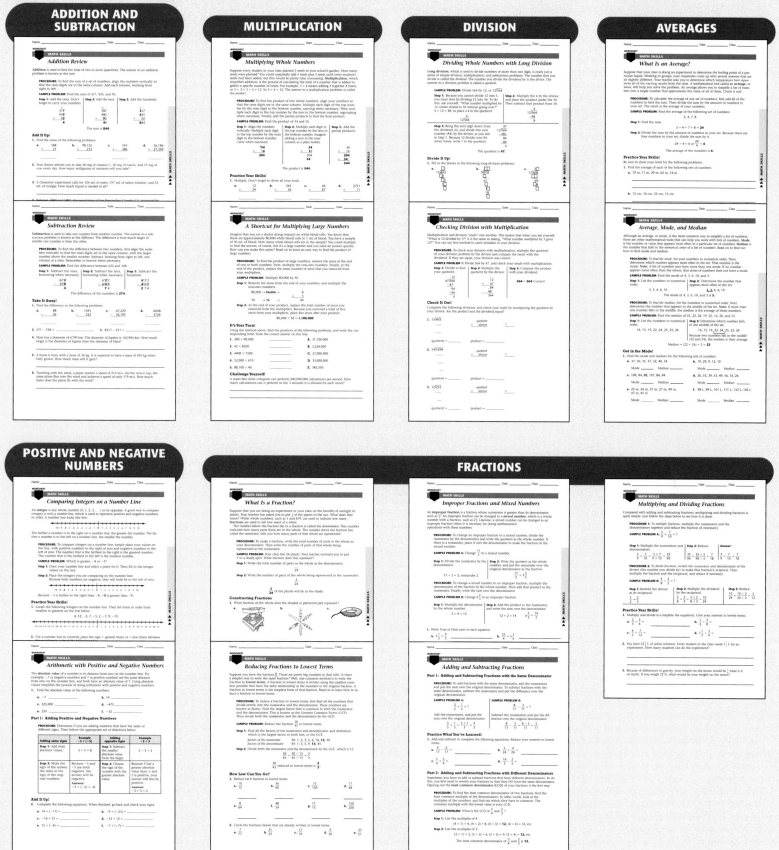

Math Skills for Science (continued)

RATIOS AND PROPORTIONS

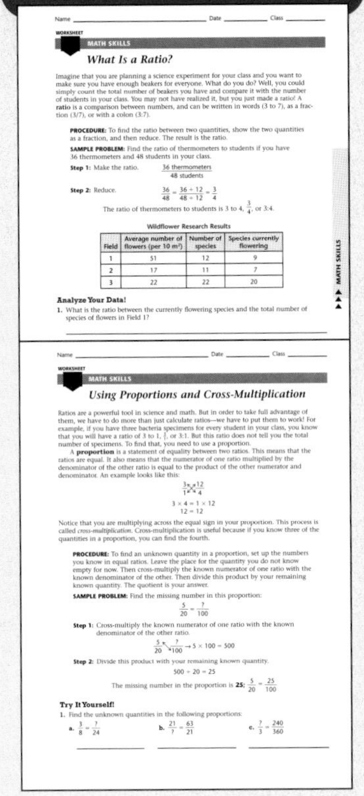

MATH SKILLS

What Is a Ratio?

MATH SKILLS

Using Proportions and Cross-Multiplication

DECIMALS

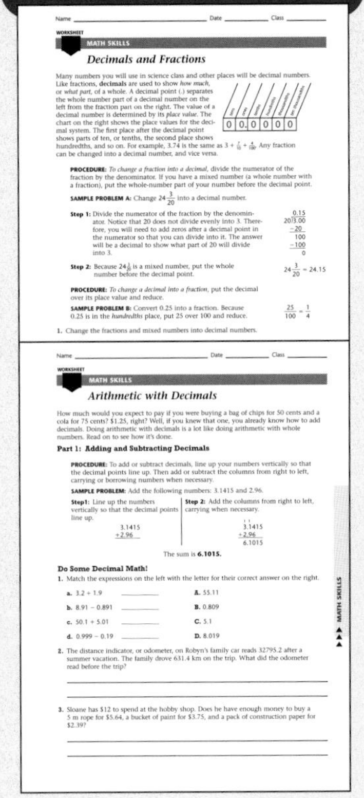

MATH SKILLS

Decimals and Fractions

MATH SKILLS

Arithmetic with Decimals

PERCENTAGES

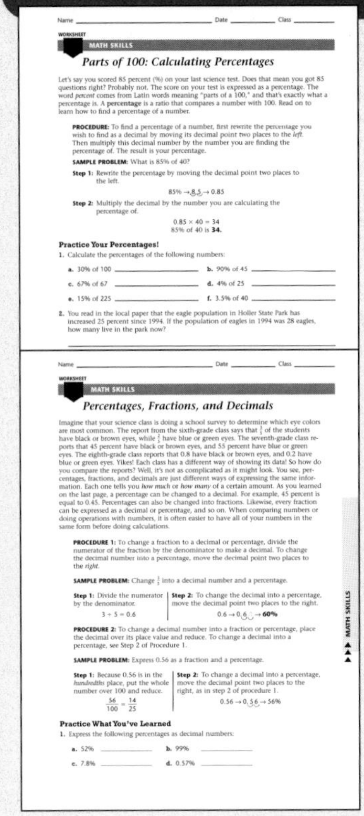

MATH SKILLS

Parts of 100: Calculating Percentages

MATH SKILLS

Percentages, Fractions, and Decimals

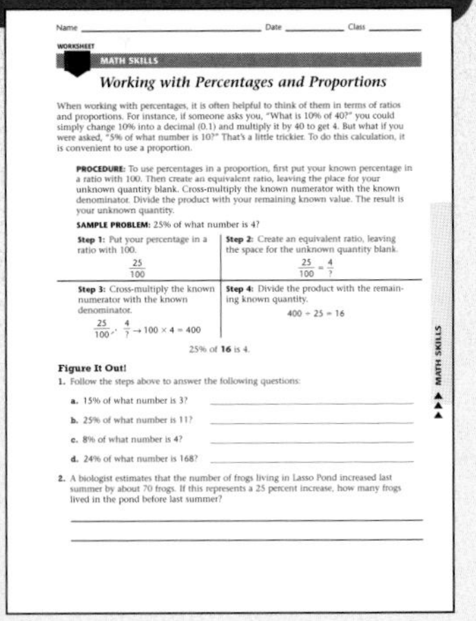

MATH SKILLS

Working with Percentages and Proportions

POWERS OF 10

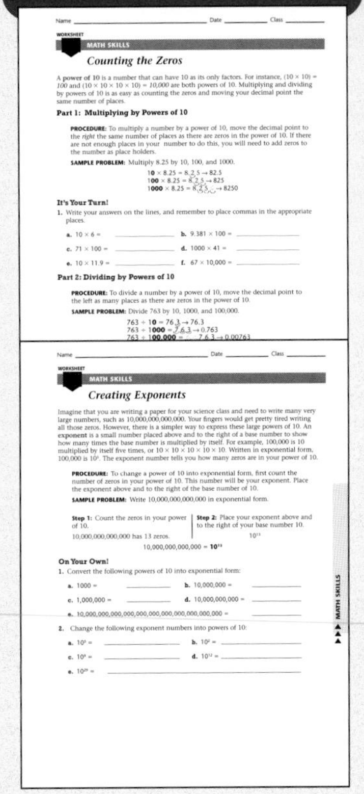

MATH SKILLS

Counting the Zeros

MATH SKILLS

Creating Exponents

SCIENTIFIC NOTATION

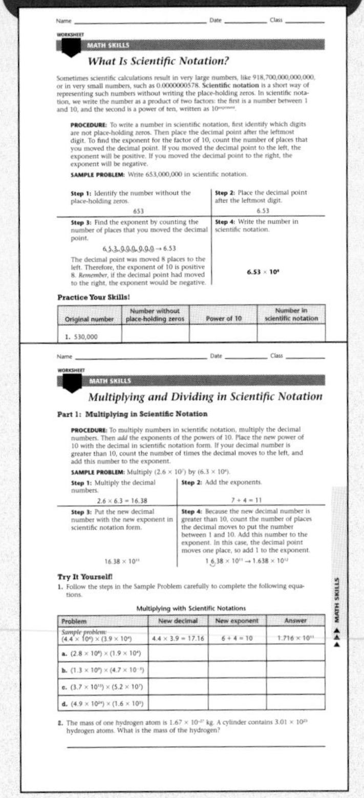

MATH SKILLS

What Is Scientific Notation?

MATH SKILLS

Multiplying and Dividing in Scientific Notation

SI MEASUREMENT AND CONVERSION

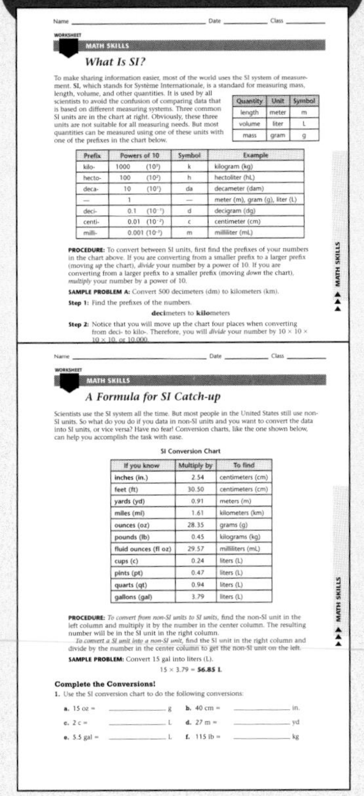

MATH SKILLS

What Is SI?

MATH SKILLS

A Formula for SI Catch-up

Math Skills for Science (continued)

GEOMETRY

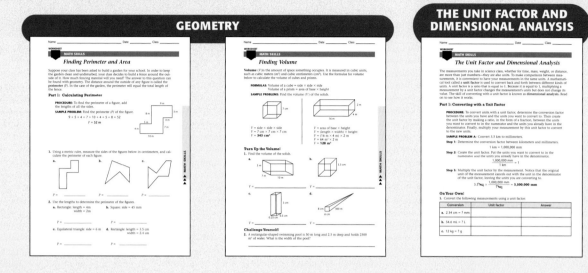

THE UNIT FACTOR AND DIMENSIONAL ANALYSIS

MATH IN SCIENCE: INTEGRATED SCIENCE

Science & Math Skills Worksheets (continued)

Math Skills for Science (continued)

MATH IN SCIENCE: LIFE SCIENCE

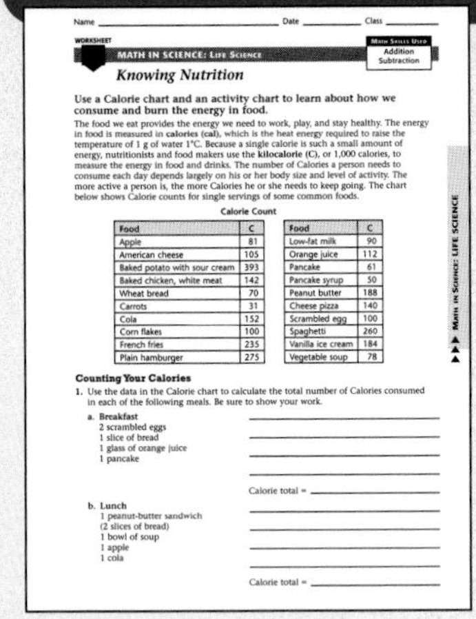

MATH IN SCIENCE: LIFE SCIENCE
Knowing Nutrition

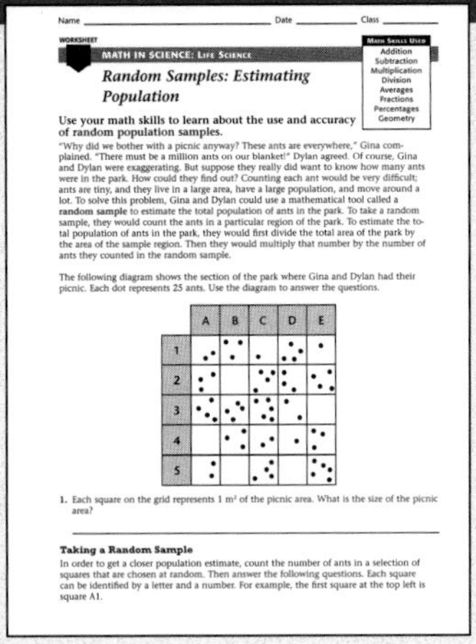

MATH IN SCIENCE: LIFE SCIENCE
Random Samples: Estimating Population

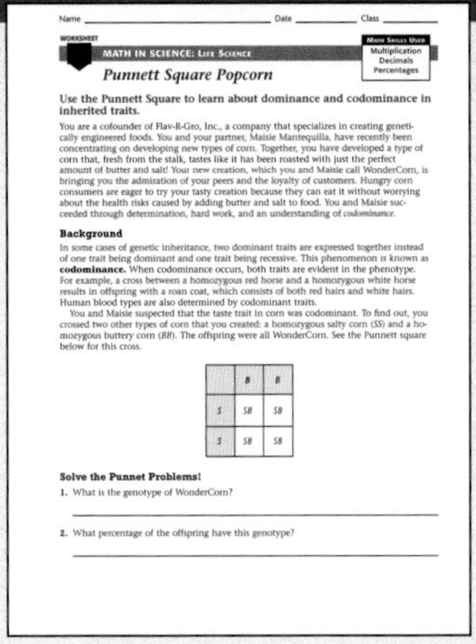

MATH IN SCIENCE: LIFE SCIENCE
Punnett Square Popcorn

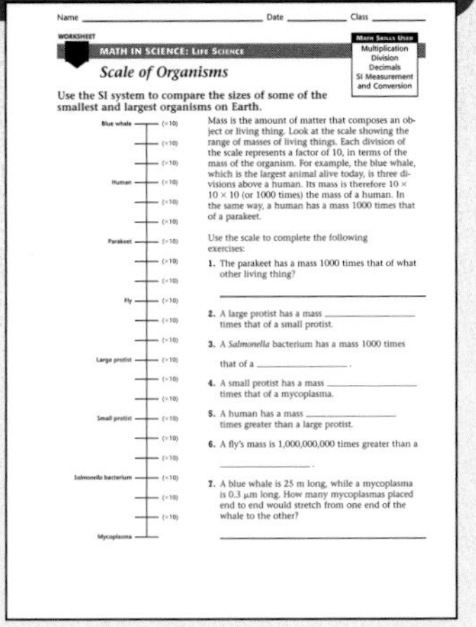

MATH IN SCIENCE: LIFE SCIENCE
Scale of Organisms

Assessment Checklist & Rubrics

The following is just a sample of over 50 checklists and rubrics contained in this booklet.

RUBRICS FOR WRITTEN WORK

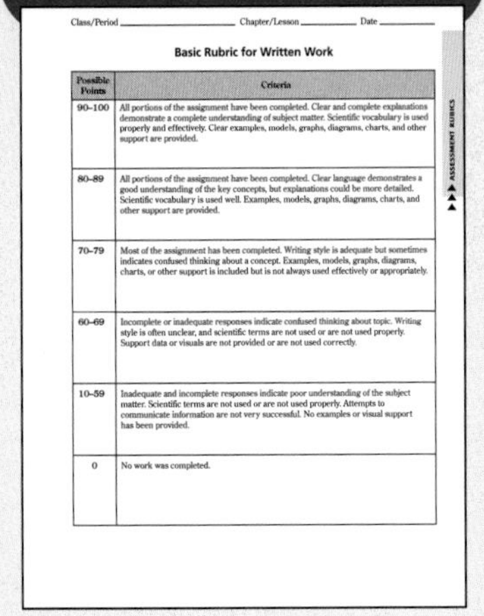

Basic Rubric for Written Work

RUBRIC FOR EXPERIMENTS

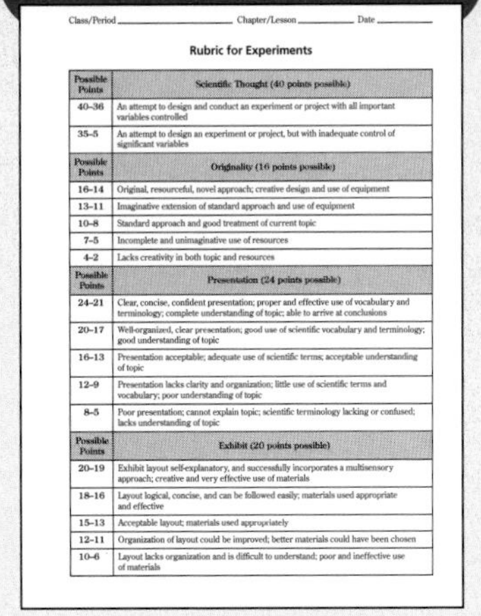

Rubric for Experiments

TEACHER EVALUATION OF COOPERATIVE LEARNING

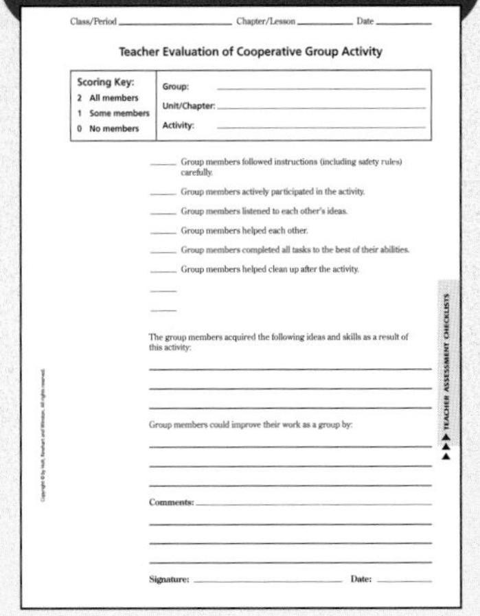

Teacher Evaluation of Cooperative Group Activity

TEACHER EVALUATION OF STUDENT PROGRESS

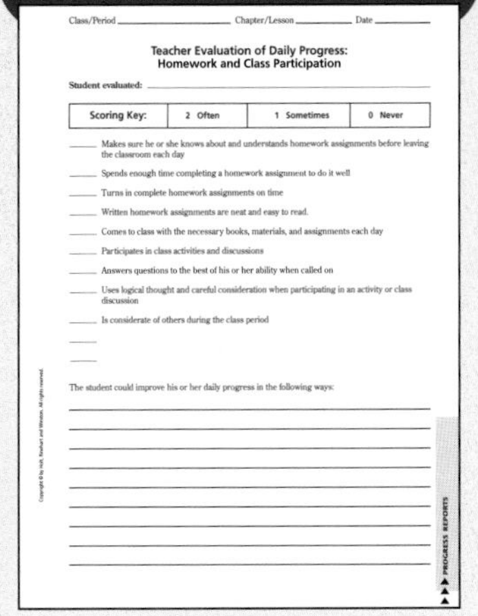

Teacher Evaluation of Daily Progress: Homework and Class Participation

LIFE SCIENCE

NATIONAL SCIENCE EDUCATION STANDARDS CORRELATIONS

The following lists show the chapter correlation of **Holt Science and Technology: Animals** with the *National Science Education Standards* (grades 5-8)

UNIFYING CONCEPTS AND PROCESSES

Standard	Chapter Correlation
Systems, order, and organization Code: UCP 1	**Chapter 1** 1.1, 1.2, 1.3 **Chapter 2** 2.1, 2.2 **Chapter 3** 3.1, 3.2, 3.3, 3.4 **Chapter 4** 4.1, 4.2
Evidence, models, and explanation Code: UCP 2	**Chapter 2** 2.2, 2.3 **Chapter 3** 3.1, 3.2, 3.3, 3.4 **Chapter 4** 4.1, 4.2
Change, constancy, and measurement Code: UCP 3	**Chapter 1** 1.2 **Chapter 2** 2.1, 2.2, 2.3 **Chapter 3** 3.1, 3.2, 3.3 **Chapter 4** 4.1, 4.2
Evolution and equilibrium Code: UCP 4	**Chapter 2** 2.1 **Chapter 3** 3.1, 3.3, 3.4 **Chapter 4** 4.2
Form and function Code: UCP 5	**Chapter 1** 1.2 **Chapter 2** 2.1, 2.2, 2.3, 2.4 **Chapter 3** 3.1, 3.2, 3.3, 3.4 **Chapter 4** 4.1, 4.2

SCIENCE AS INQUIRY

Standard	Chapter Correlation
Abilities necessary to do scientific inquiry Code: SAI 1	**Chapter 1** 1.1, 1.2, 1.3 **Chapter 2** 2.1, 2.3 **Chapter 3** 3.1, 3.2, 3.3 **Chapter 4** 4.1, 4.2
Understandings about scientific inquiry Code: SAI 2	**Chapter 1** 1.2 **Chapter 2** 2.2 **Chapter 3** 3.2

SCIENCE & TECHNOLOGY

Standard	Chapter Correlation
Abilities of technological design Code: ST 1	**Chapter 3** 3.2
Understandings about science and technology Code: ST 2	**Chapter 3** 3.2 **Chapter 4** 4.2

SCIENCE IN PERSONAL AND SOCIAL PERSPECTIVES

Standard	Chapter Correlation
Natural hazards Code: SPSP 3	**Chapter 2** 2.1
Risks and benefits Code: SPSP 4	**Chapter 2** 2.1, 2.2, 2.3
Science and technology in society Code: SPSP 5	**Chapter 3** 3.2 **Chapter 4** 4.1

HISTORY AND NATURE OF SCIENCE

Standard	Chapter Correlation
Science as a human endeavor Code: HNS 1	**Chapter 3** 3.2
Nature of science Code: HNS 2	**Chapter 1** 1.2 **Chapter 3** 3.2 **Chapter 4** 4.2
History of science Code: HNS 3	**Chapter 1** 1.1

LIFE SCIENCE NATIONAL SCIENCE EDUCATION CONTENT STANDARDS

STRUCTURE AND FUNCTION IN LIVING SYSTEMS

Standard	Chapter Correlation	
Living systems at all levels of organization demonstrate the complementary nature of structure and function. Important levels of organization for structure and function include cells, organs, tissues, organ systems, whole organisms, and ecosystems. Code: LS 1a	**Chapter 1** **Chapter 2** **Chapter 3** **Chapter 4**	1.1, 1.3 2.1, 2.2, 2.3, 2.4 3.1, 3.2, 3.3, 3.4 4.1, 4.2
Specialized cells perform specialized functions in multicellular organisms. Groups of specialized cells cooperate to form a tissue, such as a muscle. Different tissues are in turn grouped together and form larger functional units, called organs. Each type of cell, tissue, and organ has a distinct structure and set of functions that serve the organism as a whole. Code: LS 1d	**Chapter 1** **Chapter 2** **Chapter 3** **Chapter 4**	1.1 2.1, 2.3, 2.4 3.1, 3.2 4.1, 4.2
Disease is the breakdown in structures or functions of an organism. Some diseases are the result of intrinsic failures of the system. Others are the result of damage by infection by other organisms. Code: LS 1f	**Chapter 2**	2.1, 2.3

REPRODUCTION AND HEREDITY

Standard	Chapter Correlation	
Reproduction is a characteristic of all living systems; because no living organism lives forever, reproduction is essential to the continuation of every species. Some organisms reproduce asexually. Others reproduce sexually. Code: LS 2a	**Chapter 1** **Chapter 2** **Chapter 3** **Chapter 4**	1.3 2.1, 2.2 3.2, 3.4 4.2
In many species, including humans, females produce eggs and males produce sperm. Plants also reproduce sexually—the egg and sperm are produced in the flowers of flowering plants. An egg and sperm unite to begin development of a new individual. The individual receives genetic information from its mother (via the egg) and its father (via the sperm). Sexually produced offspring never are identical to either of their parents. Code: LS 2b	**Chapter 1** **Chapter 3**	1.1 3.2, 3.4
The characteristics of an organism can be described in terms of a combination of traits. Some traits are inherited and others result from interactions with the environment. Code: LS 2e	**Chapter 3**	3.4

REGULATION AND BEHAVIOR

Standard	Chapter Correlation	
All organisms must be able to obtain and use resources, grow, reproduce, and maintain stable internal conditions while living in a constantly changing external environment. Code: LS 3a	**Chapter 1** **Chapter 2** **Chapter 3** **Chapter 4**	1.2 2.1, 2.2, 2.4 3.1, 3.4 4.1, 4.2
Regulation of an organism's internal environment involves sensing the internal environment and changing physiological activities to keep conditions within the range required to survive. Code: LS 3b	**Chapter 1** **Chapter 3** **Chapter 4**	1.2 3.1 4.1
Behavior is one kind of response an organism can make to an internal or environmental stimulus. A behavioral response requires coordination and communication at many levels, including cells, organ systems, and whole organisms. Behavioral response is a set of actions determined in part by heredity and in part from experience. Code: LS 3c	**Chapter 1** **Chapter 2** **Chapter 3**	1.2, 1.3 2.3 3.1, 3.2, 3.3, 3.4
An organism's behavior evolves through adaptation to its environment. How a species moves, obtains food, reproduces, and responds to danger are based in the species' evolutionary history. Code: LS 3d	**Chapter 1** **Chapter 3**	1.2, 1.3 3.1, 3.2, 3.3, 3.4

POPULATIONS AND ECOSYSTEMS

Standard	Chapter Correlation	
A population consists of all individuals of a species that occur together at a given place and time. All populations living together and the physical factors with which they interact compose an ecosystem. Code: LS 4a	**Chapter 1**	1.2, 1.3
Populations of organisms can be categorized by the functions they serve in an ecosystem. Plants and some microorganisms are producers—they make their own food. All animals, including humans, are consumers, which obtain their food by eating other organisms. Decomposers, primarily bacteria and fungi, are consumers that use waste materials and dead organisms for food. Food webs identify the relationship among producers, consumers, and decomposers in an ecosystem. Code: LS 4b	**Chapter 1** **Chapter 2**	1.1 2.1, 2.2, 2.3, 2.4
The number of organisms an ecosystem can support depends on the resources available and abiotic factors, such as the quantity of light and water, range of temperatures, and soil composition. Given adequate biotic and abiotic resources and no disease or predators, populations (including humans) increase at rapid rates. Lack of resources and other factors, such as predation and climate, limit the growth of populations in specific niches in the ecosystem. Code: LS 4d	**Chapter 1**	1.2, 1.3

DIVERSITY AND ADAPTATIONS OF ORGANISMS

Standard	Chapter Correlation	
Biological evolution accounts for the diversity of species developed through gradual processes over many generations. Species acquire many of their unique characteristics through biological adaptation, which involves the selection of naturally occurring variations in populations. Biological adaptations include changes in structures, behaviors, or physiology that enhance survival and reproductive success in a particular environment. Code: LS 5b	**Chapter 1** **Chapter 3** **Chapter 4**	1.2 3.3, 3.4 4.1
Extinction of a species occurs when the environment changes and the adaptive characteristics of a species are insufficient to allow its survival. Fossils indicate that many organisms that lived long ago are extinct. Extinction of species is common; most of the species that have lived on Earth no longer exist. Code: LS 5c	**Chapter 1** **Chapter 3** **Chapter 4**	1.2 3.2, 3.3, 3.4 4.2

Master Materials List

For added convenience, Science Kit® provides materials-ordering software on CD-ROM designed specifically for *Holt Science and Technology*. Using this software, you can order complete kits or individual items, quickly and efficiently.

CONSUMABLE MATERIALS	AMOUNT	PAGE
Aluminum foil	1 sheet	126
Apple	1	126
Bag, heavy-plastic, sealable, 9 x 12 in.	2	126
Bag, plastic, sealable (various sizes)	2	112
Balloon, round	2	59
Balloon, slender	1	78
Birdseed	1/8 lb	112
Celery leaves	1	18
Cricket	2	126
Cricket, small, live	4	128
Earthworm	1	18
Gloves, protective	1 pair	128
Gravel, aquarium	6 oz	112
Ice, crushed	2 cups	126
Oil, cooking	100 mL	59
Oil, cooking	1 cup	44
Paper, tracing	1 sheet	92
Paper towel	1 roll	18, 50
Plastic wrap, clear, approx. 1 x 2 ft	1 sheet	126
Shoe box with lid	1	18
Soil	8 oz	18
Straw, drinking	1	92, 112
String (or yarn)	3 m	112
Tape, masking	25 cm	126
Tape, transparent	4 cm	44
Tape, transparent	1 roll	112
Water, dechlorinated	2 L	128

NONCONSUMABLE EQUIPMENT	AMOUNT	PAGE
Balance	1	50
Beaker, 400 mL	1	59
Beaker, 600 mL	1	128
Beaker, 600 mL	2	126
Binoculars	1	3
Bottle, spray	1	18
Bowl, large, plastic	1	50, 59
Calculator	1	50
Container, plastic (at least 15 cm deep)	1	78
Cork, small	1	78
Flashlight	1	18
Frog, live (in dry container)	1	128
Funnel, glass	1	50
Graduated cylinder, 100 mL	1	50
Lamp, goose-neck	1	126
Magnifying lens	1	3, 126
Pan, dissecting	1	18
Pin, straight	1	92
Pipe, PVC, 3/4 in. diam., 12 cm	1	78
Probe	1	18
Rock, large, approx., 3 lb	1	128
Rubber band	1	78
Ruler, metric	1	18
Scissors	1	112
Sponge	2	50
Sponge, natural	1	50
Stopwatch	1	12, 18
Thermometer, fever, nonglass	1	62

Answers to Concept Mapping Questions

The following pages contain sample answers to all of the concept mapping questions that appear in the
Chapter Reviews. Because there is more than one way to do a concept map, your students' answers may vary.

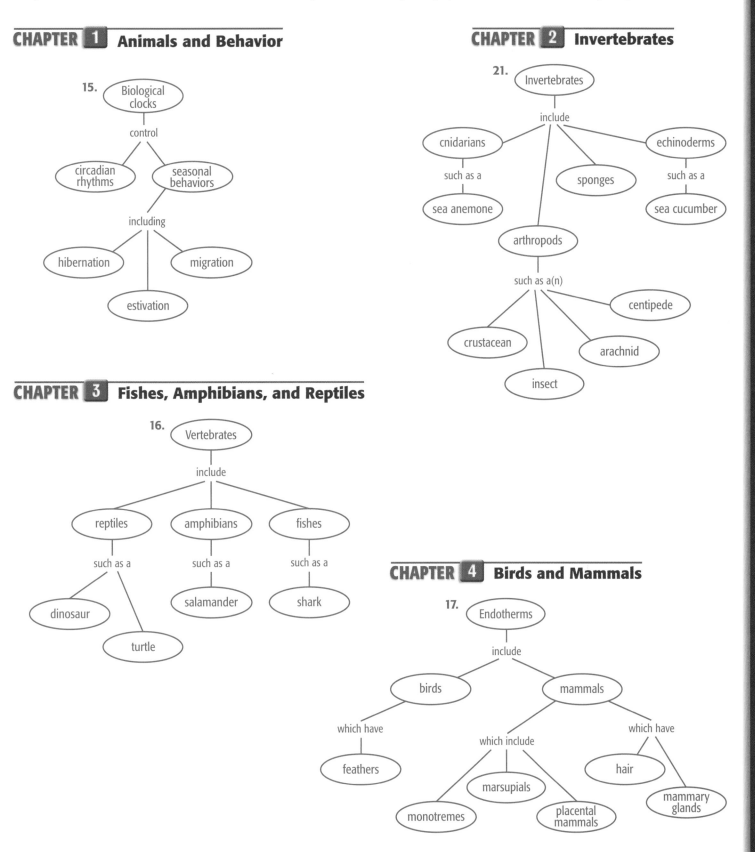

CHAPTER 1   Animals and Behavior

15.
- Biological clocks
  - control
    - circadian rhythms
    - seasonal behaviors
      - including
        - hibernation
        - migration
        - estivation

CHAPTER 3   Fishes, Amphibians, and Reptiles

16.
- Vertebrates
  - include
    - reptiles
      - such as a
        - dinosaur
        - turtle
    - amphibians
      - such as a
        - salamander
    - fishes
      - such as a
        - shark

CHAPTER 2   Invertebrates

21.
- Invertebrates
  - include
    - cnidarians
      - such as a
        - sea anemone
    - sponges
    - echinoderms
      - such as a
        - sea cucumber
    - arthropods
      - such as a(n)
        - crustacean
        - centipede
        - arachnid
        - insect

CHAPTER 4   Birds and Mammals

17.
- Endotherms
  - include
    - birds
      - which have
        - feathers
    - mammals
      - which include
        - monotremes
        - marsupials
        - placental mammals
      - which have
        - hair
        - mammary glands

To the Student

This book was created to make your science experience interesting, exciting, and fun!

Go for It!

Science is a process of discovery, a trek into the unknown. The skills you develop using *Holt Science & Technology*— such as observing, experimenting, and explaining observations and ideas— are the skills you will need for the future. There is a universe of exploration and discovery awaiting those who accept the challenges of science.

Science & Technology

You see the interaction between science and technology every day. Science makes technology possible. On the other hand, some of the products of technology, such as computers, are used to make further scientific discoveries. In fact, much of the scientific work that is done today has become so technically complicated and expensive that no one person can do it entirely alone. But make no mistake, the creative ideas for even the most highly technical and expensive scientific work still come from individuals.

Activities and Labs

The activities and labs in this book will allow you to make some basic but important scientific discoveries on your own. You can even do some exploring on your own at home! Here's your chance to use your imagination and curiosity as you investigate your world.

Keep a ScienceLog

In this book, you will be asked to keep a type of journal called a ScienceLog to record your thoughts, observations, experiments, and conclusions. As you develop your ScienceLog, you will see your own ideas taking shape over time. You'll have a written record of how your ideas have changed as you learn about and explore interesting topics in science.

Know "What You'll Do"

The "What You'll Do" list at the beginning of each section is your built-in guide to what you need to learn in each chapter. When you can answer the questions in the Section Review and Chapter Review, you know you are ready for a test.

Check Out the Internet

You will see this *sciLINKS* logo throughout the book. You'll be using *sciLINKS* as your gateway to the Internet. Once you log on to *sciLINKS* using your computer's Internet link, type in the *sciLINKS* address. When asked for the keyword code, type in the keyword for that topic. A wealth of resources is now at your disposal to help you learn more about that topic.

In addition to *sciLINKS* you can log on to some other great resources to go with your text. The addresses shown below will take you to the home page of each site.

 internet connect

This textbook contains the following on-line resources to help you make the most of your science experience.

go. hrw .com	**sciLINKS** NSTA 	**Smithsonian Institution®** Internet Connections	**CNNfyi.com**
Visit **go.hrw.com** for extra help and study aids matched to your textbook. Just type in the keyword HG2 HOME.	Visit **www.scilinks.org** to find resources specific to topics in your textbook. Keywords appear throughout your book to take you further.	Visit **www.si.edu/hrw** for specifically chosen on-line materials from one of our nation's premier science museums.	Visit **www.cnnfyi.com** for late-breaking news and current events stories selected just for you.

Chapter Organizer

CHAPTER ORGANIZATION	TIME MINUTES	OBJECTIVES	LABS, INVESTIGATIONS, AND DEMONSTRATIONS
Chapter Opener pp. 2–3	45	National Standards: UCP 1, 2, SAI 1, 2, HNS 1, 2, LS 3a, 3c	**Start-Up Activity,** Go on a Safari! p. 3
Section 1 What Is an Animal?	45	▶ Describe the differences between vertebrates and invertebrates. ▶ Explain the characteristics of animals. UCP 1, SAI 1, HNS 3, LS 1a, 1b, 1d, 2b, 4b, 5a	
Section 2 Animal Behavior	90	▶ Explain the difference between learned and innate behavior. ▶ Explain the difference between hibernation and estivation. ▶ Give examples of how a biological clock influences behavior. ▶ Describe circadian rhythms. ▶ Explain how animals navigate. UCP 1, 3, 5, SAI 1, LS 3a, 3b–3d, 4d, 5b, 5c; Labs UCP 2, 3, SAI 1, 2, HNS 2, LS 3c, 4a	**Demonstration,** Sign Language, p. 10 in ATE **QuickLab,** How Long Is a Minute? p. 12 **Discovery Lab,** Wet, Wiggly Worms! p. 18 **Datasheets for LabBook,** Wet, Wiggly Worms! **Design Your Own,** Aunt Flossie and the Bumblebee, p. 124 **Datasheets for LabBook,** Aunt Flossie and the Bumblebee **Inquiry Labs,** Follow the Leader **Whiz-Bang Demonstrations,** Six-Legged Thermometer
Section 3 Living Together	90	▶ Discuss ways that animals communicate. ▶ List the advantages and disadvantages of living in groups. UCP 1, SAI 1, LS 1a, 2a, 3c, 3d, 4a, 4d	**Long-Term Projects & Research Ideas,** Animal Myth Behaviors

See page **T23** for a complete correlation of this book with the

NATIONAL SCIENCE EDUCATION STANDARDS.

TECHNOLOGY RESOURCES

Guided Reading Audio CD
English or Spanish, Chapter 1

Science Discovery Videodiscs
Image and Activity Bank with Lesson Plans: Signaling Animals
Science Sleuths: The Plainview Park Scandals

CNN. Eye on the Environment, Monarch Migrations, Segment 4

Scientists in Action, Studying Dolphin Behavior, Segment 18
Learning the Language of Animals, Segment 19

One-Stop Planner CD-ROM with Test Generator

CLASSROOM WORKSHEETS, TRANSPARENCIES, AND RESOURCES	SCIENCE INTEGRATION AND CONNECTIONS	REVIEW AND ASSESSMENT
Directed Reading Worksheet **Science Puzzlers, Twisters & Teasers**		
Transparency 54, The Animal Kingdom **Directed Reading Worksheet,** Section 1 **Science Skills Worksheet,** Introduction to Graphs **Reinforcement Worksheet,** What Makes an Animal an Animal?		**Self-Check,** p. 6 **Homework,** pp. 6, 7 in ATE **Section Review,** p. 7 **Quiz,** p. 7 in ATE **Alternative Assessment,** p. 7 in ATE
Directed Reading Worksheet, Section 2 **Math Skills for Science Worksheet,** Percentages, Fractions, and Decimals **Math Skills for Science Worksheet,** Average, Mode, and Median **Transparency 104,** Finding Direction on Earth **Reinforcement Worksheet,** Animal Interviews **Critical Thinking Worksheet,** Masters of Navigation	**Math and More,** p. 9 in ATE **Math and More,** p. 11 in ATE **Connect to Earth Science,** p. 12 in ATE **Apply,** p. 13 **Physics Connection,** p. 13 **Eye on the Environment:** Do Not Disturb! p. 24	**Section Review,** p. 10 **Section Review,** p. 13 **Quiz,** p. 13 in ATE **Alternative Assessment,** p. 13 in ATE
Directed Reading Worksheet, Section 3 **Transparency 55,** The Dance of the Bees	**Cross-Disciplinary Focus,** p. 15 in ATE **Weird Science:** Animal Cannibals, p. 25	**Homework,** p. 16 in ATE **Review,** p. 17 **Quiz,** p. 17 in ATE **Alternative Assessment,** p. 17 in ATE

END-OF-CHAPTER REVIEW AND ASSESSMENT

Chapter Review in Study Guide
Vocabulary and Notes in Study Guide
Chapter Tests with Performance-Based Assessment, Chapter 1 Test
Chapter Tests with Performance-Based Assessment, Performance-Based Assessment 1
Concept Mapping Transparency 14

 internet connect

 go. hrw .com **Holt, Rinehart and Winston On-line Resources**
go.hrw.com

For worksheets and other teaching aids related to this chapter, visit the HRW Web site and type in the keyword: **HSTANM**

 SCILINKS **NSTA** **National Science Teachers Association**
www.scilinks.org

Encourage students to use the sciLINKS numbers listed in the internet connect boxes to access information and resources on the **NSTA** Web site.

Chapter Resources & Worksheets

Visual Resources

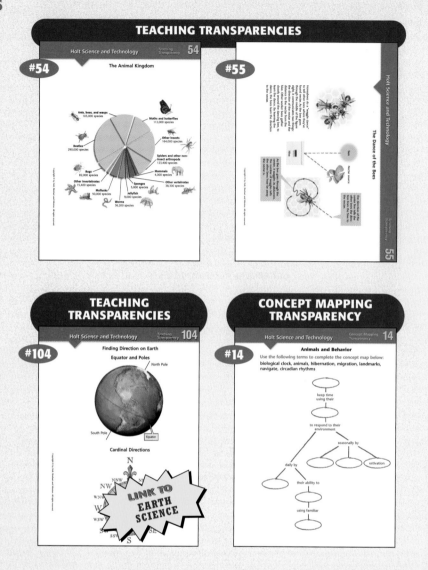

TEACHING TRANSPARENCIES

#54

Holt Science and Technology — Teaching Transparency **54**

The Animal Kingdom

- Ants, bees, and wasps 103,000 species
- Moths and butterflies 112,000 species
- Other insects 164,000 species
- Beetles 290,000 species
- Spiders and other non-insect arthropods 123,400 species
- Bugs 82,000 species
- Mammals 4,000 species
- Other invertebrates 13,400 species
- Sponges 5,000 species
- Other vertebrates 38,300 species
- Mollusks 50,000 species
- Jellyfish 9,000 species
- Worms 36,200 species

#55

Holt Science and Technology — Teaching Transparency **55**

The Dance of the Bees

TEACHING TRANSPARENCIES

#104

Holt Science and Technology — Teaching Transparency **104**

Finding Direction on Earth

Equator and Poles

North Pole

South Pole

Equator

Cardinal Directions

LINK TO EARTH SCIENCE

CONCEPT MAPPING TRANSPARENCY

#14

Holt Science and Technology — Concept Mapping Transparency **14**

Animals and Behavior

Use the following terms to complete the concept map below:
biological clock, animals, hibernation, migration, landmarks, navigate, circadian rhythms

keep time using their

to respond to their environment

seasonally by

estivation

daily by

their ability to

using familiar

Meeting Individual Needs

DIRECTED READING

#1

_____ Date _____ Class _____

DIRECTED READING WORKSHEET

Animals and Behavior

Chapter Introduction

As you begin this chapter, answer the following.

1. Read the title of the chapter. List three things that you already know about this subject.

_____

2. Write two questions about this subject that you would like answered by the time you finish this chapter.

_____

Start-Up Activity (p. 3)

3. What is the purpose of this activity?

_____

Section 1: What is an Animal? (p. 4)

4. Natural bath sponges used to be living plants. True or False? (Circle one.)

5. Describe the smallest animal you've ever seen.

_____

REINFORCEMENT & VOCABULARY REVIEW

#1

_____ Date _____ Class _____

REINFORCEMENT WORKSHEET

What Makes an Animal an Animal?

Complete this worksheet after reading Chapter 13, Section 1.

Whales, armadillos, hummingbirds, spiders . . . animals come in all sorts of shapes and sizes. Not all animals have backbones, and not all animals have hair. So what makes an animal an animal?

Complete the chart below by using the words and phrases at the bottom of the page to fill in the blank spaces.

Words and Phrases

- move
- budding
- develop from embryos
- have specialized parts
- sexually
- asexually
- multicellular
- cells have no cell walls
- division

Complete this worksheet after reading Chapter 13, Section 2.

Imagine that you work with a researcher who can really talk to the animals. Below are some sections of his taped animal interviews. Your job is to decide what animal behavior or characteristic is being described and to write it in the space provided. Possible answers are: warning coloration, migration, hibernation, estivation, and camouflage.

REINFORCEMENT & VOCABULARY REVIEW

#1

_____ Date _____ Class _____

VOCABULARY REVIEW WORKSHEET

Puzzling Animal Behavior

After you finish reading Chapter 13, give this crossword puzzle a try!
Solve the clues below, and write the answers in the appropriate spaces in the crossword puzzle.

ACROSS

3. to find the way from one place to another
4. an organism that eats other organisms
6. this type of behavior can change 17 down
7. an organism in the earliest stage of development
8. to travel from one place to another and back again
10. the internal control of natural cycles
16. an area occupied by an animal or group of animals
18. this type of behavior is the interaction between animals of the same species
19. an animal that eats other animals
20. made of many cells
21. a period of inactivity in winter1. chemicals animals use to communicate with one another

DOWN

1. chemicals animals use to communicate with one another
2. an animal without a backbone
5. blending in with the background
7. a period of reduced activity in summer
9. a collection of similar cells
11. a combination of two or more of number 9 down
12. takes place when a signal travels from one animal to another and the receiver of the signal responds
13. an object animals use to find their way
14. refers to daily rhythms
15. any animal with a skull and a backbone
16. behavior that is influenced by genes
22. an animal that is eaten by another animal

SCIENCE PUZZLERS, TWISTERS & TEASERS

#1

_____ Date _____ Class _____

SCIENCE PUZZLERS, TWISTERS & TEASERS

Animals and Behavior

Complements

1. Unscramble the words in the wheel below. Words opposite each other on the wheel are complementary terms.

Analogies

2. Give the animal-world equivalent to the human items below.

a. perfume

b. wearing a suit to the office or the team colors to a football game

c. house or bedroom

d. compass

e. the big red house on the corner or the oak tree across town

f. winking, frowning, or nodding your head

Chapter 1 • Animals and Behavior

Review & Assessment

STUDY GUIDE

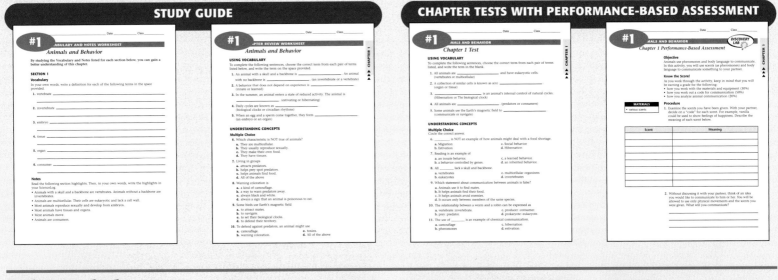

CHAPTER TESTS WITH PERFORMANCE-BASED ASSESSMENT

Lab Worksheets

INQUIRY LABS

WHIZ-BANG DEMONSTRATIONS

LONG-TERM PROJECTS & RESEARCH IDEAS

DATASHEETS FOR LABBOOK

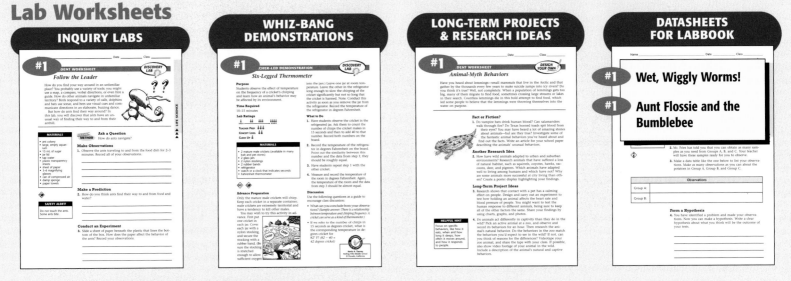

Applications & Extensions

CRITICAL THINKING & PROBLEM SOLVING

EYE ON THE ENVIRONMENT

SCIENTISTS IN ACTION

Chapter Background

SECTION 1

What Is an Animal?

▶ Animal Classifications

Zoologists classify the members of the animal kingdom on the basis of their similarities and differences. The animal kingdom has three subkingdoms (Protozoa, Parazoa, and Metazoa). The three subkingdoms are divided into phyla, and each phylum is divided into subphyla and other subgroups.

- The phylum Chordata (meaning "cord") has three subphyla, one of which is vertebrates. Vertebrates include amphibians, reptiles, birds, mammals, and three kinds of fish.

- The vast majority of animals are invertebrates. Significant invertebrate phyla include Arthropoda (meaning "jointed foot"), Porifera (meaning "hole bearers"), Nematoda (meaning "thread"), and Echinodermata (meaning "spiny skin"). Arthropoda, which includes crustaceans, spiders, millipedes, and insects, is by far the largest phylum. It includes more than 1 million living species.

▶ Animal Reproduction

Some animals can reproduce both sexually and asexually. The adult jellyfish, or medusa, releases sperm and eggs into the water, forming a planula. When the planula matures into a polyp, it reproduces asexually, duplicating itself and becoming ephyra. Ephyra then grow into adult jellyfish and start sexual reproduction once again.

▶ Moving Around

Animals use a variety of techniques to move from place to place.

- Cephalopods, which include the squid and the octopus, escape from predators by forcing a powerful jet of water from a siphon near their head. Squids have been known to swim as fast as 38 km/h (23 mph)!

- Kangaroo rats have powerful hind legs that help them quickly leap away from predators. Their tail, which acts like a rudder, enables them to change course while in midair.

SECTION 2

Animal Behavior

▶ Animal Defense Strategies

Animals use a variety of methods to defend themselves from predators. Many species inject or spray toxic chemicals. Other species have a foul odor or an unpleasant taste.

- Jellyfish eject poison-tipped barbs from nematocysts on their bodies. Although most jellyfish stings can't penetrate human skin, the stings of the Portuguese man-of-war and the box jellyfish are exceptions. Stings from both species can cause extreme pain, and in rare instances, even death. Don't ever step on a dead jellyfish. The nematocysts can still sting!

- Colorful ladybugs, also known as ladybirds, protect themselves from predators by virtue of their foul smell and terrible taste.

- A type of Chrysomelid beetle has such a toxic poison that the San, a tribe living mainly in Africa's Kalahari Desert, tip their arrows with it. The poison causes death by paralysis.

- Octopuses have beaks that are used to pierce the shells of crabs and lobsters. Once the prey is pierced, the octopus injects a poison that paralyzes its prey and helps soften the meat for easy removal.

▶ Animal Migration

What mechanisms trigger animal migration? How are birds and other animals able to find their way to destinations often thousands of miles away?

- Studies performed during the 1960s produced experiments that indicated that birds use a "celestial compass" to guide them on their migratory travels.

- Ruby-throated hummingbirds, which live as far north as Canada during the summer, fly to Central America in the fall. Their route requires them to fly 833 km (500 mi) nonstop over the Gulf of Mexico.

- Topographical features such as mountain ranges emit low-frequency sounds that some scientists believe help birds such as pigeons navigate.

▶ Human Seasonal Rhythms

Seasonal affective disorder (SAD) is a form of depression that many people, especially those in northern countries, experience during the winter. Common symptoms include fatigue, sleeping more than usual, carbohydrate craving, increased appetite, and sudden weight gain. Researchers have found that many people with SAD improve when they undergo light therapy, or phototherapy.

▶ Learned and Innate Behaviors

All behaviors, innate or learned, represent an interplay of genes and the environment. We inherit the potential for innate behavior. An innate behavior is one that appears in its fully functional form the first time it is performed. Innate behavior expresses itself without prior experience. Learned behavior depends upon experience.

SECTION 3

Living Together

▶ Animal Communication

Some kinds of animals live together, and others maintain a solitary existence. Both situations offer advantages and disadvantages. Regardless of how animals live, they communicate with each other to protect themselves, to find food, to display dominance, to find mates, and for many other reasons.

- Although octopuses and squids are both cephalopods, their social habits are quite different. Whereas the octopus is a solitary creature, squids are frequently found in schools.

- Besides using a "waggle dance" to communicate the location of nectar, honeybees also communicate information about the taste and smell of food resources. They do this through the process of trophalaxis, or the regurgitation of food into the mouths of members of the colony.

IS THAT A FACT!

- ➤ Elephants have at least 25 distinct vocal calls, including the familiar trumpet that elephants make when they are excited. Elephants can also communicate dozens of messages through low-frequency, infrasonic rumbles. Such sounds can travel up to 9.5 km.

- ➤ Antelopes raise their tail and release a warning scent to communicate danger to the herd.

For background information about teaching strategies and issues, refer to the *Professional Reference for Teachers.*

CHAPTER

1

Animals and Behavior

Sections

Pre-Reading Questions

1. What characteristics make an animal different from a plant?

2. How do animals know when to migrate?

2

Pre-Reading Questions

Students may not know the answers to these questions before reading the chapter, so accept any reasonable response.

Students may not know the answers to these questions before reading the chapter, so accept any reasonable response.

Suggested Answers

Possible answers include the following:

1. Animals are consumers, and plants are producers.

2. Biological clocks control seasonal migration. Animals also migrate when food is in short supply.

GOTCHA!

This spider needs to eat in order to survive. On the other hand, this bumblebee needs to avoid being eaten. It has to escape in order to survive. How do the spider, the bumblebee, and other animals get what they need in order to live? In this chapter you will learn what it means to be an animal. You will also learn how animals live, reproduce, and behave.

GO ON A SAFARI!

You don't have to travel far to see interesting animals. If you look closely, you are sure to find animals nearby.

Procedure

1. Go outside and find **two different animals** to observe.

2. Without disturbing the animals, sit quietly and watch them for a few minutes from a distance. You may want to use **binoculars** or a **magnifying lens.**

   Caution: Always be careful around animals that may bite or sting. Do not handle animals that are unfamiliar to you.

3. Write down everything you notice about each animal. What kind of animal is it? What does it look like? How big is it? What is it doing? You may want to draw a picture of it.

Analysis

4. Compare the animals that you studied. How are they similar? How are they different?

5. How do the animals move? Did you see them communicating with other animals or defending themselves?

6. Can you tell what each animal eats? What characteristics of each animal help it find or catch food?

3

START-UP Activity

GO ON A SAFARI!

MATERIALS
For Each Group: • binoculars or magnifying glass

Safety Caution

Remind students to review all safety cautions and icons before beginning this lab activity. Students must be careful when handling the magnifying glass. Magnified sunlight should never be focused on people, animals, or flammable materials. Injuries or a fire could result. Students should observe animals from a distance and should be especially careful with animals that could bite or sting. Students allergic to insect bites or bee stings should avoid contact with these animals and receive immediate medical attention if stung.

Students should also avoid hazards, such as poisonous plants, holes, cliffs, water, cars, glass, and other dangers.

Teacher's Notes

This activity will work best with small groups. If possible, try to have your leading science students evenly dispersed among the groups.

Answers to START-UP Activity

4. Answers will vary, but students may refer to characteristics such as the way the animals moved, what they were eating, and their body type.

5. Answers will vary.

6. Answers will vary.

Focus

What Is an Animal?

This section provides students with an introduction to the animal kingdom. Students will find out the difference between vertebrates and invertebrates and will learn how scientists classify animals. Students will also discover the characteristics that set animals apart from all other living things.

 **Bellringer**

While you are taking attendance, ask students to ponder this question:

What is the best material for washing a car—a cotton rag, a scratch pad, or an animal skeleton?

Have them take a few moments to record their answer in their ScienceLog. Before you begin the section, call on individual students to give their answer and reasoning. (It may surprise some students to learn that genuine sponges–ones that some people use for washing cars–are animal skeletons. During the process of preparing sponges, all tissue is removed from the animals, leaving only skeletal remains. Although there are about 5,000 sponge species, fewer than 20 of them are of any commercial value.)

 Teaching Transparency 54
"The Animal Kingdom"

 Directed Reading Worksheet Section 1

Terms to Learn

vertebrate	tissue
invertebrate	organ
embryo	consumer

What You'll Do

◆ Describe the differences between vertebrates and invertebrates.
◆ Explain the characteristics of animals.

Figure 1 *This natural sponge used to be alive.*

What Is an Animal?

What do you think of when you hear the word *animal*? You may think of your dog or cat. You may think about giraffes or grizzly bears or other creatures you've seen in zoos or on television. But would you think about a sponge? Natural bath sponges, like the one in **Figure 1**, are the remains of an animal that lived in the ocean!

Animals come in many different shapes and sizes. Some have four legs and fur, but most do not. Some are too small to be seen without a microscope, and others are bigger than a car. But they are all part of the fascinating world of animals.

The Animal Kingdom

Scientists have named about 1 million species of animals. How many different kinds of animals do you see in **Figure 2**? It may surprise you to learn that in addition to sponges, sea anemones and corals are also animals. So are spiders, fish, birds, and dolphins. Slugs, whales, kangaroos, and humans are animals too. Scientists have divided all these animal species into about 35 phyla and classes.

Most animals look nothing like humans. However, we do share characteristics with a group of animals called vertebrates. Any animal with a skull and a backbone is a **vertebrate.** Vertebrates include fishes, amphibians, reptiles, birds, and mammals.

Figure 2 *All of the living things in this picture are classified as animals. Do they look like animals to you?*

 **SCIENCE HUMOR**

A snail knocked on a man's door and asked for a donation to a snail charity. The man didn't like solicitors and kicked the snail off his porch. Ten years later, the snail knocked on the door again and said, "That wasn't a very nice thing to do!"

Even though you are probably most familiar with vertebrates, we are definitely the minority among living things. Less than five percent of known animal species are vertebrates. Take a look at **Figure 3.** As you can see, the great majority of known animal species are insects, snails, jellyfish, worms, and other **invertebrates,** animals without backbones. In fact, more than one-fourth of all animal species are beetles!

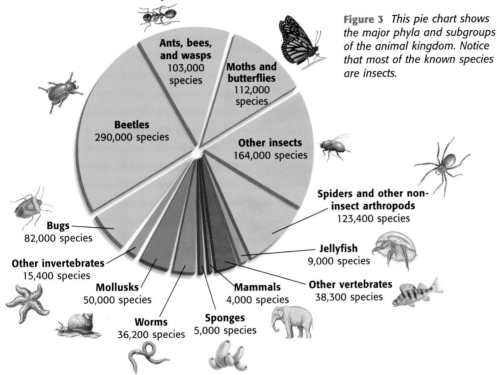

Figure 3 *This pie chart shows the major phyla and subgroups of the animal kingdom. Notice that most of the known species are insects.*

Ants, bees, and wasps
103,000 species

Moths and butterflies
112,000 species

Beetles
290,000 species

Other insects
164,000 species

Spiders and other non-insect arthropods
123,400 species

Bugs
82,000 species

Jellyfish
9,000 species

Other invertebrates
15,400 species

Mollusks
50,000 species

Mammals
4,000 species

Other vertebrates
38,300 species

Worms
36,200 species

Sponges
5,000 species

That's an Animal?

Sponges don't look like other animals. Indeed, until about 200 years ago, most people thought sponges were plants. Earthworms don't look anything like penguins, and no one would confuse a frog for a lion. So why do we say all these things are animals? What determines whether something is an animal, a plant, or something else?

There is no single answer. But all animals share characteristics that set them apart from all other living things.

Animals have many cells. All animals are *multicellular,* which means they are made of many cells. Your own body contains about 13 trillion cells. Animal cells are eukaryotic, and they do not have cell walls. Animal cells are surrounded by cell membranes only.

5

GROUP ACTIVITY

Writing To explore the diversity of the animal kingdom, have students work in groups of four. Each group will write down examples for each of the following:

- 2 Arctic animals (penguin is incorrect)
- 2 Antarctic animals (polar bear is incorrect)
- 2 animals that crawl
- 2 animals that fly
- 2 animals with no bones
- 2 African animals
- 2 North American animals
- 2 animals that live in the soil
- 2 ocean animals
- 2 animals with more than four legs

Answers should be as specific as possible. For example, they should answer "garter snake," not "snake," or "praying mantis" instead of "insect." Have each group share its answers while other groups cross out matches on their own page. How many animals did the class think of? That's diversity!

Science Skills Worksheet
"Introduction to Graphs"

internet**connect**

SC**LINKS** NSTA

TOPIC: Vertebrates and Invertebrates
GO TO: www.scilinks.org
*sci*LINKS NUMBER: HSTL330

Focus

Animal Behavior

This section introduces students to animal behavior. Students will see how animals find food and defend themselves from predators. They will discover the difference between innate and learned behavior. Finally, they will learn some of the ways animals communicate, why animal behaviors change at different times of the year, and how an animal's biological clock controls its circadian rhythms and other cycles.

Bellringer

Ask students to write a sentence for each of the following terms:

predator and *prey*

After each sentence have students list three animals that are predators and three that are prey.

- Predators hunt for their food. A list of predators might include alligators, sharks, spiders, lions, wolves, rattlesnakes, and eagles.
- Prey stay alert to avoid being eaten. A list of prey might include mice, rabbits, pigeons, flies, and deer. Sheltered English

Directed Reading Worksheet Section 2

Terms to Learn

predator	hibernation
prey	estivation
innate behavior	biological clock
learned behavior	circadian rhythm

What You'll Do

◆ Explain the difference between learned and innate behavior.
◆ Explain the difference between hibernation and estivation.
◆ Give examples of how a biological clock influences behavior.
◆ Describe circadian rhythms.
◆ Explain how animals navigate.

Animal Behavior

In the last section, you learned the characteristics that help us recognize an animal. One characteristic of most animals is that they move. Animals jump, run, fly, dart, scurry, slither, and glide. But animals don't move just for the sake of moving. They move for a reason. They run from enemies. They climb for food. They build homes. Even the tiniest mite can actively stalk its dinner, battle for territory, or migrate. All of these activities are known as behavior.

Survival Behavior

In order to stay alive, an animal has to do many things. It must find food and water, avoid being eaten, and have a place to live. Animals have many behaviors that help them accomplish these tasks.

Looking for Lunch Animals use many different methods to find or catch food. Owls swoop down on unsuspecting mice. Bees fly from flower to flower collecting nectar. Koala bears climb trees to get eucalyptus leaves. Jellyfish harpoon and lasso their prey with their tentacles. Some animals, such as the chimpanzee shown in **Figure 8,** use tools to get dinner. Whatever the meal of choice, animals have adapted to their surroundings so that they can obtain the most food using the least amount of energy.

Figure 8 *Chimpanzees make and use tools in order to get ants and other food out of hard-to-reach places.*

How to Avoid Being Eaten Animals that eat other animals are known as **predators.** The animal being eaten is the **prey.** At any given moment, an animal *diner* can become another animal's *dinner.* Therefore, animals looking for food often have to think about other things besides which food looks or tastes the best. Animals will pass up a good meal if it's too dangerous to get. But being careful is just one method of defense. Keep reading to find out what other things animals do to stay alive.

IS THAT A FACT!

Zoo keepers and pet owners have found that when they challenge their animals to search for food, the animals' appetites improve and their activity level and alertness increases. In addition, the animals genuinely seem to enjoy the search. At one zoo, the polar bears appeared downright depressed until keepers began to hide their food and freeze their fish in big buckets of solid ice. Working for their food simulated the hunting the bears would do in the wild, perhaps alleviating some of the stress of captivity.

Hiding Out One way to avoid being eaten is to be hard to see. A rabbit often "freezes" so that its natural color blends into a background of shrubs or grass. Blending in with the background is called *camouflage*. Many animals mimic twigs, leaves, stones, bark, or other materials in their environment. The insect called a walking stick looks just like a twig. Some walking sticks even sway a bit, as though a breeze were blowing. See **Figure 9** for another example of camouflage.

In Your Face The horns of a bull and the spines of a porcupine clearly signal trouble to a potential predator, but other defenses may not be as obvious. For example, animals may defend themselves with chemicals. The skunk and the bombardier beetle both spray predators with irritating chemicals. Bees, ants, and wasps inject a powerful acid into their attackers. The skin of both the South American dart-poison frog and the hooded pito-hui bird of New Guinea contains a deadly toxin. Any predator that eats, or even tries to eat, one of these animals will likely die.

Warning! Animals with a chemical defense need a way to warn predators that they should look elsewhere for a meal. Their chemical weapons are often advertised by the animal's outer covering, which has a bright design called *warning coloration*, as shown in **Figure 10**. Predators will avoid any animal with the colors and patterns they associate with pain, illness, or other unpleasant experiences. The most common warning colors are vivid shades of red, yellow, orange, black, and white.

Figure 9 *This is a picture of a caterpillar camouflaged as a twig. Can you find the caterpillar?*

Octopuses are camouflage experts. They can change the color of their entire body in less than 1 second.

Figure 10 *The warning coloration of the hooded pitohui warns predators that it is poisonous. The yellow and black stripes of the stinging yellow jacket are another example.*

9

WEIRD SCIENCE

The pitohui is one of the very few poisonous birds. This is not the only unusual thing about the colorful, foul-smelling bird, however. The poison that the bird emits—homobatrachotoxin—is the same poison made by the New World strawberry dart-poison frog. How can two species that are so different produce the same poison? Scientists are now exploring the mystery.

DEMONSTRATION

Sign Language Learn five basic signs in Sign Language, and demonstrate them for the class. Choose words such as *hungry, sad, angry, tired,* and *happy.*

Tell students that because of our innate language ability, it's possible to learn another language, even a nonvocal one. But perhaps humans aren't the only species with this ability. Koko, a gorilla, learned more than 500 different signs while in captivity. She even created some of her own signs, such as "finger bracelet" for "ring." Once, her trainer became frustrated because Koko was not cooperating. The trainer signed "bad gorilla," and Koko corrected her by signing "funny gorilla." Koko fibbed at times to avoid getting in trouble and insulted trainers when she was angry. She even had her own kitten, a tiny tailless cat that she named All Ball. **Sheltered English**

 **PG 124**

Aunt Flossie and the Bumblebee

GUIDED PRACTICE

Writing Have students observe the eating habits of animals near their home over a period of a week or so. Have them record their observations in their ScienceLog.

What did the bumblebee do to Aunt Flossie? Find out on page 124.

Why Do They Behave That Way?

How do animals know when a situation is dangerous? How do predators know which warning coloration to avoid? Sometimes animals instinctively know what to do, but sometimes they have to learn. Biologists call these two kinds of animal behavior innate behavior and learned behavior.

It's in the Genes Behavior that doesn't depend on learning or experience is known as **innate behavior.** Innate behaviors are influenced by genes. Humans inherit genes that give us the ability to walk. Puppies inherit the tendency to chew, bees the tendency to fly, and earthworms the tendency to burrow.

Some innate behaviors are present at birth. Newborn whales all have the innate ability to swim. Other innate behaviors develop months or years after birth. For example, the tendency of a bird to sing is innate. But a bird does not sing until it is nearly grown.

Figure 11 *One Japanese macaque washed the sand off a sweet potato it found on the beach. Now all of the macaques on the island wash their potatoes.*

Animal School Just because a behavior is innate does not mean that it cannot be modified. Learning can change innate behavior. **Learned behavior** is behavior that has been learned from experience or from observing other animals. Humans inherit the tendency to speak. But the language we speak is not inherited. We might learn English, Spanish, Chinese, or Tagalog.

Humans are not the only animals that modify inherited behaviors through learning. Nearly all animals can learn. For example, many young animals learn by watching their parents. **Figure 11** shows a monkey that learned a new behavior by observation.

SECTION REVIEW

1. How do innate behavior and learned behavior differ?

2. **Applying Concepts** How does the effectiveness of warning coloration for protection depend on learning?

▼ **Answers to Section Review**

1. Innate behavior is influenced by genes and does not depend on experience. Learned behavior results from experience or observation.

2. Through experience or observation of other animals, predators learn which colors are associated with painful or undesirable consequences. Once a predator learns, it can avoid animals with these warning colors.

Seasonal Behavior

In many places, animals must deal with the winter hardships of little food and bitter cold. Some avoid winter by traveling to places that are warmer. Others collect and store food. Frogs bury themselves in mud, and insects burrow into the ground.

World Travelers When food is scarce because of winter or drought, many animals migrate. To *migrate* is to travel from one place to another. Animals migrate to find food, water, or safe nesting grounds. Whales, salmon, bats, and even chimpanzees migrate. Each winter, monarch butterflies, shown in **Figure 12,** gather in central Mexico from all over North America to wait for spring. And each year, birds in the Northern Hemisphere fly thousands of kilometers south. In the spring, they return north to nest.

Slowing Down Some animals deal with food and water shortages by hibernating. **Hibernation** is a period of inactivity and decreased body temperature that some animals experience in winter. Hibernating animals survive on stored body fat. Many animals hibernate, including mice, squirrels, and skunks. While an animal hibernates, its temperature, heart rate, and breathing rate drop. Some hibernating animals drop their body temperature to a few degrees above freezing and do not wake for weeks at a time. Other animals, like the polar bears in **Figure 13,** do not enter deep hibernation. Their body temperature does not drop as severely, and they sleep for shorter periods of time.

Winter is not the only time that resources can be scarce. Many desert squirrels and mice experience a similar internal slowdown in the hottest part of the summer, when they run low on water and food. This period of reduced activity in the summer is called **estivation.**

Figure 12 *When the monarchs gather in Mexico, there can be as many as 4 million butterflies per acre!*

Don't wake the bats!
Read about the effects of humans on bat hibernation on page 24.

Figure 13 *Bears do not enter deep hibernation. However, they have periods of inactivity in which they do not eat, and their body functions slow down.*

11

MEETING INDIVIDUAL NEEDS

Writing **Learners Having Difficulty** In a given temperate region, different animals have different ways of surviving cold winters. Have students list as many behaviors or adaptations for winter survival that they can think of.
Sheltered English

MATH and MORE

It's hard not to perceive sloths as lazy. However, their slow movement makes them almost invisible to predators and saves energy, too. You may envy the sleeping patterns of sloths; they sleep 15 to 18 hours a day!

Ask: What is the average number of hours a sloth spends asleep each day? (16.5 hours)

Ask: What percentage of the day does the sloth spend asleep? (69 percent)

Math Skills Worksheet "Average, Mode, and Median"

 internetconnect

SCiLINKS
NSTA

TOPIC: Animal Behavior
GO TO: www.scilinks.org
*sci*LINKS **NUMBER:** HSTL335

WEIRD SCIENCE

Snakes are normally solitary creatures, but they will often group together in underground pits while hibernating. Hundreds or even thousands of snakes may spend the winter together in these hibernaculums. Why do they do it? Perhaps there is some protection from the cold in a group. (The protection would be limited, though, because snakes are ectotherms.) Or maybe it makes finding a mate much easier in the spring.

3) Extend

QuickLab

MATERIALS

FOR EACH PAIR:
• stopwatch

Answers to QuickLab

Answers will vary. Students should explain their answer using the concept of biological clocks.

GOING FURTHER

Writing **Maritime Navigation**
Have students write a report about maritime navigation. Tell students to include a comparison of the instruments that were used 100 years ago and their modern counterparts. Their report should also explain how ancient people navigated.

PORTFOLIO

CONNECT TO
EARTH SCIENCE

Use the following Teaching Transparency to guide a student discussion about direction, mapping, and navigation.

Teaching Transparency 104
"Finding Direction on Earth"

LINK TO EARTH SCIENCE

How Long Is a Minute?

Do you have an internal clock that helps you keep track of time? Pair up with a classmate. Your partner will start a **stopwatch** and say, "Go." When you think a minute has passed, say, "Stop!" Check the time. Try several times, and keep a record of your results. Then trade places and let your partner try. Were the recorded times close to a minute? Did your performance improve? Try again, using your pulse or your breathing as a guide. Were these times closer? Do you think you have an internal clock? Explain.

The Rhythms of Life

Humans need clocks and calendars to tell us when to get up and go to school, when a movie starts, and when it is someone's birthday. Other animals need to know when to store food and when to fly south for the winter. The internal clocks and calendars that animals use are called biological clocks. A **biological clock** is the internal control of natural cycles. Animals may use clues from their surroundings, such as the length of the day and the temperature, to set their clocks.

Some biological clocks keep track of very small amounts of time. Other biological clocks control daily cycles. These daily cycles are called **circadian rhythms.** *Circadian* means "around the day." Most animals wake up at about the same time each day and get sleepy at about the same time each night. This is an example of a circadian rhythm.

Some biological clocks control even longer cycles. Seasonal cycles are nearly universal among animals. Animals hibernate at certain times of the year and breed at other times. And every spring, migrating birds head north. Biological clocks control all of these cycles.

How Do Animals Find Their Way?

If you were planning a trip, you'd probably consult a map. If you were hiking, you might rely on a compass or trail markers to find your way. When it's time to migrate, how do animals, such as the arctic terns in **Figure 14,** know which way to go? They must *navigate,* or find their way from one place to another.

Figure 14 *Each year, arctic terns make a 38,000 km round trip from the Northern Hemisphere to Antarctica.*

internetconnect

SCiLINKS
NSTA

TOPIC: The Rhythms of Life
GO TO: www.scilinks.org
*sci*LINKS **NUMBER:** HSTL340

MISCONCEPTION
ALERT

Be sure that students understand that *hibernation* and *sleep* are not synonymous terms. Point out that animals do not hibernate continuously through the winter. They have periods that may last for days or weeks when their temperature rises to normal.

Jet Lag

When people travel to places that are in a different time zone, they frequently suffer from "jet lag." Here's an example: New York time is 6 hours behind Paris time. A traveler from New York who is staying in Paris is suffering from jet lag. She goes to bed at 10 P.M., Paris time, but she wakes up at midnight, unable to fall back asleep. She lies awake all night and finally falls asleep at about 6 A.M., one hour before her alarm rings. How might circadian rhythms explain her jet lag? When it is 10 P.M. in Paris, what time is it in New York?

Take a Left at the Post Office For short trips, many animals, including humans, use landmarks to navigate. *Landmarks* are fixed objects that an animal uses to find its way. For example, once you see the corner gas station six blocks from your house, you know how to go the rest of the way. The gas station is a landmark for you.

Bees and pigeons have a kind of mental map of landmarks in their home territory. Birds use mountain ranges, rivers, and coastlines to find their way home. Humans and other animals also navigate short distances by using a mental image of an area. Not all landmarks are visual. Blind people can navigate precisely through a familiar house because they know where everything is and how long it takes to cross a room. Pigeons navigate in their home area based on smell as well as sight.

Compass Anyone? Like human sailors, animals use the position of the sun and stars as a map. But some animals, such as migratory birds, have other methods of finding their way. They navigate using the Earth's magnetic field. You can read about this in the Physics Connection at right.

Physics
CONNECTION

Earth's core acts as a giant magnet, with magnetic north and south poles. The strength and direction of the Earth's magnetic field varies from place to place, and many birds use this variation as a map. Some migratory birds have tiny magnetic crystals of magnetite in their heads above their nostrils. Biologists think that the crystals somehow move or stimulate nerves so that a bird knows its position.

SECTION REVIEW

1. Why do animals migrate?
2. What are three methods animals use to navigate?
3. How are hibernation and estivation similar? How are they different?
4. **Applying Concepts** Some research suggests that jet lag can be overcome by getting plenty of exposure to sunlight in the new time zone. Why might this method work?

internetconnect

*sci*LINKS
NSTA

TOPIC: Animal Behavior, The Rhythms of Life
GO TO: www.scilinks.org
*sci*LINKS NUMBER: HSTL335, HSTL340

13

▼ ***Answers to Section Review***

1. Animals migrate to escape difficult conditions, such as cold weather or a shortage of food or water.
2. Animals may use landmarks, the sun and stars, or Earth's magnetic field to help them navigate.
3. Both hibernation and estivation are periods of inactivity that allow some animals to survive when food is scarce. Hibernation occurs in the winter, but estivation occurs in the summer.
4. Spending time in sunlight may act as an environmental cue that helps the body's biological clock adjust to the cycles of day and night in the new time zone and overcome jet lag.

SECTION 3
READING WARM-UP

Living Together

Focus

Living Together

In this section students will discover some of the ways that animals communicate with each other. They will explore how animals signal intentions and information to other animals through smell, sound, sight, and touch. Students will also learn about the advantages and disadvantages of living in a group.

Bellringer

As you are taking attendance, play a tape of humpback-whale songs. Ask students to offer suggestions related to what information the whales might be communicating. Your library might be a good source for whale tapes. Examples of whale songs can also be found on the Internet.

Terms to Learn

social behavior
communication
territory
pheromone

What You'll Do

- Discuss ways that animals communicate.
- List the advantages and disadvantages of living in groups.

Most animals do not live alone; they associate with other animals. When animals interact, it may be in large groups or one on one. Animals may work together, or they may compete with one another. All of this behavior is called social behavior. **Social behavior** is the interaction between animals of the same species. Whether friendly or hostile, all social behavior requires communication.

Communication

Imagine what life would be like if people could not talk or read. There would be no telephones, no televisions, no books, and no Internet. The world would certainly be a lot different! Language is an important way for humans to communicate. In **communication,** a signal must travel from one animal to another, and the receiver of the signal must respond in some way.

Communication helps animals live together, find food, avoid enemies, and protect their homes. Animals communicate to warn others of danger, to identify family members, to frighten predators, and to find mates. Some of the most dramatic uses of communication are courtship displays. *Courtship* is special behavior by animals of the same species that leads to mating. **Figure 15** shows two cranes performing a courtship display.

Animals also communicate to protect their living space. Many animals defend a **territory,** an area that is occupied by one animal or a group of animals and that other members of the species are excluded from. Many species, such as the wolves in **Figure 16,** use their territories for mating, finding food, and raising young.

Figure 15 *Japanese ground cranes perform an elaborate courtship dance.*

Figure 16 *These wolves are howling to discourage neighboring wolves from invading their territory.*

14

1 Motivate

ACTIVITY

Nonverbal Communication
Play a game of charades with students to demonstrate the importance of nonverbal communication among humans and other animals. Allow the class to provide feedback after a student guesses successfully.
Sheltered English

 Directed Reading Worksheet Section 3

IS THAT A FACT!

Vampire bats are one of the few animals in the world that will share a meal with unrelated colony members—a truly altruistic behavior. These bats must consume 50–100 percent of their weight in blood each night (usually from cows or horses). If a bat misses a meal two nights in a row, it will die. As many as a third of the bats go without eating each night, yet few bats starve. A hungry bat will lick the wings of another bat, which in response usually regurgitates some of its meal to help the other bat survive.

How Do Animals Communicate?

Animals communicate by signaling intentions and information to other animals through smell, sound, vision, and touch. Most animal signals tend to be simple compared with those that we use. But no matter which signal is used, it must convey specific information.

Do You Smell Trouble? One method of communication is chemical. Even single-celled organisms communicate with one another by means of chemicals. In animals, these chemicals are called **pheromones** (FER uh MOHNZ).

Ants and other insects secrete a variety of pheromones. For example, alarm substances released into the air alert other members of the species to danger. Trail substances are left along a path so that others can follow to find food and return to the nest. Recognition odors on an ant's body announce which colony an ant is from. Such a message signals both friends and enemies, depending on who is receiving the message.

Many animals, including vertebrates, use pheromones to attract or influence members of the opposite sex. Amazingly, elephants and insects use some of the same pheromones to attract mates. Queen butterflies, like the one in **Figure 17,** use pheromones during their courtship displays.

Do You Hear What I Hear? Animals also communicate by making noises. Wolves howl. Dolphins and whales use whistles and complex clicking noises to communicate with others. Male birds may sing songs in the spring to claim their territory or attract a mate.

Sound is a signal that can reach a large number of animals over a large area. Elephants communicate with other elephants kilometers away using rumbles at a frequency too low for most humans to hear, as described in **Figure 18.** Humpback whales sing songs that can be heard for kilometers.

Figure 17 *Queen butterflies use pheromones as part of their courtship display.*

Figure 18 *Elephants communicate with low-pitched sounds that humans cannot hear. When an elephant is communicating this way, the skin on its forehead flutters.*

15

IS THAT A FACT!

Research shows that baleen-whale sounds, which scientists believe are produced by the larynx, may be the loudest sounds produced by any animal on land or in the sea. Such sounds may carry hundreds of kilometers underwater.

internetconnect

SCiLINKS **NSTA**

TOPIC: Communication in the Animal Kingdom
GO TO: www.scilinks.org
***sci*LINKS NUMBER:** HSTL345

2 Teach

CROSS-DISCIPLINARY FOCUS

Geography Dolphins are usually thought of as ocean animals, but there is a group of small dolphins that live in fresh water in many of the world's largest rivers. River dolphins are different from their marine relatives in that they have poor eyesight and huge numbers of pointed teeth. In addition, they swim on their sides or even upside down. Have students locate on a map or globe the following rivers and coastal areas where river dolphins live: the Ganges River (India), the Indus River (Pakistan), the Yangtze River (China), the Amazon River (Brazil), the estuaries of the La Plata River (the Atlantic coast of South America) and of the Tucuxi River (the northeastern coast of South America).

MEETING INDIVIDUAL NEEDS

Learners Having Difficulty
Some students may not realize how often humans use nonverbal communication or the importance of such methods in negotiating even the mundane events of everyday life. Ask students how each of these nonverbal communication methods provides essential information:

smell (what's cooking, dangerous fumes, spoiled food)

facial expressions (friend or foe, surprise, fear, apprehension)

sound (someone approaching, a train's warning whistle, school bells, fire alarms) **Sheltered English**

ACTIVITY

Investigate Grooming Tell students that grooming, or cleaning behavior, represents another way that animals communicate with each other through touch. Encourage students to do research about animals that communicate in this fashion. Examples include birds (preening), many mammals (mutual grooming), and certain fish (cleaning symbiosis). Students can use their research to create illustrated booklets that they can then share with the class.

GUIDED PRACTICE

Poster Project Tell students that wolves use body language called posturing to communicate with members of the pack. Have small groups of students research wolf posturing and then create illustrated charts showing various postures and what they mean. After posting the charts on the bulletin board, lead a discussion about wolf communication. Encourage students who have a pet dog to talk about the similarities and the differences between the body language used by their pet and the body language used by wolves. Sheltered English

[Teaching Transparency 55]
"The Dance of the Bees"

Figure 19 *When dogs want to play, they drop down on their forelegs.*

Showing Off Many forms of communication are visual. When we wink at a friend or frown at an opponent, we are communicating with *body language.* Other animals are no different. **Figure 19** shows one way dogs use body language.

An animal that wants to scare another animal may do something that makes it appear larger. It may ruffle its feathers or fur or open its mouth and show its teeth. Visual displays are also important in courtship. Fireflies blink complex signals in the dark to attract one another.

Getting in Touch An animal may also use touch to communicate, like the honeybee does. A honeybee that finds a patch of flowers rich in nectar returns to its hive to tell fellow workers where the flowers are. Inside the dark hive, the bee communicates by performing a complex figure-eight dance, as shown below, which the other bees learn by observation and touch.

The Dance of the Bees

Honeybees do a "waggle dance" to tell other bees where they've found nectar. As the bee goes through the middle of the figure eight, it communicates two things: the direction of the nectar and the distance to the nectar from the hive. Other worker bees gather closely around the dancing bee to learn the dance. By learning the dance, the bees learn the direction to the nectar.

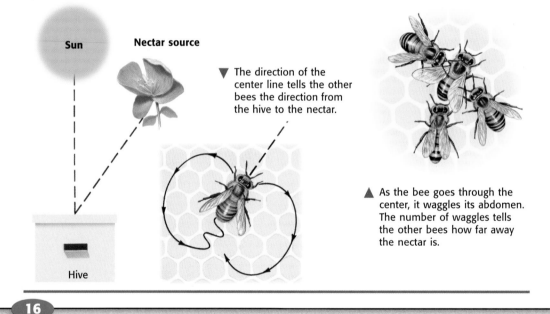

Sun

Nectar source

▼ The direction of the center line tells the other bees the direction from the hive to the nectar.

Hive

▲ As the bee goes through the center, it waggles its abdomen. The number of waggles tells the other bees how far away the nectar is.

Homework

Writing **Research Ant Behavior** Have students research the behavior of ants. How do they organize the work of their colony? Several species of ants enslave other species. Have students investigate how one species of ant manages to capture and control another species.

Part of the Family

Tigers live alone. Except for the time a mother tiger spends with her cubs, a tiger meets other tigers rarely and for very short periods. Yet the tiger's closest relative, the lion, is rarely alone. Lions live in groups called prides. The members of a pride sleep together, hunt together, and raise their cubs together. **Figure 20** shows two lions at work. Why do some animals live in groups, while others live apart?

Figure 20 *This pair of lions cooperates to hunt a gazelle.*

The Benefits of Living in a Group Living with other animals is much safer than living alone. Large groups can spot a predator or other dangers quickly, and groups of animals can cooperate to defend themselves. For example, if a predator threatens them, a herd of musk oxen will circle their young with their horns pointed outward. Honeybees attack by the thousands when another animal tries to take their honey.

Living together can also help animals find food. Tigers and other animals that hunt alone can usually kill only animals that are smaller than themselves. In contrast, lions, wolves, hyenas, and other predators that hunt cooperatively can kill much larger prey.

The Downside of Living in a Group Living in groups causes problems as well. Animals living in groups attract predators, so they must always be on the lookout, as shown in **Figure 21**. Groups of animals need more food, and animals in groups compete with each other for food and for mates. Individuals in groups can also give each other diseases.

Figure 21 *A ground squirrel whistles a loud alarm to alert other ground squirrels that danger is near.*

SECTION REVIEW

1. Scientists have discovered pheromones in humans. Name three other types of animal communication used by humans.

2. Why is communication important? Name three reasons.

3. **Applying Concepts** Considering what you have learned about group living, list two advantages and two disadvantages to living in a group of humans.

internetconnect

SC*LINKS*.
NSTA

TOPIC: Communication in the Animal Kingdom
GO TO: www.scilinks.org
*sci*LINKS NUMBER: HSTL345

17

▼ *Answers to Section Review*

1. Answers will vary. Humans communicate with sound when we speak and listen. We use visual displays (sight) to interpret sign language, body language, and facial expressions. We use touch when we hug and tap someone on the shoulder.

2. Communication allows members of a species to share information important

to survival. Reasons may include finding food, avoiding enemies, protecting territory, and courtship.

3. Answers will vary. Some possible advantages are protection and the ability to work together. Some possible disadvantages are increased competition, fighting, and the spread of disease.

3 Extend

MEETING INDIVIDUAL NEEDS

Writing **Advanced Learners**
Students might enjoy researching social weavers of the family Ploceidae. These small African birds cooperatively build and maintain huge, thatched-roof, apartment-like structures with as many as 300 chambers. Each chamber is occupied by one pair of birds. Students can prepare an illustrated report of their findings or write a fictional story about the cooperative efforts of the birds and the value of cooperation.

4 Close

Quiz

1. What two things must happen for communication to occur? (a signal and a response)

2. What are two of the most important kinds of animal communication? (courtship and territorial displays)

ALTERNATIVE ASSESSMENT

Concept Mapping Have students create a concept map, including all necessary linking words, using the following concepts:

communication, identify family members, pheromones, making noises, touch, courtship, defend a territory, warn about danger, body language

Discovery Lab

Wet, Wiggly Worms!
Teacher's Notes

Time Required

One 45-minute class period

Lab Ratings

EASY ——————— HARD

TEACHER PREP
STUDENT SET-UP
CONCEPT LEVEL
CLEAN UP

MATERIALS

The materials listed on the student page are enough for a group of 4–5 students.

Safety Caution

Remind students to review all safety cautions and icons before beginning this lab activity. Students may wish to wear protective gloves while handling the worms.

Gladys Cherniak
St. Paul's Episcopal School
Mobile, Alabama

Wet, Wiggly Worms!

Earthworms have been digging in the earth for more than 100 million years! Earthworms fertilize the soil with their waste and loosen the soil when they tunnel through the moist dirt of a garden or lawn. Worms are food for many animals, such as birds, frogs, snakes, rodents, and fish. Some say they are good food for people, too!

In this activity, you will observe the behavior of a live earthworm. Remember that earthworms are living animals that deserve to be handled gently. Be sure to keep your earthworm moist during this activity. The skin of the earthworm must stay moist so that the worm can get oxygen. If the earthworm's skin dries out, the worm will suffocate and die. Use a spray bottle to moisten the earthworm with water.

MATERIALS

- spray bottle
- dissecting pan
- paper towels
- water
- live earthworm
- probe
- celery leaves
- flashlight
- shoe box with lid
- clock
- soil
- metric ruler

Procedure

1. Place a wet paper towel in the bottom of a dissecting pan. Put a live earthworm on the paper towel, and observe how the earthworm moves. Record your observations in your ScienceLog.

2. Use the probe to carefully touch the anterior end (head) of the worm. Gently touch other areas of the worm's body with the probe. Record the kinds of responses you observe.

3. Shine a flashlight on the anterior end of the earthworm. Record the earthworm's reaction to the light.

4. Place celery leaves at one end of the pan. Record how the earthworm responds to the presence of food.

5. Line the bottom of the shoe box with a damp paper towel. Cover half of the shoe box with the box top.

6. Place the worm on the uncovered side of the shoe box in the light. Record your observations of the worm's behavior for 3 minutes.

7. Place the worm in the covered side of the box. Record your observations for 3 minutes.

8. Repeat steps 6–7 three times.

9. Spread some loose soil evenly in the bottom of the shoe box so that it is about 4 cm deep. Place the earthworm on top of the soil. Observe and record the earthworm's behavior for 3 minutes.

10. Dampen the soil on one side of the box, and leave the other side dry. Place the earthworm in the center of the box between the wet and dry soil. Cover the box, and wait 3 minutes. Uncover the box, and record your observations. Repeat this procedure 3 times. (You may need to search for the worm!)

Analysis

11. How did the earthworm respond to being touched? Were some areas more sensitive than others?

12. How is the earthworm's behavior influenced by light? Based on your observations, describe how an animal's response to a stimulus might provide protection for the animal.

13. How did the earthworm respond to the presence of food?

14. When the worm was given a choice of wet or dry soil, which did it choose? Explain this result.

Going Further

Based on your observations of an earthworm's behavior, draw a conclusion about where you might expect to find earthworms. Prepare a poster that illustrates your conclusion. Draw a picture with colored markers, or cut out pictures from magazines. Include all the variables that you used in your experiment, such as soil or no soil, wet or dry soil, light or dark, and food. At the bottom of your poster, write a caption describing where earthworms might be found in nature.

Lab Notes

Earthworms are scientifically classified as animals belonging to the order Oligochaeta, class Chaetopoda, and phylum Annelida. There are about 1,800 species of earthworms. Only two of these are grown commercially. Earthworms have setae, or bristles, located on each segment that help them move. Earthworms have both male and female reproductive organs. They usually do not self-fertilize, but they do exchange sperm as they pass in their burrows. Eggs are deposited in the burrow in a cocoon. The cocoon is manufactured by the clitellum that encircles the body of the worm. Different segments of the earthworm perform different functions, just as each of our body parts do. Earthworms have from 95 to 150 segments, depending on the species.

 Datasheets for LabBook

19

Answers

11–14. Students' answers will vary according to their own observations. They will probably observe that the worm squirms when touched and that some areas are more sensitive than others, such as the clitellum. Students will probably observe that earthworms avoid light. Students should describe the worm's behavior as self-protective.

Going Further

Students' posters should describe warm, wet soil, darkness, and partially decayed organic matter for food.

Chapter Highlights

Chapter Highlights

VOCABULARY DEFINITIONS

SECTION 1

vertebrate an animal with a skull and a backbone; examples include mammals, birds, reptiles, amphibians, and fish

invertebrate an animal without a backbone

embryo an organism in the earliest stage of development

tissue a group of similar cells that work together to perform a specific job in the body

organ a combination of two or more tissues that work together to perform a specific function in the body

consumer organisms that eat producers or other organisms for energy

SECTION 2

predator an animal that eats other animals

prey an organism that is eaten by another organism

innate behavior a behavior that is influenced by genes and does not depend on learning or experience

SECTION 1

Vocabulary

   vertebrate *(p. 4)*
   invertebrate *(p. 5)*
   embryo *(p. 6)*
   tissue *(p. 6)*
   organ *(p. 6)*
   consumer *(p. 7)*

Section Notes

- Animals with a skull and a backbone are vertebrates. Animals without a backbone are invertebrates.

- Animals are multicellular. Their cells are eukaryotic and lack a cell wall.

- Most animals reproduce sexually and develop from embryos.

- Most animals have tissues and organs.

- Most animals move.

- Animals are consumers.

SECTION 2

Vocabulary

   predator *(p. 8)*
   prey *(p. 8)*
   innate behavior *(p. 10)*
   learned behavior *(p. 10)*
   hibernation *(p. 11)*
   estivation *(p. 11)*
   biological clock *(p. 12)*
   circadian rhythm *(p. 12)*

Section Notes

- Many animals use camouflage, chemicals, or both to defend themselves against predators.

- Behavior may be classified as innate or learned. The potential for innate behavior is inherited. Learned behavior depends on experience.

- Some animals migrate to find food, water, or safe nesting grounds.

- Some animals hibernate in the winter, and some estivate in the summer.

☑ Skills Check

Math Concepts

TIME DIFFERENCE In the Apply on page 13, you considered how the time difference between New York and Paris could explain jet lag. Paris time is 6 hours later than New York time. If it is 10 P.M. in Paris, subtract 6 hours to get New York time.

$$10 - 6 = 4$$

It is 4 P.M. in New York. Similarly, when it is 7 A.M. in Paris, it is 1 A.M. in New York.

Visual Understanding

THE DANCE OF THE BEES The illustration on page 16 shows how bees use the waggle dance to communicate the location of a nectar source. Notice the position of the sun in relation to the hive and the nectar source. The bee communicates this information by the direction of the center line in the dance.

20

Lab and Activity Highlights

Wet, Wiggly Worms! `PG 19`

Aunt Flossie and the Bumblebee `PG 124`

Datasheets for LabBook (blackline masters for these labs)

learned behavior a behavior that has been learned from experience or observation

hibernation a period of inactivity that some animals experience in winter; allows them to survive on stored body fat

estivation a period of reduced activity that some animals experience in the summer

biological clock an internal control of natural cycles

circadian rhythm daily cycle

SECTION 3

social behavior the interaction between animals of the same species

communication a transfer of a signal from one animal to another that results in some type of response

territory an area occupied by one animal or a group of animals from which other members of the species are excluded

pheromone a chemical produced by animals for communication

SECTION 2

- Animals have internal biological clocks to control natural cycles.

- Daily cycles are called circadian rhythms.

- Some biological clocks are regulated by cues from an animal's environment.

- Animals navigate close to home using landmarks and a mental image of their home area.

- Some animals use the positions of the sun and stars or Earth's magnetic field to navigate.

Labs

Aunt Flossie and the Bumblebee *(p. 124)*

SECTION 3

Vocabulary

social behavior *(p. 14)*

communication *(p. 14)*

territory *(p. 14)*

pheromone *(p. 15)*

Section Notes

- Communication must include both a signal and a response.

- Two important kinds of communication are courtship and territorial displays.

- Animals communicate through sight, sound, touch, and smell.

- Group living allows animals to spot both prey and predators more easily.

- Groups of animals are more visible to predators than are individuals, and animals in groups must compete with one another for food and mates.

---

 internetconnect

GO TO: go.hrw.com

Visit the **HRW** Web site for a variety of learning tools related to this chapter. Just type in the keyword:

KEYWORD: HSTANM

SCiLINKS
NSTA

GO TO: www.scilinks.org

Visit the **National Science Teachers Association** on-line Web site for Internet resources related to this chapter. Just type in the *sci*LINKS number for more information about the topic:

TOPIC: Vertebrates and Invertebrates   *sci*LINKS NUMBER: HSTL330
TOPIC: Animal Behavior   *sci*LINKS NUMBER: HSTL335
TOPIC: The Rhythms of Life   *sci*LINKS NUMBER: HSTL340
TOPIC: Communication in the Animal Kingdom   *sci*LINKS NUMBER: HSTL345

21

 Vocabulary Review Worksheet

Blackline masters of these Chapter Highlights can be found in the **Study Guide.**

Lab and Activity Highlights

LabBank

Inquiry Labs, Follow the Leader

Whiz-Bang Demonstrations, Six-Legged Thermometer

Long-Term Projects & Research Ideas, Animal-Myth Behaviors

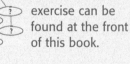
Chapter Review

To complete the following sentences, choose the correct term from each pair of terms listed below:

1. An animal with a skull and a backbone is __?__. An animal with no backbone is __?__. *(an invertebrate or a vertebrate)*

2. A behavior that does not depend on experience is __?__. *(innate or learned)*

3. In the summer, an animal enters a state of reduced activity. The animal is __?__. *(estivating or hibernating)*

4. Daily cycles are known as __?__. *(biological clocks or circadian rhythms)*

5. When an egg and a sperm come together, they form __?__. *(an embryo or an organ)*

UNDERSTANDING CONCEPTS

Multiple Choice

6. Which characteristic is not true of animals?
   a. They are multicellular.
   b. They usually reproduce sexually.
   c. They make their own food.
   d. They have tissues.

7. Living in groups
   a. attracts predators.
   b. helps prey spot predators.
   c. helps animals find food.
   d. All of the above

8. Warning coloration is
   a. a kind of camouflage.
   b. a way to warn predators away.
   c. always black and white.
   d. always a sign that an animal is poisonous to eat.

9. Some birds use Earth's magnetic field
   a. to attract mates.
   b. to navigate.
   c. to set their biological clocks.
   d. to defend their territory.

10. To defend against predators, an animal might use
    a. camouflage.   c. toxins.
    b. warning coloration. d. All of the above

Short Answer

11. How are pheromones used in communication?

12. What is a territory? Give an example of a territory from your own environment.

13. What landmarks help you navigate your way home from school?

14. What do migration and hibernation have in common?

Concept Mapping

15. Use the following terms to create a concept map: estivation, circadian rhythms, seasonal behaviors, hibernation, migration, biological clocks.

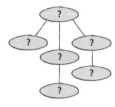

CRITICAL THINKING AND PROBLEM SOLVING

Write one or two sentences to answer the following questions:

16. If you smell a skunk while riding in a car and you shut the car window, has the skunk communicated with you? Explain.

17. Flying is an innate behavior in birds. Is it an innate behavior or a learned behavior in humans? Why?

18. Ants depend on pheromones and touch for communication, but birds depend more on sight and sound. Why might these two types of animals communicate differently?

INTERPRETING GRAPHICS

The pie chart below shows the major phyla of the animal species on Earth. Use the chart to answer the questions that follow.

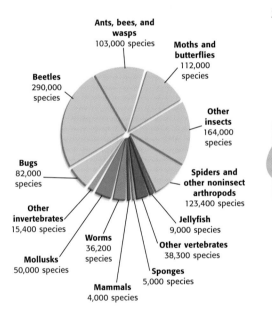

Ants, bees, and wasps
103,000 species

Moths and butterflies
112,000 species

Beetles
290,000 species

Other insects
164,000 species

Bugs
82,000 species

Spiders and other noninsect arthropods
123,400 species

Other invertebrates
15,400 species

Jellyfish
9,000 species

Worms
36,200 species

Other vertebrates
38,300 species

Mollusks
50,000 species

Sponges
5,000 species

Mammals
4,000 species

19. What group of animals has the most species? How is this shown on the chart?

20. How many species of beetles are on Earth? How does that compare with the number of mammal species?

21. How many species of vertebrates are known?

22. Scientists are still discovering new species. Which pie wedges are most likely to increase? Why do you think so?

MATH IN SCIENCE

Use the data from the pie chart to answer the following questions:

23. What is the total number of animal species on Earth?

24. How many different species of moths and butterflies are on Earth?

25. What percentage of all animal species are moths and butterflies?

26. What percentage of all animal species are vertebrates?

Reading Check-up

Take a minute to review your answers to the Pre-Reading Questions found at the bottom of page 2. Have your answers changed? If necessary, revise your answers based on what you have learned since you began this chapter.

23

Blackline masters of this Chapter Review can be found in the **Study Guide.**

CRITICAL THINKING AND PROBLEM SOLVING

16. Yes; even though you were not the intended recipient of the message, the skunk communicated with you. The skunk has sent a signal (its smell), and you have responded (by shutting the window).

17. It is a learned behavior. Humans are not born with the ability to fly, but we have learned to fly using airplanes.

18. Ants are much smaller and cannot see or hear over great distances, so they must depend on pheromones and touch for communication. Birds have better eyesight, and they can hear well and sing, so they can communicate by sound and sight.

INTERPRETING GRAPHICS

19. Beetles have the greatest number of species. Students may also list the group arthropods, which includes beetles, bugs, insects, and spiders—all of the wedges that are colored yellow. On the pie chart, this is shown by the largest wedge (or group of wedges) and by the label.

20. There are 290,00 species of beetles. There are only 4,000 species of mammals.

21. There are 42,300 vertebrate species (4,000 mammals + 38,300 other vertebrates).

22. Answers will vary, but students may suggest that new species of insects and beetles will be found. Because there are so many species in these groups, there is a greater chance that they have not all been found.

MATH IN SCIENCE

23. 1,032,300
24. 112,000
25. 10.9 percent
26. 4.1 percent

Background

Bats make up the order Chirop-tera, which means "hand wing." Bats are considered the best bug control around. For example, 20 million Mexican free-tail bats live in Bracken Cave, Texas. Each night they eat 250 tons of insects. Bats are also responsible for pollinating flowers and dispersing seeds for many plants. In Arizona, nectar-feeding bats pollinate giant cacti, such as the saguaro and organ pipe. In the rain forest, many trees and shrubs depend on bats to pollinate flowers and to disperse their seeds.

There are nearly 1,000 different species of bats. The smallest bat, the bumblebee bat of Thailand (*Craseonycteris thonglongyai*), weighs less than a penny. The largest bat, the Indonesian flying fox (*Pteropus vampyrus*), boasts a wingspan of nearly 1.8 m. Only three bats are considered vampire bats—the common vampire (*Desmodus rotundus*), the hairy-legged vampire (*Diphylla ecaudata*), and the white-winged vampire (*Diaemus youngi*). All three are found in Latin America.

EYE ON THE ENVIRONMENT

Do Not Disturb!

Did you know that bats are the only mammals that can fly? Unlike many birds, most bat species in the northern and central parts of the United States don't fly south for the winter. Instead of migrating, many bat species go into hibernation. But if their sleep is disturbed too often, the bats may die.

Long Winter's Nap

Most bats eat insects, but winter is a time of food shortage. In late summer, many North American bats begin to store up extra fat. These fat reserves help them survive the winter. For the stored fat to last until spring, bats must hibernate. They travel to caves where winter temperatures are low enough—0°C to 9.5°C—and stable enough for the bats to hibernate comfortably.

Hibernating bats' body temperature drops to almost the same temperature as the surrounding cave. Their heart rate, normally about 400 beats per minute, slows to about 25 beats per minute. With these changes, the stored fat will usually last all winter, unless human visitors wake the bats from their deep sleep. If that happens, the bats may starve to death.

No Admittance!

Even with their slowed metabolism, bats must wake up occasionally. They still need to drink water every so often. Sometimes they move to a warmer or cooler spot in the cave. But bats usually have enough fat stored so that they can wake up a few times each winter and then go back to sleep.

People visiting the caves force the bats to wake up unnecessarily. This causes the bats to use up the fat they have stored faster than they can afford. For example, a little brown bat consumes 67 days worth of stored fat each time it awakes. And with no insects around to eat, it cannot build up its fat reserve again.

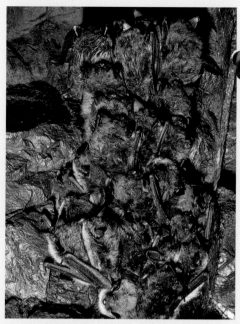

▲ *These little brown bats are roosting in a cave.*

Most species of hibernating bats can survive the winter after waking about three extra times. But frequent intrusions can lead to the death of a whole colony of bats. Thousands of these interesting and extremely beneficial mammals may die when people carelessly or deliberately disturb them as they hibernate.

Increase Your Knowledge

▶ Using the Internet or the library, find out more about bats. Learn how they are beneficial to the environment and what threatens their survival. Discuss with your classmates some ways to protect bats and their habitats.

24

Answer to Increase Your Knowledge

Answers will vary. Among other services, bats help keep insect populations under control, pollinate some plants, disperse seeds, and fertilize soil. Habitat destruction and human ignorance endanger bats. Solutions might include passing laws to protect bats and educating people about what bats do and don't do.

WEIRD SCIENCE

ANIMAL CANNIBALS

Competing, surviving, and reproducing are all part of life. And in some species, so is *cannibalism* (eating members of one's own species). But how does cannibalism relate to competing, surviving, and reproducing? It turns out that sometimes an animal's choice of food is a factor in whether its genes get passed on or not.

Picky Eaters

Tiger salamanders start life by eating zooplankton, aquatic insect larvae, and sometimes tadpoles. If conditions in their small pond include intense competition with members of their own species, some of the larger salamanders become cannibals!

Scientists are not sure why tiger salamanders become cannibals or why they usually eat nonrelatives. Scientists hypothesize that this behavior eliminates competition. By eating other salamanders, a tiger salamander reduces competition for food and improves the chances of its own survival. That increases the chances its genes will be passed on to the next generation. And eating nonrelatives helps to ensure that genes coming from the same family are more likely to be passed on to the next generation.

The Ultimate Sacrifice

Male Australian redback spiders take a different approach to making sure their genes are

▲ *During mating, male Australian redback spiders offer themselves as food to their mates.*

passed on. During mating, the male spider tumbles his body over, does a handstand, and waves his abdomen near the female's mouth, offering himself to her as a meal. The female accepts the dinner invitation if she is hungry. And it seems that about 65 percent of the time she is hungry!

Male spiders want to pass on their genes, so they compete fiercely for the females. A female redback spider wants to make sure that as many of her eggs are fertilized as possible, so she often mates with two different males. If the female eats the first male, studies show that she will not mate with a second male as often as she would if she had not eaten the first suitor. Because eating the male takes some time, more eggs are fertilized by the mate who also becomes dinner. The male spider who offers himself as a meal may then have more of his genes passed to the next generation.

On Your Own

▶ Other animals devour members of their own species. Scientists believe there are a variety of reasons for the behavior. Using the Internet or the library, research cannibalism in different animals, such as praying mantises, blue crabs, stickleback fish, black widow spiders, spadefoot toad tadpoles, and lions. Present your findings to the class.

25

Background

In a behavior related to cannibalism, some animals attempt to improve their chances of reproductive success by interfering with the reproductive cycle of their fellow species members. For example, consider a female stickleback fish that attacks the nest of a male (it is the male stickleback that tends the nest) and eats the embryos. She is more likely to have greater reproductive success because her own offspring will have less competition for food. When a lion takes over a pride, it kills the cubs so that it doesn't spend time raising and protecting young that don't carry its genes. The female lion, on the other hand, will try to protect the cubs in order to protect her genes.

Answer to On Your Own

Scientists think that cannibalism, a behavior that might appear to be detrimental to a species, may be part of a behavior adaptation called the "lifeboat strategy." Under adverse conditions, such as a scarcity of food, animals are more likely to practice cannibalism not only to feed themselves individually but also to reduce the population searching for food, which reduces competition. A good example is the blue crab, which feeds on soft-shell clams in normal circumstances. When the clams are in short supply, however, the crabs begin to eat one another. This reduces the number of crabs competing for clams and increases the chance that the species as a whole will survive.

Chapter Organizer

CHAPTER ORGANIZATION	TIME MINUTES	OBJECTIVES	LABS, INVESTIGATIONS, AND DEMONSTRATIONS
Chapter Opener pp. 26–27	45	National Standards: UCP 1, SAI 2, ST 2, SPSP 5	**Start-Up Activity,** p. 27
Section 1 Simple Invertebrates	90	▶ Describe the difference between radial and bilateral symmetry. ▶ Describe the function of a coelom. ▶ Explain how sponges are different from other animals. ▶ Describe the differences in the simple nervous systems of the cnidarians and the flatworms. UCP 1, 4, 5, SPSP 3, 4, LS 1a, 1d, 1f, 2a, 3a–3c, 4b, 5a; LabBook UCP 3, SAI 1	**Demonstration,** Sponges, p. 30 in ATE **Demonstration,** Stinging Cells, p. 33 in ATE **Skill Builder,** Porifera's Porosity, p. 50 **Datasheets for LabBook,** Porifera's Porosity
Section 2 Mollusks and Annelid Worms	90	▶ Describe the body parts of a mollusk. ▶ Explain the difference between an open circulatory system and a closed circulatory system. ▶ Describe segmentation. UCP 1–3, 5, SAI 2, SPSP 4, LS 1a, 2a, 3a, 4b, 5a;	**Inquiry Labs,** At a Snail's Pace **Labs You Can Eat,** Here's Looking at You, Squid!
Section 3 Arthropods	90	▶ List the four main characteristics of arthropods. ▶ Describe the different body parts of the four kinds of arthropods. ▶ Explain the two types of metamorphosis in insects. UCP 2, 3, 5, SAI 1, SPSP 4, LS 1a, 1d, 1f, 4b, 5a; LabBook SAI 1, LS 3c	**QuickLab,** Sticky Webs, p. 44 **Discovery Lab,** The Cricket Caper, p. 126 **Datasheets for LabBook,** The Cricket Caper
Section 4 Echinoderms	90	▶ Describe three main characteristics of echinoderms. ▶ Describe the water vascular system. UCP 5, LS 1a, 1d, 3a, 4b, 5a	**Long-Term Projects & Research Ideas,** Creepy, Crawly Food?

See page **T23** for a complete correlation of this book with the

NATIONAL SCIENCE EDUCATION STANDARDS.

TECHNOLOGY RESOURCES

Guided Reading Audio CD
English or Spanish, Chapter 2

One-Stop Planner CD-ROM with Test Generator

 CNN. **Scientists in Action,** Stopping the Termite Attack, Segment 21

CLASSROOM WORKSHEETS, TRANSPARENCIES, AND RESOURCES	SCIENCE INTEGRATION AND CONNECTIONS	REVIEW AND ASSESSMENT
Directed Reading Worksheet **Science Puzzlers, Twisters & Teasers**		
Directed Reading Worksheet, Section 1 **Critical Thinking Worksheet,** A New Form of Danger in the Deep **Reinforcement Worksheet,** Life Without a Backbone	**Multicultural Connection,** p. 28 in ATE **Real-World Connection,** p. 30 in ATE **Environment Connection,** p. 33 **Real-World Connection,** p. 34 in ATE **Weird Science:** Water Bears, p. 56	**Section Review,** p. 31 **Self-Check,** p. 33 **Homework,** p. 34 in ATE **Section Review,** p. 35 **Quiz,** p. 35 in ATE **Alternative Assessment,** p. 35 in ATE
Directed Reading Worksheet, Section 2	**MathBreak,** Speeding Squid, p. 36 **Multicultural Connection,** p. 37 in ATE **Apply,** p. 39 **Eye on the Environment:** Sizable Squid, p. 57	**Section Review,** p. 38 **Section Review,** p. 40 **Quiz,** p. 40 in ATE **Alternative Assessment,** p. 40 in ATE
Directed Reading Worksheet, Section 3 **Math Skills for Science Worksheet,** Dividing Whole Numbers with Long Division **Math Skills for Science Worksheet,** Checking Division with Multiplication **Transparency 56,** Incomplete Metamorphosis **Transparency 57,** Changing Form—Complete Metamorphosis	**Math and More,** p. 42 in ATE **Connect to Chemistry,** p. 43 in ATE	**Self-Check,** p. 43 **Section Review,** p. 46 **Quiz,** p. 46 in ATE **Alternative Assessment,** p. 46 in ATE
Directed Reading Worksheet, Section 4 **Transparency 155,** The Three Groups of Marine Life **Transparency 58,** Water Vascular System **Reinforcement Worksheet,** Spineless Variety	**Connect to Earth Science,** p. 48 in ATE	**Section Review,** p. 49 **Quiz,** p. 49 in ATE **Alternative Assessment,** p. 49 in ATE

internet connect

go.hrw.com

Holt, Rinehart and Winston On-line Resources

go.hrw.com

For worksheets and other teaching aids related to this chapter, visit the HRW Web site and type in the keyword: **HSTINV**

SCiLINKS
NSTA

National Science Teachers Association

www.scilinks.org

Encourage students to use the *sci*LINKS numbers listed in the internet connect boxes to access information and resources on the **NSTA** Web site.

END-OF-CHAPTER REVIEW AND ASSESSMENT

Chapter Review in Study Guide
Vocabulary and Notes in Study Guide
Chapter Tests with Performance-Based Assessment, Chapter 2 Test
Chapter Tests with Performance-Based Assessment, Performance-Based Assessment 2
Concept Mapping Transparency 15

Chapter Resources & Worksheets

Visual Resources

TEACHING TRANSPARENCIES

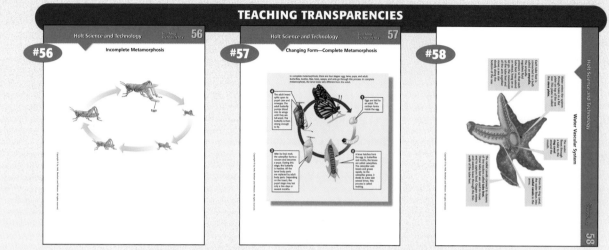

#56 — Holt Science and Technology — Teaching Transparency 56 — Incomplete Metamorphosis

#57 — Holt Science and Technology — Teaching Transparency 57 — Changing Form—Complete Metamorphosis

#58 — Holt Science and Technology — Water Vascular System — 58

TEACHING TRANSPARENCIES

#155 — Holt Science and Technology — The Three Groups of Marine Life — Phytoplankton — 155

LINK TO EARTH SCIENCE

CONCEPT MAPPING TRANSPARENCY

#15 — Holt Science and Technology — Concept Mapping 15 — **Invertebrates**

Use the following terms to complete the concept map below:
Porifera, symmetry, invertebrates, Mollusca, Annelida, snails, bilateral, sponges, coral, asymmetry

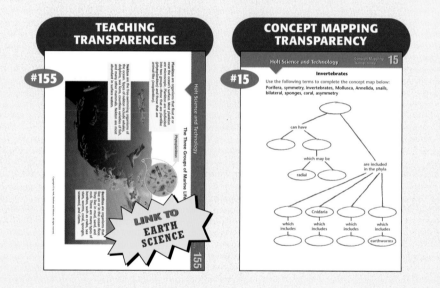

Meeting Individual Needs

DIRECTED READING

#2 — DIRECTED READING WORKSHEET — *Invertebrates*

Chapter Introduction

As you begin this chapter, answer the following.

1. Read the title of the chapter. List three things that you already know about this subject.

2. Write two questions about this subject that you would like answered by the time you finish this chapter.

Start-Up Activity (p. 27)

3. What is the purpose of this activity?

Section 1: Simple Invertebrates (p. 28)

4. There are _____ 1 million species of invertebrates on Earth. (more than or less than)

No Backbones Here! (p. 28)

5. List three features scientists use to compare different animals.

REINFORCEMENT & VOCABULARY REVIEW

#2 — REINFORCEMENT WORKSHEET — *Life Without a Backbone*

Complete this worksheet after you finish reading Chapter 14, Section 1.

What do a butterfly, a spider, a jellyfish, a worm, a snail, an octopus, and a lobster have in common? All of these animals are invertebrates. Clearly, there are many differences between these animals. Yet the most important characteristic these animals share is something none of them have—a backbone!

Despite their obvious differences, all invertebrates share some basic characteristics. Using the list of words provided, fill in the boxes with the correct answers. There will be some words that you will not use at all.

Characteristics

spicules
asymmetrical
ganglia
gut
nerve cord
bilateral symmetry
coelom
neuron
uniform
nerve networks
radial symmetry

All About Invertebrates

An invertebrate has a body plan that can have

An invertebrate might use these structures to digest its food.

An invertebrate might use one or more of the following structures to control its body movement.

#2 — VOCABULARY REVIEW WORKSHEET — *Searching for a Backbone*

After you finish Chapter 14, give this puzzle a try! Identify the word described by each clue, and write the word in the space provided. Then circle the word in the puzzle on the next page. The word may appear horizontally, vertically, or diagonally.

1. external support made of protein and chitin

2. combination of head and thorax

3. circulatory system in which blood is pumped through network of vessels

4. symmetry in which body has two similar halves

5. groups of nerve cells

6. identical or almost identical repeating body parts

7. swimming form of cnidarian

8. an animal without a backbone

9. vase-shaped form of cnidarian

10. circulatory system in which blood is pumped through sinuses

11. the change in form through which an insect grows while becoming an adult

12. without symmetry

13. three segments of arthropods

14. symmetry in which body parts are arranged in a circle

15. eye made of many identical units

16. where almost all animals digest food

17. jaws

18. the space in the body where the gut is located

19. an organism that feeds off another organism without killing it

SCIENCE PUZZLERS, TWISTERS & TEASERS

#2 — SCIENCE PUZZLERS, TWISTERS & TEASERS — *Invertebrates*

Odd One Out

1. For each group of terms, circle the one that doesn't belong and explain why not.

   a. earthworm, bristle worm, roundworm, leech

   b. dog, sponge, planarian, human

   c. lobster, squid, crab, pillbug

   d. hydra, clam, sea urchin, centipede

   e. spineless, asymmetrical, invertebrate, without backbone

Analogies

2. In the analogies below, the first word is related to the second word in the same way that the third word is related to a fourth. For instance, the example below can be read, "Lemon is to yellow as lime is to green." Lemons are yellow in color, while limes are green. Fill in the blanks to complete the following analogies.

   Example: lemon : yellow :: lime : _____green_____

   a. blood vessels : cats :: _____ : mollusks

   b. skin : echinoderm :: _____ : arthropod

   c. ladybug : 6 :: tarantula : _____

   d. ganglia : nervous :: coelom : _____

Review & Assessment

STUDY GUIDE

CHAPTER TESTS WITH PERFORMANCE-BASED ASSESSMENT

Lab Worksheets

INQUIRY LABS

LABS YOU CAN EAT

LONG-TERM PROJECTS & RESEARCH IDEAS

DATASHEETS FOR LABBOOK

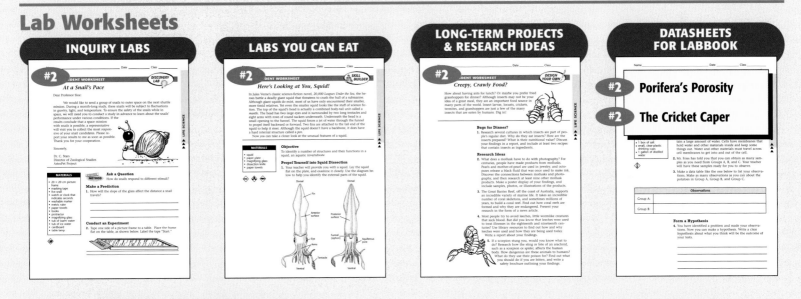

Porifera's Porosity

The Cricket Caper

Applications & Extensions

CRITICAL THINKING & PROBLEM SOLVING

SCIENTISTS IN ACTION

Chapter Background

SECTION 1

Simple Invertebrates

▶ **Aristotle**

The Greek philosopher Aristotle (384–322 B.C.) made the first recorded distinctions between invertebrate and vertebrate animals. He even organized invertebrates into a number of different groups.

- Aristotle was particularly interested in marine invertebrates; he made detailed observations of sea stars, crustaceans, and mollusks—especially cuttlefish, which are related to squids.

▶ **Sponges as Animals**

Sponges were not completely accepted as animals until the early 1800s, when Scottish zoologist R. E. Grant conducted experiments in which he added fine, colored particles to the water around sponges.
Grant watched under a microscope as the particles were taken into the sponges through microscopic pores and then "vomited forth" from the central cavity.

IS THAT A FACT!

- Of roughly 5,000 living species of sponges, only about 150 species live in fresh water. All the rest live in marine habitats.

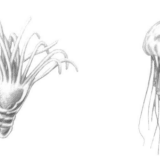

▶ **Medusa**

The tentacle-bearing medusa form of cnidarians gets its name from Medusa, a character in Greek mythology. Medusa was a monster whose long, curly "hair" was made up of snakes.

SECTION 2

Mollusks and Annelid Worms

▶ **Useful, Edible Mollusks**

Mollusks, more than any other invertebrates, are consumed as food by people worldwide. Oysters, mussels, clams, snails, squids, and octopuses are just a few edible mollusks.

IS THAT A FACT!

- Giant clams are the largest living bivalves. Shells of the giant clam *Tridacna gigas* can be 1.5 m long and weigh more than 225 kg.

▶ **Earth-Movers**

Charles Darwin (1809–1882) spent many years studying earthworms and calculating their remarkable earth-moving abilities.

- Scientists estimate that the amount of soil brought to the surface by earthworms each year can be as much as 90 metric tons per hectare in temperate regions and considerably more in tropical regions. This activity helps aerate the soil and improve growing conditions for plants.

IS THAT A FACT!

- Australia is home to the world's longest earthworms, which can exceed 3 m in length.

▶ **Terrestrial Leeches**

Most leeches are aquatic, but tropical rain forests are home to terrestrial leeches. The body heat of mammals attracts these tiny blood-sucking leeches. They will quickly move over vegetation to converge on any unlucky animal that stands in one place for more than a few minutes.

SECTION 3

Arthropods

▶ Diversity

Nearly 1 million species of arthropods have been identified. Scientists estimate that between 2 million and 30 million species are yet to be named. As a group, arthropods are more densely and widely distributed than members of any other animal group.

- Arthropods are found in every imaginable type of environment, from mountain peaks to deep-sea trenches, from equatorial rain forests to polar regions. Some arthropods are adapted for life on land, others for life in the air, and still others in salty, brackish, or fresh water.

▶ Beetles

The order Coleoptera (meaning "sheathed wings"), containing beetles, fireflies, and weevils, is the largest order in the animal kingdom. There are at least 250,000 known species of beetles.

IS THAT A FACT!

➤ All known species of spiders are predators. Their chelicerae (anterior pair of appendages) end in fangs that inject venom that kills or paralyzes their prey. When spiders bite, they also pump digestive enzymes into their victims. A spider can then suck up the resulting predigested "broth" from its prey.

SECTION 4

Echinoderms

▶ How Sea Stars Feed

The mouth of a sea star is located on the underside of its body. A short esophagus leads to a large stomach that, in many species, can be pushed out, or everted, through the sea star's mouth.

- When a sea star, such as *Asterias,* comes upon a clam, for example, it uses its tube feet and muscular arms to pull the clam's shell apart just enough so that the sea star can push its everted stomach through the opening. The stomach then wraps around the soft parts of the clam's body, and digestion begins.

▶ Class Crinoidea

The fifth class of echinoderms, Crinoidea, is less familiar to most people than are the other classes in the phylum Echinodermata. Crinoids include sea lilies and feather stars.

- Sea lilies have a stalked body topped by feathery arms that are used to snare small plankton from the water. Most sea lilies live in deep water. Feather stars are colorful, free-moving animals with long, many-branched arms. Feather stars are common inhabitants of coral reefs.

IS THAT A FACT!

➤ When disturbed, many types of sea cucumbers will expel parts of their internal organs through the anus. This defense mechanism is quite effective in discouraging potential predators. The lost parts are quickly regenerated.

For background information about teaching strategies and issues, refer to the *Professional Reference for Teachers.*

Invertebrates

CHAPTER 2

Invertebrates

Sections

Pre-Reading Questions

1. How are sponges different from other invertebrates?

2. How are you different from an octopus? How are you similar?

26

A SCI-FI SLUG?

No, this isn't an alien! It's a sea slug, a close relative of garden slugs and snails. This sea slug lives in the cold Pacific Ocean near the coast of California. Its bright coloring comes from the food that the slug eats. This animal doesn't breathe with lungs. Instead, it brings oxygen into its body through the spikes on its back.

Sea slugs don't have a backbone. In this chapter, you will discover many other animals that have no backbones. You will also learn about the structure and function of their bodies.

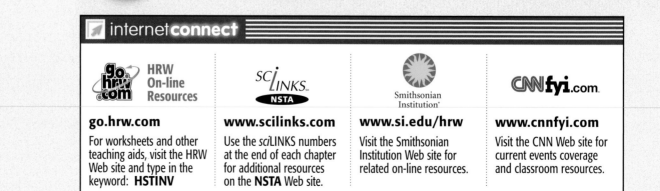

internet connect

go.hrw.com

HRW On-line Resources

For worksheets and other teaching aids, visit the HRW Web site and type in the keyword: **HSTINV**

SCiLINKS NSTA

www.scilinks.com

Use the *sci*LINKS numbers at the end of each chapter for additional resources on the **NSTA** Web site.

Smithsonian Institution®

www.si.edu/hrw

Visit the Smithsonian Institution Web site for related on-line resources.

CNNfyi.com

www.cnnfyi.com

Visit the CNN Web site for current events coverage and classroom resources.

START-UP Activity

CLASSIFY IT!

Animals are classified according to their different characteristics, including their internal and external features. In this activity, you will try your hand at classification.

Procedure

1. Look at the **pictures** that your teacher has provided. Scientists group all of these animals together because these animals do not have a backbone.

2. Which animals are the most alike? Put them in the same group.

3. For each group, decide which animals within the group are the most alike. Put these animals into smaller groups inside of their larger group.

4. In your ScienceLog or using a computer, construct a table that organizes your classification groups.

Analysis

5. What features did you use to classify these animals into groups? Explain why you think these features are the most important.

6. What features did you use to place the animals in smaller groups? Explain your reasoning.

7. Compare your table with those of your classmates. What similarities or differences do you find?

27

CLASSIFY IT!

MATERIALS
FOR EACH STUDENT: • pictures of invertebrates

Teacher's Notes

Biological classification, in which organisms are named and organized according to their relatedness, is also known as taxonomy. Researchers who specialize in this area of biology are called taxonomists.

Answers to START-UP Activity

2. Answers will vary according to the animals provided to students. Sample answer: The lobster, the spider, and the grasshopper are the most alike.

4. Look for logical grouping of animals. Animals within each group should share some characteristic(s) that is (are) not seen in other groups.

5. Answers will vary according to the animals provided to students. Students should explain the logic of their groupings. Sample answer: I grouped animals by their number of legs and wings, as well as their type of body covering.

6. Answers will vary according to the animals provided to students. Students should explain the logic of their groupings. Sample answer: I grouped animals by how many legs, antennae, wings, and eyes they have, as well as by where they live and what their body shape is.

7. Answers will vary. Look for logical, well-reasoned answers.

Focus

Simple Invertebrates

This section introduces students to simple invertebrates—sponges, cnidarians, flatworms, and roundworms. Students learn about the different body plans of these animals and important characteristics of their sensory, nervous, and digestive systems.

Bellringer

Pose the following questions to your students:

- What is an invertebrate? (an animal without a backbone)

- What is your favorite invertebrate?

- What special features does this invertebrate have that help it survive in its environment?

Have students write their answers in their ScienceLog.

1 Motivate

ACTIVITY

Determining Symmetry Divide students into cooperative groups of three or four. Distribute to each group copies of simple, top-view drawings of a butterfly and a sea urchin and a small, rectangular hand mirror (mirrors without frames work best). Challenge students to use the mirror to demonstrate that the butterfly is bilaterally symmetrical and that the sea urchin is radially symmetrical. Encourage students to discuss their findings as a class.

Sheltered English

READING WARM-UP

Terms to Learn

invertebrate	ganglia
bilateral symmetry	gut
radial symmetry	coelom
asymmetrical	

What You'll Do

- ◆ Describe the difference between radial and bilateral symmetry.
- ◆ Describe the function of a coelom.
- ◆ Explain how sponges are different from other animals.
- ◆ Describe the differences in the simple nervous systems of the cnidarians and the flatworms.

Morpho butterfly

Horned flatworm

Harlequin shrimp

28

Simple Invertebrates

Animals without backbones, also known as **invertebrates,** make up an estimated 97 percent of all animal species. So far, more than 1 million invertebrates have been named. Most biologists think that millions more remain undiscovered.

Tiger beetle

No Backbones Here!

Invertebrates come in many different shapes and sizes. Grasshoppers, clams, earthworms, and jellyfish are all invertebrates, and they are all very different from each other. But one thing invertebrates have in common is that they don't have backbones.

The differences and similarities among all animals, including invertebrates, can be compared by looking at several characteristics. These characteristics include the type of body plan, the presence or absence of a head, and the way food is digested and absorbed.

Body Plans Invertebrates have two basic body plans, or types of *symmetry*. Symmetry can be bilateral or radial. Animal body plans are shown on the next page.

Most animals have bilateral symmetry. An animal with **bilateral symmetry** has a body with two similar halves. For example, if you draw an imaginary line down the middle of an ant, you see the same features on each side of the line.

Some invertebrates have radial symmetry. In an animal with **radial symmetry,** the body parts are arranged in a circle around a central point. If you were to draw an imaginary line across the top of a sea anemone, you would see that both halves look the same. But you could draw the line in any direction and still see two similar halves.

The simplest invertebrates, the sponges, have no symmetry at all. Animals without symmetry are **asymmetrical.**

Multicultural CONNECTION

The silica spicules from many freshwater sponges are very sharp, abrasive, and strong. In Russia, dried freshwater sponges have long been used to polish silver, brass, and other metals. Indians who live along the Amazon River, in South America, add sponge spicules to clay to strengthen the pots they make from it. Have students research other uses of sponge spicules or entire sponges and create a poster based on their findings.

Animal Body Plans

This ant has **bilateral symmetry.**
The two halves of its body mirror
each other. On each side you see
one eye, one antenna, and three
legs.

This sea anemone has **radial
symmetry.** Animals with radial
symmetry have a body organized
around the center, like spokes on
a wheel.

This sponge is **asymmetrical.**
You cannot draw a straight
line so that its body is divided
into two equal halves.

Getting a Head All animals except sponges have fibers
called *nerves* that carry signals to control the movements
of their body. Simple invertebrates have nerves arranged
in networks or in nerve cords throughout their body.
These simple animals have no brain or head.

In some invertebrates, dozens of nerve cells come
together in groups called **ganglia** (singular, *ganglion*).
Ganglia occur throughout the body, controlling different body parts. **Figure 1** shows one of the ganglia, the
brain, and nerve cords of a leech.

More-complex animals have a brain and a head,
where the brain is stored. The brain controls many different nerves in different parts of the body.

Don't You Have Any Guts? Almost all animals digest
food in a central gut. The **gut** is a pouch lined with cells
that release powerful enzymes. These enzymes break
down food into small particles that cells can then absorb.
Your gut is your digestive tract.

Complex animals have a special space in the body
for the gut. This space is the **coelom** (SEE luhm), shown
in **Figure 2.** The coelum allows the gut to move food
without interference from the movements of the body.
Other organs, such as the heart and lungs, are also in
the coelom, but they are separated from the gut.

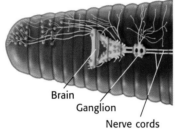

Brain
Ganglion
Nerve cords

Figure 1 *Leeches have a simple brain
and ganglia. A pair of nerve cords connects the brain and ganglia.*

Coelom   Gut

Figure 2 *This is the coelom of an
earthworm. The gut and organs are
in this special cavity.*

29

2 Teach

USING THE FIGURE

Have students study the three
invertebrates in the "Animal
Body Plans" illustration and
note their different habitats. Tell
students that being bilaterally
symmetrical is an advantage
for animals that travel through
their environment and that
being radially symmetrical is
an advantage for animals who
live attached to a substrate and
whose environment meets
them on all sides. Ask students
whether they think the organisms pictured in the figure support that statement. Point out
to students that there is no way
to divide the sponge to get two
equal halves. Sheltered English

DISCUSSION

Digestion Have students discuss
the advantages of having a central gut specialized for digestion.

Sample answers:

1. Powerful digestive enzymes are
   isolated from cells and tissues
   that might be harmed by those
   enzymes.

2. The breakdown of food particles
   takes place more rapidly in a
   centralized gut than it does in
   individual, unspecialized body
   cells.

3. Wastes are isolated from other
   parts of the body.

**Directed Reading
Worksheet** Section 1

IS THAT A FACT!

The discovery of a new species of carnivorous sponge in the Mediterranean Sea has
amazed marine biologists and confused
taxonomists. A typical sponge is a filter
feeder, filtering out organic matter from
the ocean water. This newly discovered
sponge does not eat that way. Investigators
discovered that it eats crustaceans by
growing thin filaments that cover its prey.
The prey is dissolved and digested by the
sponge in a matter of days. Now scientists
are rethinking the definition of *sponge*.
This newly discovered creature resembles
a sponge except in its feeding habits.

REAL-WORLD CONNECTION

Sponges have few predators. The sharp spicules—or tough fibers—in their bodies discourage fish and other aquatic organisms from eating them. Many sponges also produce toxic chemicals that deter predators and keep other sponges from growing too close. A chemical isolated from a Caribbean sponge, *Cryptotethya crypta*, was one of the first marine compounds to be used in chemotherapy. Currently, many other chemical compounds produced by sponges are being tested as anticancer and antiviral drugs.

DEMONSTRATION

Sponges Place a thin, dry slice of a natural sponge under a microscope, and allow students to examine the spongin-fiber network. Next, add a few drops of water to the sponge, and have students examine the slice again. Students should be able to see clearly how the water is taken up by the fibers (the fibers will swell slightly) as well as into the spaces between the fibers.
Sheltered English

Sponges

Sponges are the simplest animals. They have no symmetry, no head or nerves, and no gut. Although sponges can move, they are so slow that their movement is very difficult to see. In fact, sponges were once thought to be plants. But sponges cannot make their own food and must eat other organisms. That's one reason they are classified as animals.

Kinds of Sponges All sponges live in water, and most are found in the ocean. As shown in **Figure 3,** they come in beautiful colors and a variety of shapes.

Most sponges have a skeleton made of needlelike splinters called *spicules,* as shown in **Figure 4.** Spicules come in many shapes, from simple, straight needles to curved rods and complex star shapes. The skeleton supports the body of the sponge and helps protect it from predators.

Sponges are divided into classes according to the type of spicules they have. The largest class of sponges contain spicules made of silicate, the material we use to make glass. Bath sponges are similar to silica sponges, but they lack spicules. Instead of spicules, they have a skeleton made of a protein called *spongin.* That is why they are soft. Another group of sponges have spicules made of calcium carbonate, the material that makes up the shells of shellfish.

Re-form and Replace If a sponge's body is broken apart by being forced through a sieve, the separate cells will come back together and re-form the same sponge. In addition, new sponges can form from pieces broken off another sponge. Unlike most animals, a sponge can also replace its body parts, or *regenerate.*

Giant barrel sponge

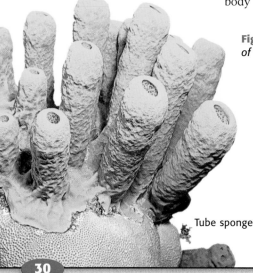

Tube sponge

Figure 3 Sponges come in a variety of shapes, sizes, and colors.

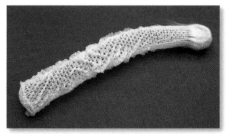

Figure 4 This is the skeleton of a glass sponge.

WEIRD SCIENCE

Nearly all sponges are sessile—they live attached to a surface and cannot move from place to place. *Tethya seychellensis,* which lives in the Red Sea, is an exception. Young sponges of this species can move very slowly—about 10 to 15 mm a day—by extending long, sticky projections from their body wall. The projections attach to the substrate and then contract, pulling the sponge forward.

How Do Sponges Eat? Sponges belong to the phylum Porifera. The name refers to the thousands of holes, or *pores,* on the outside of sponges. The sponge sweeps water into its body through these pores. Inside the body, cells called *collar cells* filter food particles and microorganisms from the water. The rest of the water flows into a central cavity and out a hole at the top of the sponge, like smoke going up a chimney. The hole at the top is called the *osculum.* **Figure 5** shows this process.

Sponges don't have a gut. Instead, each collar cell digests its own particles of food. No other animal has anything like collar cells.

Collar cells line the central cavity of a sponge. Each collar cell filters particles of food from the water and digests them.

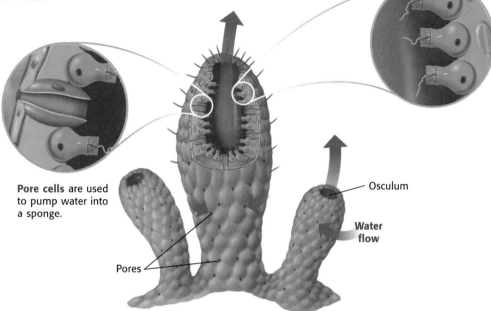

Pore cells are used to pump water into a sponge.

Osculum

Water flow

Pores

Figure 5 *A sponge filters particles of food from water using collar cells and then pumps the water out the osculum. A sponge can filter up to 22 L of water a day.*

SECTION REVIEW

1. Why are collar cells important in classifying sponges as animals?

2. What is a coelom?

3. **Interpreting Graphics** Does the animal shown at right have radial symmetry, bilateral symmetry, or no symmetry? Explain your answer.

▼ *Answers to Section Review*

1. All animals must get and digest food. Collar cells filter food particles from the water and digest food.

2. A coelom is a space in the body where the gut and other organs are found.

3. The slug has bilateral symmetry; if you draw an imaginary line through it, you get two halves that are mirror images of each other.

Mnemonics Write the words *medusa* and *polyp* on the chalkboard. Point out that *medusa* contains the letter *d* and that the medusa form of a cnidarian has tentacles that hang **d**own from the animal's body. By the same token, the word *polyp* contains the letter *p*, and the polyp form of a cnidarian has tentacles that project u**p** from the animal's body. Tell students they can use this letter association to remember the different body forms.

GUIDED PRACTICE

Writing | Have students research the jellyfish *Aurelia*. Then have students write a story about an *Aurelia* jellyfish in which they describe the jellyfish's life cycle, how it moves, what it eats, and how it senses its environment.

ACTIVITY

Observing Hydras Obtain live hydras and water fleas (*Daphnia*) from a biological supply house. Distribute the hydras in water-filled specimen dishes, and have students work in pairs to study the hydras under a dissecting microscope. Then add several water fleas to the water in each specimen dish, and have students observe how hydras use their nematocyst-equipped tentacles to capture and subdue prey. Encourage students to make drawings of the hydras and to record their observations about how hydras move and manipulate captured prey into their mouths.
Sheltered English

Jellyfish

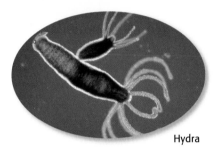
Hydra

Figure 6 *These three organisms are cnidarians. Why are they in the same phylum?*

Sea anemone

Cnidarians

Take a look at the organisms shown in **Figure 6**. They look very different, but all of these animals belong to the phylum Cnidaria (ni DER ee uh).

The word *cnidaria* comes from the Greek word for "nettle." Nettles are plants that release stinging barbs into the skin. Cnidarians do the same. All cnidarians have stinging cells. Do you know anyone who has been stung by a jellyfish? It is a very painful experience!

Cnidarians are more complex than sponges. Cnidarians have complex tissues, a gut for digesting food, and a nervous system. However, some species of cnidarians do share a characteristic with sponges. If the cells of the body are separated, they can come back together to form the cnidarian.

The Medusa and the Polyp Cnidarians come in two forms, the medusa and the polyp. They are shown in **Figure 7**. The *medusa* looks like a mushroom with tentacles streaming down from below. A well-known medusa is the jellyfish. As a medusa's body, or bell, contracts and relaxes, the medusa swims through the water.

The other cnidarian body form is the *polyp*. Polyps are shaped like vases and usually live attached to a surface.

Some cnidarians are polyps and medusas at different times in their life. But most cnidarians spend their life as a polyp.

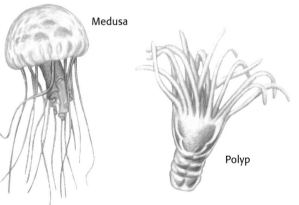
Medusa

Polyp

Figure 7 *Both the medusa and the polyp have radial symmetry. Can you see why?*

WEIRD SCIENCE

The tentacles of some cnidarians are capable of stinging even if they are detached from the main body or after the animal itself is dead. *Physalia*, the Portuguese man-of-war, is a colonial cnidarian that frequently washes ashore along temperate and tropical beaches.

Barefoot beachgoers who happen to step on these stranded cnidarians quickly discover that the stinging cells can still deliver a painful sting, even if the animals themselves have been dead for several days.

Kinds of Cnidarians There are three classes of cnidarians: hydras, jellyfish, and sea anemones and corals. Hydras are common cnidarians that live in fresh water. They spend their entire life in the polyp form. Jellyfish spend most of their life as a medusa.

Sea anemones and corals are polyps all their life. They look like brightly colored flowers. Corals are tiny cnidarians that live in colonies. These colonies build huge skeletons of calcium carbonate. Each new generation of corals builds on top of the last generation. Over thousands of years, these tiny animals build massive underwater reefs. Coral reefs can be found in warm tropical waters throughout the world.

Catching Lunch All cnidarians have long tentacles covered with special stinging cells. When a small fish or other organism brushes against the tentacles of a cnidarian, hundreds of stinging cells fire into the organism and release a paralyzing toxin. Each stinging cell uses water pressure to fire a tiny barbed spear called a *nematocyst* (ne MA toh sist). **Figure 8** shows a nematocyst before and after firing.

Environment
CONNECTION

Coral reefs, some of which are more than 2.5 million years old, are home to one-fourth of all marine fish species. Unfortunately, living coral reefs are threatened by overfishing, pollution, mining, and accidental damage from swimmers and boats. Scientists are now looking for ways to help protect coral reefs.

DEMONSTRATION

Stinging Cells After students have studied **Figure 8,** perform the following demonstration. Invert the fingers of a rubber glove, and use duct tape to attach the top of the glove securely to the head of a water faucet. Tell students that the inverted fingers of the glove represent nematocysts coiled within stinging cells. Scientists have discovered that nematocysts "fire" as a result of a sudden change in water pressure inside stinging cells. When a nematocyst is stimulated to discharge, the nematocyst membrane becomes highly permeable to water. As water rushes in, the sudden increase in water pressure pushes the nematocyst out with explosive force, turning it inside out in the process. Demonstrate this phenomenon by briefly turning on the faucet. The sudden pressure increase will cause the inverted fingers of the rubber glove to evert quickly and forcefully.
Sheltered English

Figure 8 *Each stinging cell contains a nematocyst.*

Before firing Coiled inside each stinging cell is a tiny barbed harpoon.

After firing When the nematocyst is fired, the long barbed strand ejects into the water. Larger barbs also cover the base of the strand.

You've Got Some Nerve Cnidarians have a simple network of nerve cells called a *nerve net*. The nerve net controls the movements of the body and the tentacles.

A medusa has a *nerve ring* in the center of its nerve net. This ring of nerve cells coordinates the swimming of a jellyfish in the same way that our spinal cord coordinates walking. The nerve ring is not a brain, however. Cnidarians do not think or plan in the way that more-complex animals do.

> ✔ **Self-Check**
>
> Medusas have a nerve ring, but polyps do not. How does the way medusas move explain their more complex nervous system? *(See page 152 to check your answer.)*

BRAIN FOOD

Many jellyfish that capture and eat small fish have transparent or nearly transparent bodies and long, trailing tentacles that are very difficult to see in the water. Ask students to speculate about how these features are an advantage to jellyfish as predators.

33

Answer to Self-Check

Because medusas swim through the water by contracting their bodies, they must have a nervous system that can control these actions. Polyps move very little, so they don't need as complex a nervous system.

REAL-WORLD CONNECTION

Schistosomiasis is an infectious disease caused by blood flukes of the genus *Schistosoma*. About 200 million people are afflicted by schistosomiasis worldwide, primarily in Africa, Latin America, tropical Asia, and the Middle East. Encourage students to research the *Schistosoma* blood fluke and, as a class, to create a bulletin-board display in which they describe and illustrate the fluke's complex life cycle, the symptoms of the disease, and steps that can be taken to reduce the chance of infection.

MISCONCEPTION
ALERT

Students may think that tapeworm infections are relatively rare among people living in developed countries. Even in the United States, however, tapeworms from pigs and cattle can infect humans. Researchers estimate that about 1 percent of American cattle are infected with beef tapeworm. About 20 percent of all beef consumed in the United States is not federally inspected; lightly infected beef is frequently missed during inspections. As a result, if a person eats rare roast beef, hamburgers, or steaks, the chance of becoming infected with beef tapeworm is significant.

Critical Thinking Worksheet
"A New Form of Danger in the Deep"

Flatworms

When you think of worms, you probably think of earthworms. But there are many other types of worms, and most of them are too tiny to see. The simplest group of worms are the flatworms.

Look at the flatworm shown in **Figure 9.** Unlike the invertebrates you have studied so far, flatworms have bilateral symmetry. Most flatworms also have a clearly defined head and two large, unblinking eyespots. Even though the eyespots cannot focus, a flatworm knows the direction that light is coming from. A flatworm also has two bumps on each side of its head. These are *sensory lobes* and are used for detecting food.

Figure 9 *This flatworm is called a planarian. It has a head with eyespots and sensory lobes.*

Planarians Flatworms are divided into three classes. The big-eyed flatworms we have been discussing are called *planarians*. Most of these flatworms are small; their length is less than the length of a fingernail. They live in water and on land. Most planarians are predators. They eat other animals or parts of other animals and digest food in their gut. The planarian's head, eyespots, and sensory lobes are clues that it has a brain for processing information. **Figure 10** shows a diagram of the nervous system of a planarian.

Flukes and Tapeworms The two other groups of flatworms are *flukes* and *tapeworms*. A fluke is shown in **Figure 11.** These animals are parasites. A *parasite* is an organism that feeds on another living creature, called the *host*. The host is usually not killed. Most flukes and all tapeworms find their way inside the bodies of other animals, where they live and reproduce. Fertilized eggs pass out of the host's body with the body's waste. If these fertilized eggs end up in drinking water or on food, they can be eaten by another host, where they will develop into a new fluke or tapeworm.

Ganglia

Eyespot

Nerve cords

Nerve

Figure 10 *The nervous system of a flatworm has nerves connecting two parallel nerve cords. Ganglia make up a primitive brain.*

Figure 11 *Flukes use suckers to attach to their host.*

Homework

Writing Have students research the life cycle of the roundworm parasite *Trichinella spiralis* and write a persuasive paragraph in their ScienceLog on the importance of cooking pork thoroughly to prevent contracting trichinosis.

IS THAT A FACT!

The adult broad-fish tapeworm, which can infect humans, grows 10 to 20 m in length and may consist of 3,000 to 4,000 sections. A mature fish tapeworm can shed a million eggs a day.

Flukes and tapeworms have tiny heads without eyespots or sensory lobes. They have special suckers and hooks for attaching to the host. Those flatworms that live inside the gut of their host have special skin that resists digestion by the stomach enzymes of the host. Tapeworms are so specialized that they have no gut at all. These creatures simply absorb nutrients from the intestines of their host. **Figure 12** shows a tapeworm that can infect humans.

Roundworms

Roundworms, or nematodes, are round when viewed in cross section and are long and slender. Like other worms, they have bilateral symmetry. Most species of roundworms are tiny. A single rotten apple lying on the ground in an orchard could contain 100,000 roundworms. These tiny creatures break down the dead tissues of plants and animals and help build rich soils. **Figure 13** shows a roundworm.

Roundworms have a simple nervous system. A ring of ganglia forms a primitive brain, and parallel nerve cords run the length of their body.

Most roundworms are parasites. Roundworms that infect humans include pinworms and hookworms. Another roundworm is passed from infected pork to humans and causes trichinosis (TRIK i NOH sis), a severe illness. Cooking pork thoroughly will kill the roundworms.

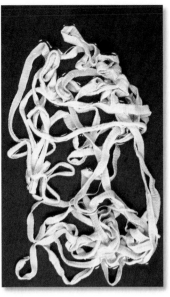
Figure 12 *Tapeworms can reach enormous sizes. Some can grow longer than a school bus!*

Figure 13 *Roundworms have a fluid-filled body cavity.*

SECTION REVIEW

1. What characteristic gives cnidarians their name?

2. What are two characteristics of flatworms that make them different from cnidarians?

3. **Analyzing Relationships** Both predators and parasites live off the tissues of other animals. Explain the difference between a predator and a parasite.

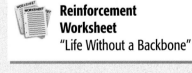

internet**connect**

SC*i*LINKS.
NSTA

TOPIC: Sponges, Roundworms
GO TO: www.scilinks.org
*sci*LINKS NUMBER: HSTL355, HSTL360

35

▼ *Answers to Section Review*

1. stinging cells

2. Flatworms have bilateral symmetry, and they have ganglia (and a brain). Cnidarians do not.

3. Both feed on other living organisms, but a predator kills its prey (or feeds on dead prey), and a parasite feeds on a host, usually without killing it.

Quiz

Ask students to answer the following questions:

1. Describe the nervous system of most simple invertebrates. (Simple invertebrates have nerves arranged in networks or in nerve cords throughout their body. In some invertebrates, nerve cells are grouped into ganglia that control different body parts.)

2. List three different kinds of cnidarians. (Possible answers: corals, hydras, jellyfish, sea anemones)

3. What is the relationship between a parasite and its host? (A parasite is an organism that feeds on another living creature; the organism it feeds on is its host.)

ALTERNATIVE ASSESSMENT

PORTFOLIO Ask students to create an illustrated book about the way sponges, cnidarians, and flatworms obtain food. Students should label body structures on their illustrations and may wish to draw internal views or cross sections in order to show special cells, internal organs, or body systems. Extensive text in which students discuss the feeding adaptations of these different invertebrates should accompany the illustrations.

Reinforcement Worksheet
"Life Without a Backbone"

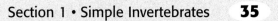
internet**connect**

SC*i*LINKS.
NSTA
TOPIC: Roundworms
GO TO: www.scilinks.org
*sci*LINKS NUMBER: HSTL360

Focus

Mollusks and Annelid Worms

In this section, students are introduced to three major classes of the phylum Mollusca—gastropods, bivalves, and cephalopods. Students learn about the main parts of a mollusk's soft body, the way they feed, and the diversity in their circulatory and nervous systems. They will also explore annelid worms, including earthworms, bristle worms, and leeches.

Bellringer

Have students unscramble the following words, and write a sentence using them in their ScienceLog:

gluss (slugs)

isalns (snails)

sdusqi (squids)

klomssul (mollusks)

(Slugs, snails, and squids are all mollusks.)

1) Motivate

GROUP ACTIVITY

Writing Divide students into cooperative groups of four or five. Challenge each group to investigate how people in different countries use mollusks for food. Students can look for recipes on how to prepare and serve snails, clams, squids, and other mollusks. Ask each group to create a menu consisting of an appetizer and a main dish in which mollusks are the primary ingredient.

Answer to MATHBREAK

$\frac{30 \text{ km/h}}{60 \text{ min/h}} = 0.5$ km/min

SECTION 2
READING WARM-UP

Terms to Learn

open circulatory system
closed circulatory system
segment

What You'll Do

◆ Describe the body parts of a mollusk.
◆ Explain the difference between an open circulatory system and a closed circulatory system.
◆ Describe segmentation.

Mollusks and Annelid Worms

Have you ever eaten clam chowder or calamari? Have you ever seen worms on the sidewalk after it rains? If you have, then you have encountered the invertebrates discussed in this section—mollusks and annelid worms. These invertebrates are more complex than the invertebrates you have read about so far. Mollusks and annelid worms have a coelom and a circulatory system. And they have more-complex nervous systems than those of the flatworms and roundworms.

Earthworm

Mollusks

The phylum Mollusca includes snails, slugs, clams, oysters, squids, and octopuses. The mollusks are the second largest phylum of animals. Most mollusks are in three classes: *gastropods* (slugs and snails), *bivalves* (clams and other two-shelled shellfish), and *cephalopods* (squids and octopuses). **Figure 14** shows some of the variety of mollusks.

Snails

Squid

Clam

Figure 14 *A snail, a squid, and a clam are all mollusks. Snails are gastropods; squids are cephalopods; and clams are bivalves.*

$\div \ 5 \ \div \ \Omega \ \le \ \infty \ +\Omega \ ^\sqrt{} \ 9 \ _\infty^\le \ \Sigma \ 2$

MATH **BREAK**

Speeding Squid

If a squid is swimming at 30 km/h, how far can it go in 1 minute?

36

Most mollusks live in the ocean, but some live in freshwater habitats. Other mollusks, such as slugs and snails, have adapted to life on land.

Mollusks range in size from 1 mm long snails to the giant squid, which can reach up to 18 m in length. Most mollusks move slowly, but some squids can swim up to 40 km/h and leap more than 4 m above the water.

WEIRD SCIENCE

The blue-ringed octopus, found in the waters of the South Pacific, is deadly. When it is provoked, the blue rings on its skin turn so blue that they almost glow. The saliva in its bite contains a powerful toxin for which there is no known antidote! This toxin paralyzes the victim and shuts down all its life systems. If a person bitten by this octopus arrives at the hospital in time, he or she is put on a respirator for a few days until the toxin wears off.

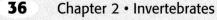

How Do You Know a Mollusk When You See One? A snail, a clam, and a squid look quite different from one another. Yet on closer inspection, the bodies of all mollusks are almost the same. The body parts shared by mollusks are described in **Figure 15.**

KEY
- Foot
- Visceral mass
- Mantle
- Shell

Figure 15 *A mollusk has a soft body, usually covered by a shell. All mollusks also have a foot, a visceral mass, and a mantle.*

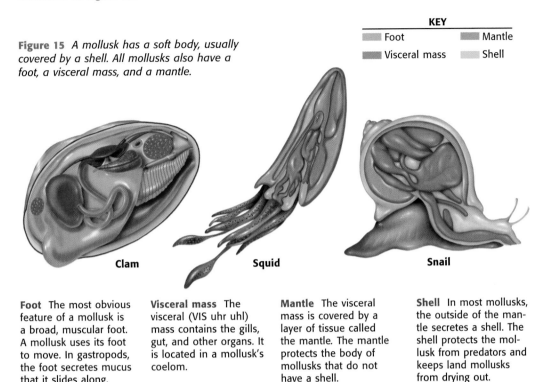

Clam   **Squid**   **Snail**

Foot The most obvious feature of a mollusk is a broad, muscular foot. A mollusk uses its foot to move. In gastropods, the foot secretes mucus that it slides along.

Visceral mass The visceral (VIS uhr uhl) mass contains the gills, gut, and other organs. It is located in a mollusk's coelom.

Mantle The visceral mass is covered by a layer of tissue called the mantle. The mantle protects the body of mollusks that do not have a shell.

Shell In most mollusks, the outside of the mantle secretes a shell. The shell protects the mollusk from predators and keeps land mollusks from drying out.

How Do Mollusks Eat? Each type of mollusk has its own way of eating. Clams and other bivalves sit in one place and filter tiny plants, bacteria, and other particles from the water around them. Snails and slugs eat with a ribbonlike tongue covered with curved teeth, called a *radula* (RAJ oo luh). **Figure 16** shows a close-up of a slug's radula. Slugs and snails use the radula to scrape algae off rocks, chunks of tissue from seaweed, or pieces from the leaves of plants. Predatory snails and slugs often have large teeth on their radula that they use to attack their prey. And parasitic snails pierce their victims much as a mosquito does. Octopuses and squids use tentacles to grab their prey and place it in their powerful jaws, just as we can use our fingers to eat.

Figure 16 *The rows of teeth on a slug's radula help to scrape food from surfaces.*

37

Science Bloopers

Nearly 30 cm long, the giant African snail, *Achatina fulica,* is native to east Africa, where it eats decaying vegetation. When these African snails were introduced to many Pacific islands, they munched crops instead and quickly became agricultural pests. In a misguided attempt to solve that problem, several kinds of predatory snails were released on the islands in the hope that they would kill off the African snails. Unfortunately, the predatory snails ignored the African snails and ate the islands' native snail species, some of which are now nearly extinct.

MEETING INDIVIDUAL NEEDS

Learners Having Difficulty
Visual learners and students with limited English proficiency may have trouble understanding the difference between closed and open circulatory systems. Distribute copies of illustrations showing the closed circulatory system in a human and the open circulatory system in a clam. (A college-level biology textbook is a good source for illustrations of the clam circulatory system.) Encourage students to trace the path that blood takes in a clam. Call attention to the blood sinuses in the clam's body, and tell students that these irregular channels and spaces in the clam's tissues are filled and drained by blood vessels. Contrast this situation with the human circulatory system, in which blood is completely contained in vessels throughout the body. **Sheltered English**

COOPERATIVE LEARNING

Writing Have students work in pairs to research how cephalopods have been used in experimental studies of behavior and nerve function. Students may present their research in the form of a written report or as an oral interview, with one student acting as a magazine reporter who is gathering information for an article and the other student playing the role of a research scientist who has conducted experiments on cephalopods.

BRAIN FOOD

An octopus has three hearts! Two of them are near the gills and are called *gill hearts*.

Have a Heart Unlike simpler invertebrates, mollusks have a circulatory system. Most mollusks have an **open circulatory system.** In this system, a simple heart pumps blood through blood vessels that empty into spaces in the animal's body called *sinuses*. This is very different from our own circulatory system, which is a **closed circulatory system.** In a closed circulatory system, a heart circulates blood through a network of blood vessels that form a closed loop. Cephalopods (squids and octopuses) also have a closed circulatory system, although it is much simpler than ours.

It's a Brain! Mollusks have complex ganglia. In most mollusks, these ganglia occur throughout the body. Mollusks have ganglia that control breathing, ganglia that move the foot, and ganglia that control digestion.

Cephalopods, like the one in **Figure 17,** have a more complex nervous system than the other mollusks have. In fact, octopuses and squids have the most advanced nervous system of all invertebrates. They have a brain, where all of their ganglia are connected. Not surprisingly, these animals are the smartest of all invertebrates. Octopuses, for example, can learn to navigate a maze and can distinguish between different shapes and colors. If they are given bricks or stones, they will build a cave to hide in.

Figure 17 *An octopus has a large brain. The brain coordinates the movement of its eight long arms.*

SECTION REVIEW

1. What are the four main parts of a mollusk's body?

2. What is the difference between an open circulatory system and a closed circulatory system?

3. **Analyzing Relationships** What two features do cephalopods share with humans that other mollusks do not?

▼ **Answers to Section Review**

1. foot, visceral mass, mantle, and shell

2. In an open circulatory system, the heart pumps blood through vessels into sinuses. In a closed circulatory system, the blood is pumped through a closed network of vessels.

3. Like humans, cephalopods have a closed circulatory system and a brain.

Annelid Worms

You have probably seen earthworms, like the one in **Figure 18.** Earthworms belong to the phylum Annelida. Annelid worms are often called segmented worms because their body has segments. **Segments** are identical, or almost identical, repeating body parts.

These worms are much more complex than flatworms and roundworms. Annelid worms have a coelom and a closed circulatory system. They also have a nervous system that includes ganglia in each segment and a brain in the head. A nerve cord connects the brain and the ganglia.

Kinds of Annelid Worms The annelid worms include three classes: earthworms, bristle worms, and leeches. Annelid worms live in salt water, in fresh water, or on land. They may scavenge anything edible, or they may prey on other organisms as predators or as parasites.

More than Just Bait Earthworms are the most common annelid worms. An earthworm has 100 to 175 segments, most of which are identical. Some segments are specialized for eating and reproduction. Earthworms eat soil. They break down organic matter in the soil and excrete wastes called *castings*. Castings provide nutrients that plants can use. Earthworms also improve the soil by burrowing tunnels, which allow air and water to reach deep into the soil.

Earthworms have stiff bristles on the outside of their body to help them move. The bristles hold one part of the worm in place while the other part pushes through the soil.

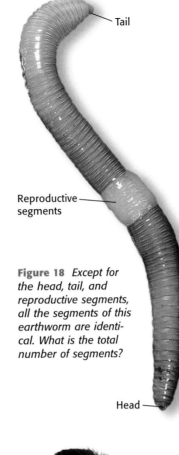

Tail

Reproductive segments

Figure 18 *Except for the head, tail, and reproductive segments, all the segments of this earthworm are identical. What is the total number of segments?*

Head

Do Worms Make Good Neighbors?

A friend of yours is worried because his garden is full of earthworms. He wants to find a way to get rid of the worms. Do you think this is a good idea? Why? Write a letter to your friend explaining what you think he should do.

39

SCIENCE HUMOR

Q: What is worse than biting into an apple and finding a worm?

A: biting into an apple and finding half a worm

IS THAT A FACT!

The large fleshy lobe to the right of the octopus's eyes in **Figure 17** is not the head. It contains the visceral mass.

Quiz

Have students answer the following questions:

1. What are the three main classes of mollusks? (gastropods, bivalves, and cephalopods)

2. How do herbivorous snails and slugs use their radula to obtain food? (These mollusks use their radula to scrape algae off rocks, chunks of tissue from seaweed, or pieces from plant leaves.)

ALTERNATIVE ASSESSMENT

Writing Have students select a mollusk or annelid worm that interests them and research its life cycle, habitat, food, and unique structural or behavioral adaptations. Then ask students to write a rhyming or free-verse poem in their ScienceLog about the invertebrate based on the information gathered in their research.

Figure 19 *This bristle worm feeds by filtering particles from the water with its bristles. Can you see the segments on this worm?*

Bristles Can Be Beautiful If there were a beauty contest for worms, bristle worms would win. These remarkable worms come in many varieties and in brilliant colors. **Figure 19** shows a bristle worm. All bristle worms live in water. Some burrow through soggy sand and mud, eating whatever small creatures and particles they meet. Others crawl along the bottom, eating mollusks and other small animals.

Blood Suckers and More Leeches are known mostly as parasites that suck other animals' blood. This is true of some leeches, but not all. Other leeches are scavengers that eat dead animals. Still others are predators that prey on insects, slugs, and snails. Leeches that are parasites feed on the blood of other animals.

But leeches aren't all bad. Until the twentieth century, doctors regularly used leeches in medical treatments. Doctors attached leeches to a sick person to drain "bad" blood from the body. Although this practice is not accepted today, leeches are still used in medicine. After surgery, doctors sometimes use leeches to prevent dangerous swelling near a wound, as shown in **Figure 20.** Leeches also make a chemical that keeps blood from forming clots. Modern doctors give heart attack patients medicines that contain this chemical to keep blood clots from blocking arteries.

Figure 20 *Modern doctors sometimes use leeches to reduce swelling after surgery.*

internet**connect**
SCI*LINKS*
NSTA
TOPIC: Mollusks and Annelid Worms
GO TO: www.scilinks.org
*sci*LINKS **NUMBER:** HSTL365

SECTION REVIEW

1. Name the three types of annelid worms. How are they alike? How are they different?

2. **Making Inferences** Why would a chemical that keeps blood from clotting be beneficial to leeches?

3. **Analyzing Relationships** How are annelid worms different from flatworms and roundworms? What characteristics do all worms share?

▼ *Answers to Section Review*

1. Earthworms, bristle worms, and leeches; all are segmented, and all are annelid worms; earthworms live in soil, and bristle worms live in the water; some leeches and some bristle worms are predators, but all earthworms are scavengers; only leeches are parasites.

2. Because they feed on the blood of fish and other animals, leeches have to keep the blood flowing (not clotting) from their hosts.

3. Annelid worms are segmented. They have a coelom and a closed circulatory system. All of the worms have bilateral symmetry.

Terms to Learn

exoskeleton   mandible
compound eye   metamorphosis
antennae

What You'll Do

◆ List the four main characteristics of arthropods.
◆ Describe the different body parts of the four kinds of arthropods.
◆ Explain the two types of metamorphosis in insects.

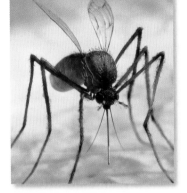
Mosquito

Tarantula

Arthropods

Fiddler crab

They have lived here for hundreds of millions of years and have adapted to nearly all environments. An acre of land contains millions of them. You know them by more common names, such as insects, spiders, crabs, and centipedes. They are _arthropods,_ the largest group of animals on Earth.

Seventy-five percent of all animal species are arthropods. The world population of humans is about 6 billion. Biologists estimate the world population of arthropods to be about a billion billion.

Characteristics of Arthropods

All arthropods share four characteristics: jointed limbs, a segmented body with specialized parts, an exoskeleton, and a well-developed nervous system.

Jointed Limbs Jointed limbs give arthropods their name. _Arthro_ means "joint," and _pod_ means "foot." Jointed limbs are arms, legs, or other similar body parts that bend at joints. Jointed limbs allow arthropods to move easily.

Segmented and Specialized Like annelid worms, arthropods are _segmented._ In some arthropods, such as the centipedes, nearly every segment is identical. Only the segments at the head and tail are different from the rest. Most other species of arthropods have segments that include very specialized parts, such as wings, antennae, gills, pincers, and claws. Many of these special parts form during the animal's development, when two or three segments grow together to form a _head,_ a _thorax,_ and an _abdomen._ These parts are labeled on the grasshopper pictured in **Figure 21.**

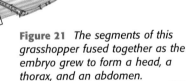
Head

Thorax

Abdomen

Figure 21 _The segments of this grasshopper fused together as the embryo grew to form a head, a thorax, and an abdomen._

41

WEIRD SCIENCE

Mantis shrimp have powerful forelegs. They use them to smash the shells of prey such as snails and crabs. This "smasher" can deliver a blow with a force equal to that of a small-caliber bullet, which is enough to break through a glass tank!

Directed Reading Worksheet Section 3

Focus

Arthropods

In this section, students learn that arthropods have the following characteristics: jointed limbs, a segmented body, a chitinous exoskeleton, and a well-developed brain and specialized sense organs. Students are introduced to four major groups of arthropods—centipedes and millipedes, crustaceans, arachnids, and insects. Insect bodies and patterns of development are examined in detail.

Bellringer

Have students pretend that, like a caterpillar, they can undergo metamorphosis and emerge from a cocoon in a new form. Ask students the following questions about their metamorphosis:

• How long will you be inside a cocoon?
• What will you look like when you emerge?
• How will you find food, and what will you eat?
• What physical or behavioral adaptations will you have after metamorphosis that you do not have now?

1 Motivate

DISCUSSION

Characteristics of Arthropods
After introducing the general characteristics of arthropods, have students discuss how these characteristics may have helped arthropods adapt to nearly all environments and to diversify to make up the largest group of animals on Earth.

The compound eyes of insects are made up of tiny bundles of light-sensitive cells called ommatidia (singular: ommatidium). The huge eyes of dragonflies contain about 28,000 ommatidia. The eyes of butterflies contain around 14,000, while those of houseflies have about 4,000. Ask students to calculate roughly how many times more ommatidia dragonflies have than butterflies or houseflies. (Dragonflies have roughly twice as many ommatidia as butterflies and seven times as many as houseflies.)

Then ask students to speculate on the relationship between the number of ommatidia and the ways these three types of arthropods get food. (Possible answer: Dragonflies are fast-flying predators and need acute vision to spot potential prey and maneuver at high speeds; many butterflies feed on flowers and must distinguish between flower types (shapes and color); houseflies rely more on odor detection than vision to find their food, which often consists of dead or stationary organisms.)

Math Skills Worksheet "Dividing Whole Numbers with Long Division"

Math Skills Worksheet "Checking Division with Multiplication"

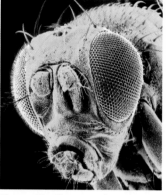

Figure 22 *Compound eyes consist of many individual light-sensitive cells that work together.*

Knights in Shining . . . Chitin? Arthropods have a hard **exoskeleton,** an external skeleton made of protein and a special substance called *chitin* (KIE tin). The exoskeleton does some of the same things an internal skeleton does. It provides a stiff frame that supports the animal's body. The exoskeleton also allows the animal to move. All of the muscles attach to different parts of the skeleton. When the muscles contract, they move the exoskeleton, which moves the parts of the animal.

But the exoskeleton also does things that internal skeletons don't do well. The exoskeleton acts like a suit of armor to protect internal organs and muscles. It also allows arthropods to live on land without drying out.

They've Got Smarts All arthropods have a head and a well-developed brain. The brain coordinates information from many sense organs, including eyes and bristles on the exoskeleton. Bristles sense movement, vibration, pressure, and chemicals. The eyes of some arthropods are very simple; they can detect light but cannot form an image. But most arthropods have compound eyes, which allow them to see images, although not as well as we do. A **compound eye** is made of many identical light-sensitive cells, as shown in **Figure 22**.

Kinds of Arthropods

Arthropods are classified according to the kinds of body parts they have. You can also tell the difference between arthropods by looking at the number of legs, eyes, and antennae they have. **Antennae** are feelers that respond to touch, taste, and smell.

Centipedes and Millipedes Centipedes and millipedes have a single pair of antennae, jaws called **mandibles,** and a hard *head capsule.* The easiest way to tell a centipede from a millipede is to count the number of legs per segment. Centipedes have one pair of legs per segment. Millipedes have two pairs of legs per segment. Take a look at **Figure 23.** How many legs can you count?

Figure 23 *Centipedes have one pair of legs per segment. The number of legs can range from 30 to 354. Millipedes have two pairs of legs per segment. The record number of legs on a millipede is 752!*

42

WEIRD SCIENCE

Did you know that compass termites from the outback of Australia are able to air-condition their mounds? Their towers are up to 2.5 m long and 3 m high but are very narrow and tall. As many as 2 million termites may be living inside. When the nest becomes too hot, worker termites rush to open a valve made of dried mud at the top of the mound. Cooler air enters the nest and sinks to the bottom of the tower. By opening and closing the mud valve in their nest, the termites have complete control over the temperature of their mound!

Crustaceans Crustaceans include shrimps, barnacles, crabs, and lobsters. Nearly all crustaceans are aquatic and have *gills* for breathing underwater. All crustaceans have mandibles and two pairs of antennae. Crustaceans have two compound eyes, usually on the end of stalks. The lobster in **Figure 24** shows all of these traits. The double antennae of crustaceans set them apart from all other arthropods.

✓ **Self-Check**

What is the difference between a segmented worm and a centipede? *(See page 152 to check your answer.)*

Answer to Self-Check

Segmented worms belong to the phylum Annelida. Centipedes are arthropods. Centipedes have jointed legs, antennae, and mandibles. Segmented worms have none of these characteristics.

Figure 24 *A lobster is a crustacean. It has compound eyes on the end of eye stalks.*

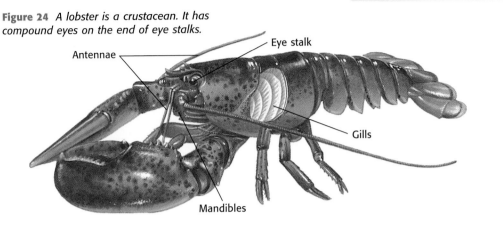

Antennae

Eye stalk

Gills

Mandibles

Arachnids Spiders, scorpions, mites, ticks, and daddy long-legs are all arachnids. **Figure 25** shows that an arachnid has two main body parts, the cephalothorax (SEF uh loh THOR AKS) and the abdomen. The *cephalothorax* consists of both a head and a thorax and usually has four pairs of walking legs. Arachnids have no antennae and no mandibles. Instead of mandibles, they have special mouthparts called *chelicerae* (kuh LIS uh ree), as illustrated in Figure 25. Some chelicerae look like pincers or fangs.

The eyes of arachnids are distinctive. While crustaceans and insects have compound eyes, arachnids do not. Spiders, for example, have eight simple eyes arranged in two rows at the front of the head. Count the eyes for yourself in **Figure 26.**

Abdomen

Cephalothorax

Chelicerae

Figure 25 *Arachnids have two main body parts and special mouthparts called chelicerae.*

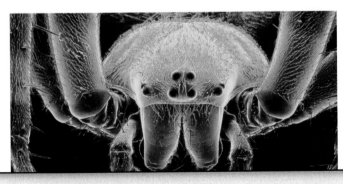

Figure 26 *In addition to eight legs, spiders have eight eyes!*

43

RETEACHING

Writing In their ScienceLog, have students describe a lobster and list the characteristics it exhibits that make it a crustacean.

ACTIVITY

Making Models

MATERIALS
FOR EACH STUDENT:
• modeling clay
• pipe cleaners

It is a common misconception that spiders are insects. Challenge students to disprove this misconception by using modeling clay and pipe cleaners to create models of a spider and an insect. Have students read this section before they begin. Students' models should reflect the fact that spiders have two main body parts, four pairs of legs, and no antennae, whereas insects have three main body parts, three pairs of legs, and one pair of antennae. Sheltered English

GROUP ACTIVITY

Have students work in cooperative groups of three or four to research web-building spiders. Each group should investigate a different spider species. Using string or yarn, have each group create an example of the type of web their chosen species builds. Guide students in a class discussion in which they compare and contrast the different web shapes and designs. Sheltered English

CONNECT TO
CHEMISTRY

Chitin is a strong, flexible, waterproof polysaccharide (a polymer of glucose). Chitin molecules bond readily with proteins, such as those found in the exoskeletons of arthropods. A Japanese textile and fiber manufacturing company has exploited chitin's unique chemical properties to create chitin sutures for surgery and chitin-based artificial skin. Chitin sutures don't have to be removed because they dissolve in the body; they also bind so well with proteins that they may promote healing.

Trapdoor spiders construct silk-lined burrows topped with a hinged lid that acts like a trapdoor. They lurk beneath the door, waiting for isopods, crickets, or other prey to pass by, then they bound up from below with remarkable speed. If the trapdoor is disturbed, the spiders pull their burrow doors shut with their chelicerae. Using a small spring scale, researchers have found that a trapdoor spider can exert an inward pull on its trapdoor that is 140 times its body weight. Calculate what your pulling strength would be if you could exert a force 140 times your weight.

(Example: 40 kg student × 140 = pulling strength of 5,600 kg)

MATERIALS

FOR EACH STUDENT:
• tape
• cooking oil

Answers to QuickLab

Fingers will not stick to tape when they have oil on them. Spiders secrete an oily substance in their legs that keeps them from sticking to their webs.

Figure 27 American Dog Tick

QuickLab

Sticky Webs

Some spiders spin webs of sticky silk to trap their prey. Why don't spiders stick to their own webs? This experiment will show you the answer. Place a piece of **tape** on your desk sticky side up. The tape represents a web. Your fingers will represent an insect. Holding the tape in place by the edges, "walk" your fingers across the tape. What happens? Dip your fingers in **cooking oil**, and "walk" them across the tape again. What happens this time? Why? How might this experiment explain why spiders don't get stuck in their webs?

TRY at HOME

44

Spiders and Ticks   Spiders do not carry diseases and are enormously useful to humans. They kill more insect pests than any other animal, including birds. Several arachnids have painful bites or stings. But the fangs of small garden spiders cannot pierce human skin. In the United States, just three species of spiders—the black widow and two species of brown spider—have bites poisonous enough to kill a person. However, with proper medical treatment, they are not fatal.

Ticks live in forests, brushy areas, and even country lawns. **Figure 27** shows an American dog tick. Ticks that bite humans sometimes carry Lyme disease, Rocky Mountain spotted fever, and other diseases. Many people wear long pants and hats when going into areas where ticks live, and they check themselves for ticks after being outdoors. Fortunately, most people who are bitten by ticks do not get sick.

Insects   The largest group of arthropods is insects. If you put all of the insects in the world together, they would weigh more than all other animals combined! **Figure 28** shows some of the wide variety of insects.

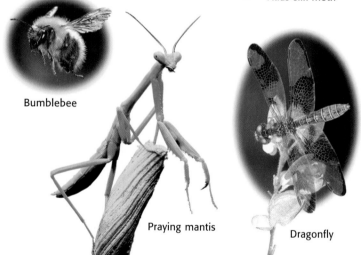

Figure 28 *These are a few of the many varieties of insects. Can you see what they have in common?*

Atlas silk moth

Bumblebee

Praying mantis

Dragonfly

internetconnect

SCILINKS
NSTA

TOPIC: Arthropods
GO TO: www.scilinks.org
*sci*LINKS NUMBER: HSTL370

IS THAT A FACT!

The hind legs of the human flea, *Pulex irritans*, are especially adapted for jumping. How high can a flea jump? *Pulex* can leap 33 cm horizontally and 20 cm vertically—that's equal to an 85 m high jump for a human!

Insects Are Everywhere (Almost) Insects live on land, in every freshwater environment, and at the edges of the sea. The only place on Earth insects do not live is in the ocean.

Many insects are beneficial. Most flowering plants depend on bees, butterflies, and other insects to carry pollen from one plant to another. Farmers depend on insects to pollinate hundreds of fruit crops, such as apples, cherries, tomatoes, and pumpkins.

Many insects are also pests. Fleas, lice, mosquitoes, and flies burrow into our flesh, suck our blood, or carry diseases. Plant-eating insects consume up to one-third of crops in this country, despite the application of pesticides.

Insect Bodies An insect's body has three parts: the head, the thorax, and the abdomen, as shown in **Figure 29.** On the head, insects have one pair of antennae and two compound eyes. They also have three pairs of mouthparts, including one pair of mandibles. The thorax is made of three segments, each with one pair of legs.

In many insects, the second and third segments of the thorax have a pair of wings. Some insects have no wings, and some have two pairs of wings.

Insect Development As an insect develops from an egg to an adult, it changes form. This process is called **metamorphosis.** There are two main types of metamorphosis, incomplete and complete. Primitive insects, such as grasshoppers and cockroaches, go through incomplete metamorphosis. In this metamorphosis there are only three stages: egg, nymph, and adult, as shown in **Figure 30.**

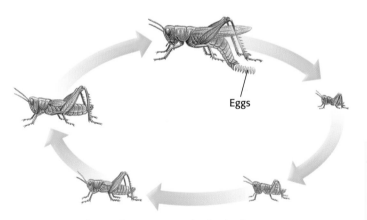

Eggs

Figure 30 *In incomplete metamorphosis, the larvae, called nymphs, look like smaller adults.*

BRAIN FOOD

A cockroach can live for a week without its head! It finally dies of thirst because it has no mouth to drink water with.

Figure 29 *Wasps have the same body parts as all other insects.*

Head
Thorax
Abdomen

LabBook

Does a cricket like cold climates? Find out on page 126 of your LabBook.

---

3) Extend

ACTIVITY

Poster Project Insecticides are routinely sprayed on lawns and gardens to kill insect pests. Unfortunately, these chemicals also kill many beneficial insects, persist in the environment, and accumulate in the bodies of animals (including people) higher up the food chain. In recent years, a variety of biological controls for insect pests have been developed that are much more environmentally safe. Have students investigate different biological controls and create a poster on the topic that could be displayed at a local garden center.

GOING FURTHER

Encourage students with limited English proficiency to make flashcards of the vocabulary words in this chapter. You may wish to pair English-proficient students with ESL students for vocabulary practice. In addition, encourage students from other countries to share information about interesting arthropods that they remember seeing in their country. Sheltered English

LabBook PG 126
The Cricket Caper

Teaching Transparency 56 "Incomplete Metamorphosis"

Science Bloopers

In 1869, the gypsy moth was introduced into the United States in an attempt to breed a better silkworm. The results were disastrous. Some moths escaped, and the species spread throughout the northeastern part of the country. Gypsy moth caterpillars eat the leaves of deciduous trees. In years when there are especially large numbers of caterpillars, millions of acres of forest can be stripped of their leaves.

Quiz

Ask students whether the following statements are true or false:

1. The cephalothorax of a spider consists of both a head and a thorax. (true)

2. The legs of most insects arise from the abdomen. (false)

3. A few types of insects live in the ocean. (false)

4. The three stages of complete metamorphosis are egg, nymph or larva, and adult. (false)

ALTERNATIVE ASSESSMENT

Writing Have students write a narrative in which they describe a walk along a rocky ocean shore or through a tropical rain forest. Have them describe at least a dozen different arthropods that they are likely to encounter. Students should research the two different ecosystems before they begin writing. Some students may wish to create illustrations or collages to accompany their narratives.

Teaching Transparency 57 "Changing Form—Complete Metamorphosis"

Changing Form—Complete Metamorphosis

In complete metamorphosis, there are four stages: egg, larva, pupa, and adult. Butterflies, beetles, flies, bees, wasps, and ants go through this process. In complete metamorphosis, the larva looks very different from the adult.

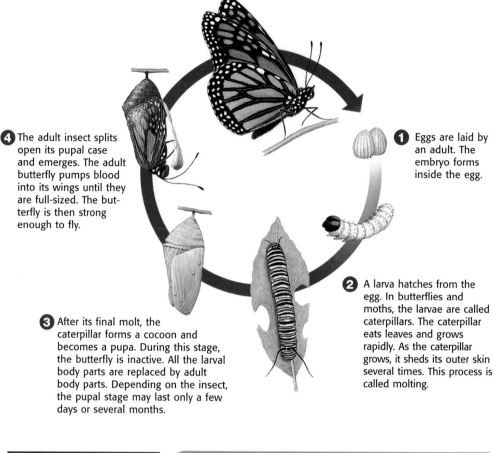

4 The adult insect splits open its pupal case and emerges. The adult butterfly pumps blood into its wings until they are full-sized. The butterfly is then strong enough to fly.

1 Eggs are laid by an adult. The embryo forms inside the egg.

3 After its final molt, the caterpillar forms a cocoon and becomes a pupa. During this stage, the butterfly is inactive. All the larval body parts are replaced by adult body parts. Depending on the insect, the pupal stage may last only a few days or several months.

2 A larva hatches from the egg. In butterflies and moths, the larvae are called caterpillars. The caterpillar eats leaves and grows rapidly. As the caterpillar grows, it sheds its outer skin several times. This process is called molting.

internet connect

SCI LINKS
NSTA

TOPIC: Arthropods
GO TO: www.scilinks.org
sciLINKS NUMBER: HSTL370

SECTION REVIEW

1. Name the four kinds of arthropods. How are their bodies different?

2. What is the difference between complete metamorphosis and incomplete metamorphosis?

3. **Applying Concepts** Suppose you have found an arthropod in a swimming pool. The creature has compound eyes, antennae, and wings. Is it a crustacean? Why or why not?

▼ **Answers to Section Review**

1. **centipedes and millipedes**—one pair of antennae, mandibles, many segments, head capsules
   crustaceans—mandibles, compound eyes on stalks, two pairs of antennae
   arachnids—two main body parts: cephalothorax and abdomen, four pairs of legs, no antennae, no mandibles, chelicerae
   insects—one pair of antennae, three pairs of legs, head, thorax, abdomen; may or may not have wings

2. incomplete metamorphosis—three stages: egg, nymph, adult; larvae (nymphs) look like smaller adults
   complete metamorphosis—four stages: egg, larva, pupa, adult; larvae look much different than adults

3. No; crustaceans do not have wings.

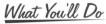

What You'll Do

◆ Describe three main characteristics of echinoderms.
◆ Describe the water vascular system.

Echinoderms

The last major phylum of invertebrates is Echinodermata. All echinoderms (ee KI noh DUHRMS) are marine animals. They include sea stars (starfish), sea urchins, sea lilies, sea cucumbers, brittle stars, and sand dollars. The smallest echinoderms are only a few millimeters across. The largest is a sea star that grows to 1 m in diameter.

Echinoderms live on the sea floor in all parts of the world's oceans. Some echinoderms prey on oysters and other shellfish, some are scavengers, and others scrape algae off rocky surfaces.

Brittle star

Sea star

Feather star

Spiny Skinned

The name *echinoderm* means "spiny skinned." The surface of the animal is not the spiny part, however. The body of the echinoderm contains an **endoskeleton,** an internal skeleton similar to the kind that vertebrates have. The hard, bony skeleton is usually covered with spines. The spines may be no more than sharp bumps, as in many sea stars. Or they may be long and pointed, as in sea urchins. All of the spines are covered by the outer skin of the animal.

Bilateral or Radial?

Adult echinoderms have radial symmetry. But sea stars, sea urchins, sand dollars, and other echinoderms all develop from larvae with bilateral symmetry. **Figure 31** shows a sea urchin larva. Notice how the two sides are similar.

When echinoderm embryos first begin to develop, they form a mouth in the same way the embryos of vertebrates do. This is one of the reasons biologists think that vertebrates are more closely related to echinoderms than to other invertebrates.

Adult

Larva

Figure 31 *The sea urchin larva has bilateral symmetry. The adult sea urchin has radial symmetry.*

47

Most adult echinoderms either are sessile (remain in one place) or move slowly over the sea floor. Echinoderm larvae, however, are able to swim, and with the help of ocean currents, they often travel great distances before they settle to the bottom and metamorphose into their adult form. Challenge students to speculate about why it is an advantage for echinoderm larvae to be bilaterally symmetrical and for echinoderm adults to be radially symmetrical.

READING 📖 STRATEGY

Prediction Guide Before students read this page, ask the following question:

How does a starfish move from place to place?

a. It curls up its arms and rolls across the sea floor.

b. It uses suction-cup-like tube feet that systematically attach and release to move along.

c. It uses its spines to dig into the sea floor and pull itself forward.

d. With its long arms, a starfish can swim slowly through the water.

(b)

INDEPENDENT PRACTICE

Writing **Concept Mapping** Have students make a concept map in their ScienceLog using the terms that describe echinoderms' physical characteristics and nervous and water vascular systems. Students should connect at least 12 terms, and link them with meaningful phrases. Encourage students to share their concept maps with the class.

CONNECT TO EARTH SCIENCE

Echinoderms are members of the *benthos,* the organisms that live on the ocean floor. Use the following Teaching Transparency to illustrate the ocean context of echinoderms.

Teaching Transparency 155 "The Three Groups of Marine Life" *LINK TO EARTH SCIENCE*

The Nervous System

All echinoderms have a simple nervous system similar to that of a jellyfish. Around the mouth is a circle of nerve fibers called the *nerve ring*. In sea stars, a *radial nerve* runs from the nerve ring to the tip of each arm, as shown in **Figure 32**. The radial nerves control the movements of the sea star's arms.

At the tip of each arm is a simple eye that senses light. The rest of the body is covered with cells that are sensitive to touch and to chemical signals in the water.

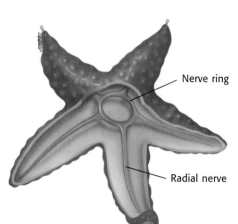

Nerve ring

Radial nerve

Figure 32 *Sea stars have simple nervous systems.*

Water Vascular System

One system that is unique to echinoderms is the **water vascular system.** This system uses water pumps to help the animal move, eat, breathe, and sense its environment. **Figure 33** shows the water vascular system of a sea star. Notice how water pressure from the water vascular system is used for a variety of functions.

Figure 33 *A water vascular system allows sea stars and all echinoderms to move, eat, and breathe.*

The water flows through a tube to the **ring canal** around the mouth.

Water enters the system through holes in a flat plate on top of the sea star. This plate is called the **sieve plate.**

From the ring canal, the water flows into **radial canals** in the arms.

Each tube foot is connected to a bulb called an **ampulla.** The ampulla regulates fluid pressure so that each tube foot may extend or retract, hang on or let go. The movement of the tube feet and of the arm together move a sea star slowly along the bottom of the sea.

The radial canals connect to dozens of tiny suckers called **tube feet.** These tube feet are used to move and to capture food. Oxygen enters and wastes leave through the thin walls of the tube feet.

48

Teaching Transparency 58 "Water Vascular System"

Reinforcement Worksheet "Spineless Variety"

IS THAT A FACT!

Sea stars typically have five arms, but some species may have 40 or even 50 arms!

Kinds of Echinoderms

Scientists divide echinoderms into several classes. Sea stars are the most familiar echinoderms, and they make up one class. But there are three classes of echinoderms that may not be as familiar to you.

Brittle Stars and Basket Stars The brittle stars and basket stars look like sea stars with long slender arms. These delicate creatures tend to be smaller than sea stars. **Figure 34** shows a basket star.

Sea Urchins and Sand Dollars Sea urchins and sand dollars are round, and their skeletons form a solid internal shell. They have no arms, but they use their tube feet to move in the same way as sea stars. Some sea urchins also walk on their spines. Sea urchins feed on algae they scrape from the surface of rocks and other objects and chew with special teeth. Sand dollars burrow into soft sand or mud, as shown in **Figure 35,** and eat tiny particles of food they find in the sand.

Sea Cucumbers Like sea urchins and sand dollars, sea cucumbers lack arms. A sea cucumber has a soft, leathery body. Unlike sea urchins, sea cucumbers are long and have a wormlike shape. **Figure 36** shows a sea cucumber.

Figure 34 *Basket stars have longer arms than sea stars.*

Figure 35 *Sand dollars burrow in the sand.*

Figure 36 *Like other echinoderms, sea cucumbers move with tube feet.*

SECTION REVIEW

1. How are sea cucumbers different from other echinoderms?

2. What is the path taken by water as it flows through the parts of the water vascular system?

3. **Applying Concepts** How are echinoderms different from other invertebrates?

internetconnect

SCI*LINKS*
NSTA

TOPIC: Echinoderms
GO TO: www.scilinks.org
*sci***LINKS NUMBER:** HSTL375

49

▼ *Answers to Section Review*

1. Sea cucumbers have a leathery body and a wormlike shape.

2. Water enters through a sieve plate and flows into a ring canal. From there, water flows down radial canals that are connected

to tube feet. Water pressure in the tube feet is regulated by bulbs called ampullae.

3. Echinoderms have an endoskeleton.

Extend

GOING FURTHER

Writing Have students investigate and report on a fifth class of echinoderms mentioned but not discussed in the text. Class Crinoidea includes sea lilies and feather stars. Crinoids are the most ancient of living echinoderms.

4 Close

Quiz

Have students answer the following questions in their ScienceLog:

1. Name four major groups of echinoderms. (any four: sea stars, brittle stars and basket stars, sea urchins and sand dollars, sea cucumbers, sea lilies and feather stars)

2. What does the water vascular system enable echinoderms to do? (Echinoderms use the water vascular system to move, eat, breathe, and sense their environment.)

ALTERNATIVE ASSESSMENT

Writing Have students compare and contrast the members of the four main classes of echinoderms discussed in the text. Students may wish to create a chart to accompany their narrative that lists characteristics that all echinoderms have in common and those that are unique to each class.

internetconnect

SCI*LINKS*
NSTA

TOPIC: Echinoderms
GO TO: www.scilinks.org
*sci***LINKS NUMBER:** HSTL375

Porifera's Porosity
Teacher's Notes

Time Required
One 45-minute class period

Lab Ratings

EASY ———————————> HARD

TEACHER PREP ▲▲
STUDENT SET-UP ▲
CONCEPT LEVEL ▲
CLEAN UP ▲

MATERIALS

Students may choose a very light absorbent material, such as a tissue, for the Going Further. You may need to have access to an electronic scale.

Safety Caution

Remind students to review all safety cautions and icons before beginning this lab activity.

Preparation Notes

Many students have never touched a natural sponge. Allow them a few moments to experience the feel of a natural sponge, and help them identify the structures. Tell them that the sponges are animals even though they don't appear animal-like. Review the life cycle of a sponge, and discuss how sponges obtain food.

Answers

7. Answers will vary. Students should subtract the mass of the dry sponge from the mass of the wet sponge.

Skill Builder Lab

USING SCIENTIFIC METHODS

Porifera's Porosity

Early biologists thought that sponges were plants because sponges are like plants in some ways. In many species, the adults stick to a surface and stay there. They cannot chase their food. Sponges absorb and filter a lot of water to get food.

In this activity, you will observe the structure of a sponge. You will also think about how a sponge's structure affects its ability to hold water and catch food. You will think about how the size of the sponge's holes affects the amount of water the sponge can hold.

MATERIALS

* natural sponge
* kitchen sponge
* paper towel
* balance
* bowl (large enough for sponge and water)
* water
* graduated cylinder
* funnel
* calculator (optional)

Make Observations

1. Put on your safety goggles and lab apron. Observe the natural sponge. Identify the pores on the outside of the sponge. See if you can find the central cavity and oscula. Record your data in your ScienceLog.

2. Notice the size and shape of the holes. Look at the holes in the kitchen sponge and the holes in the paper towel. How do their holes compare with the sponge's natural holes?

Form a Hypothesis

3. Which item do you think can hold the most water per gram of dry mass? Formulate a testable hypothesis and record it in your ScienceLog.

Test the Hypothesis

4. Read steps 5–9. Using a computer or your ScienceLog, design and draw a data table. Remember, you will collect data for the natural sponge, the kitchen sponge, and the paper towel.

5. Use the balance to measure the mass of your sponge. Record the mass.

6. Place the sponge in the bowl. Use the graduated cylinder to add water to the sponge. Add 10 mL at a time until the sponge is completely soaked. Record the amount of water added.

7. Gently remove the sponge from the bowl. Use the funnel and the graduated cylinder to measure the amount of water left in the bowl. How much water did the sponge absorb? Record your data.

50

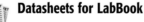
Datasheets for LabBook

Kathy LaRoe
East Valley Middle School
East Helena, Montana

8 Calculate how many milliliters of water your sponge holds per gram of dry sponge. For example, if your sponge's dry mass is 12 g and your sponge holds 59.1 mL of water, then your sponge holds 4.9 mL of water per gram.

$$\left(\frac{59.1 \text{ mL}}{12 \text{ g}} = 4.9 \text{ mL/g}\right)$$

9 Repeat steps 5–8 using the kitchen sponge and the paper towel.

Analyze the Results

10 Which item held the most water per gram of dry mass?

11 Did your results support your hypothesis?

12 Do you see a connection between the size of an item's holes and the item's ability to hold water?

Draw Conclusions

13 What can you conclude about how the size and shape of a sponge's holes affect the feeding ability of a sponge?

Going Further

You have just studied how a sponge's body structure complements its feeding function. Now collect a few different types of live insects. Using good animal safety, observe how they eat and examine the structure of their mouthparts. How does the structure of their mouthparts complement the mouthparts' function? Record your answers in your ScienceLog.

Going Further

Students will probably find that very few other materials hold as much water as a natural sponge. Students may want to measure the absorbency of disposable diapers. In those, liquid is chemically converted to a gel.

51

Chapter Highlights

Chapter Highlights

SECTION 1

invertebrate an animal without a backbone

bilateral symmetry a body plan in which two halves of an organism's body are mirror images of each other

radial symmetry a body plan in which the parts of a body are arranged in a circle around a central point

asymmetrical without symmetry

ganglia groups of nerve cells

gut the pouch where food is digested in animals

coelom a cavity in the body of some animals where the gut and organs are located

SECTION 2

open circulatory system a circulatory system consisting of a heart that pumps blood through spaces called sinuses

closed circulatory system a circulatory system in which a heart circulates blood through a network of vessels that forms a closed loop

segment one of many identical or almost identical repeating body parts

---

SECTION 1

Vocabulary

invertebrate (p. 28)
bilateral symmetry (p. 28)
radial symmetry (p. 28)
asymmetrical (p. 28)
ganglia (p. 29)
gut (p. 29)
coelom (p. 29)

Section Notes

- Invertebrates are animals without a backbone.
- Most animals have radial symmetry or bilateral symmetry.

- Unlike other animals, sponges have no symmetry.
- A coelom is a space inside the body. The gut hangs inside the coelom.
- Ganglia are clumps of nerves that help control the parts of the body.
- Sponges have special cells called collar cells to digest their food.
- Cnidarians have special stinging cells to catch their prey.
- Cnidarians have two body forms, the polyp and the medusa.
- Tapeworms and flukes are parasitic flatworms.

SECTION 2

Vocabulary

open circulatory system (p. 38)
closed circulatory system (p. 38)
segment (p. 39)

Section Notes

- All mollusks have a foot, a visceral mass, and a mantle. Most mollusks also have a shell.
- Mollusks and annelid worms have both a coelom and a circulatory system.
- In an open circulatory system, the heart pumps blood through vessels into spaces called sinuses. In a closed circulatory system, the blood is pumped through a closed network of vessels.
- Segments are identical or nearly identical repeating body parts.

☑ Skills Check

Math Concepts

SPEED AND DISTANCE If a snail is moving at 30 cm/h, how far can it travel in 1 minute? There are 60 minutes in 1 hour:

$$\frac{30 \text{ cm}}{60 \text{ min}} = 0.5 \text{ cm/min}$$

In 1 minute the snail will travel 0.5 cm.

Visual Understanding

METAMORPHOSIS Some insects go through incomplete metamorphosis, and some go through complete metamorphosis. Look at the illustrations on pages 45 and 46 to see the difference between these two types of metamorphosis.

Lab and Activity Highlights

Porifera's Porosity   PG 50

The Cricket Caper   PG 126

 Datasheets for LabBook (blackline masters for these labs)

SECTION 3

Vocabulary

exoskeleton *(p. 42)*
compound eye *(p. 42)*
antennae *(p. 42)*
mandible *(p. 42)*
metamorphosis *(p. 45)*

Section Notes

• Seventy-five percent of all animals are arthropods.

• The four main characteristics of arthropods are jointed limbs, an exoskeleton, segments, and a well-developed nervous system.

• Arthropods are classified by the type of body parts they have.

• The four kinds of arthropods are centipedes and millipedes, crustaceans, arachnids, and insects.

• Insects can undergo complete or incomplete metamorphosis.

Labs

The Cricket Caper *(p. 126)*

SECTION 4

Vocabulary

endoskeleton *(p. 47)*
water vascular system *(p. 48)*

Section Notes

• Echinoderms are marine animals that have an endoskeleton and a water vascular system.

• Most echinoderms have bilateral symmetry as larvae and radial symmetry as adults.

• The water vascular system allows echinoderms to move around by means of tube feet, which act like suction cups.

• Echinoderms have a simple nervous system consisting of a nerve ring and radial nerves.

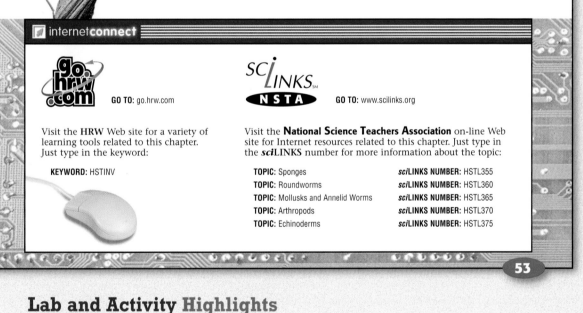

Vocabulary Review Worksheet

Blackline masters of these Chapter Highlights can be found in the **Study Guide**.

---

internetconnect

GO TO: go.hrw.com

Visit the **HRW** Web site for a variety of learning tools related to this chapter. Just type in the keyword:

KEYWORD: HSTINV

*SCI*LINKS.
N S T A

GO TO: www.scilinks.org

Visit the **National Science Teachers Association** on-line Web site for Internet resources related to this chapter. Just type in the *sci*LINKS number for more information about the topic:

TOPIC: Sponges   *sci*LINKS NUMBER: HSTL355
TOPIC: Roundworms   *sci*LINKS NUMBER: HSTL360
TOPIC: Mollusks and Annelid Worms   *sci*LINKS NUMBER: HSTL365
TOPIC: Arthropods   *sci*LINKS NUMBER: HSTL370
TOPIC: Echinoderms   *sci*LINKS NUMBER: HSTL375

53

Lab and Activity Highlights

LabBank

Labs You Can Eat, Here's Looking at You, Squid!

Inquiry Labs, At a Snail's Pace

Long-Term Projects & Research Ideas, Creepy, Crawly Food?

Chapter Review
Answers

Chapter Review

USING VOCABULARY

1. invertebrates
2. pores, an osculum
3. radial, bilateral
4. mantle
5. segments
6. water pressure in a tube foot

UNDERSTANDING CONCEPTS

Multiple Choice

7. d
8. c
9. c
10. b
11. d
12. b
13. c
14. c
15. b
16. b

USING VOCABULARY

To complete the following sentences, choose the correct term from each pair of terms listed below:

1. Animals without a backbone are called ___?___ . (*invertebrates* or *vertebrates*)

2. A sponge uses ___?___ to pull water in and releases water out through ___?___ . (*an osculum* or *pores*)

3. Cnidarians have ___?___ symmetry and flatworms have ___?___ symmetry. (*radial* or *bilateral*)

4. The shell of a snail is secreted by the ___?___ . (*radula* or *mantle*)

5. Annelid worms have ___?___ . (*jointed limbs* or *segments*)

6. An ampulla regulates ___?___ . (*water pressure in a tube foot* or *blood pressure in a closed circulatory system*)

UNDERSTANDING CONCEPTS

Multiple Choice

7. Invertebrates make up what percentage of all animals?
  a. 4 percent   **c.** 85 percent
  b. 50 percent   **d.** 97 percent

8. Which of the following describes the body plan of a sponge:
  a. radial symmetry   **c.** asymmetry
  b. bilateral symmetry   **d.** partial symmetry

9. What cells do sponges have that no other animal has?
  a. blood cells
  b. nerve cells
  c. collar cells
  d. none of the above

10. Which of the following animals do not have ganglia?
  a. annelid worms   **c.** flatworms
  b. cnidarians   **d.** mollusks

11. Which of the following animals has a coelom?
  a. sponge   **c.** flatworm
  b. cnidarian   **d.** mollusk

12. Both tapeworms and leeches are
  a. annelid worms.   **c.** flatworms.
  b. parasites.   **d.** predators.

13. Some arthropods do not have
  a. jointed limbs.
  b. an exoskeleton.
  c. antennae.
  d. segments.

14. Echinoderms live
  a. on land.   **c.** in salt water.
  b. in fresh water.   **d.** All of the above

15. *Echinoderm* means
  a. "jointed limbs."   **c.** "endoskeleton."
  b. "spiny skinned."   **d.** "shiny tube foot."

16. Echinoderm larvae have
  a. radial symmetry.
  b. bilateral symmetry.
  c. no symmetry.
  d. radial and bilateral symmetry.

Short Answer

17. What is a gut?

18. How are arachnids different from insects?

19. Which animal phylum contains the most species?

20. How does an echinoderm move?

Concept Mapping

21. Use the following terms to create a concept map: insect, sponges, sea anemone, invertebrates, arachnid, sea cucumber, crustacean, centipede, cnidarians, arthropods, echinoderms.

Write one or two sentences to answer the following questions:

22. You have discovered a strange new animal that has bilateral symmetry, a coelom, and nerves. Will this animal be classified in the Cnidaria phylum? Why or why not?

23. Unlike other mollusks, cephalopods can move rapidly. Based on what you know about the body parts of mollusks, why do you think cephalopods have this ability?

24. Roundworms, flatworms, and annelid worms belong to different phyla. Why aren't all the worms grouped in the same phylum?

MATH IN SCIENCE

25. If 75 percent of all animals are arthropods and 40 percent of all arthropods are beetles, what percentage of all animals are beetles?

INTERPRETING GRAPHICS

Below is an evolutionary tree showing how the different phyla of animals may be related to one another. The "trunk" of the tree is on the left. Use the tree to answer the questions that follow.

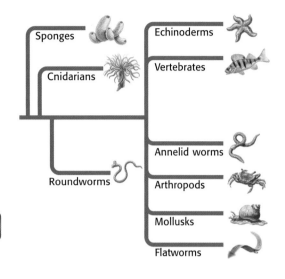

26. Which phylum is the oldest?

27. Are mollusks more closely related to roundworms or flatworms?

28. What phylum is most closely related to the vertebrates?

Reading Check-up

Take a minute to review your answers to the Pre-Reading Questions found at the bottom of page 26. Have your answers changed? If necessary, revise your answers based on what you have learned since you began this chapter.

Concept Mapping Transparency 15

Blackline masters of this Chapter Review can be found in the **Study Guide.**

Short Answer

17. a pouch lined with cells that release enzymes to digest food

18. Arachnids have two body parts—a cephalothorax and abdomen—and eight legs. Insects have three body parts—a head, a thorax, an abdomen—and six legs. Arachnids have chelicerae. Insects have antennae.

19. arthropods

20. with tube feet and the water vascular system

Concept Mapping

21. An answer to this exercise can be found at the front of this book.

CRITICAL THINKING AND PROBLEM SOLVING

22. No; cnidarians have radial symmetry and do not have coeloms.

23. Because cephalopods do not have a shell, they need to move rapidly to avoid predators. They can move rapidly because they have a large brain.

24. All of the worms are not grouped in the same phylum because they have different characteristics. Annelid worms are segmented; the others are not. Annelid worms also have a coelom and a closed circulatory system. Roundworms have a round cross section, and flatworms do not. Roundworms have a more complex digestive system than flatworms. Flatworms are the only worms with eyespots and sensory lobes.

MATH IN SCIENCE

25. $0.75 \times 0.40 = 0.30 = 30$ percent

INTERPRETING GRAPHICS

26. the sponges

27. flatworms

28. the echinoderms

Background

Tardigrades are also known as moss piglets and can be placed in history by the fact that they were some of the first organisms Antony van Leeuwenhoek examined with his spectacular invention, the microscope.

This is of interest especially because these creatures are not well represented in the fossil record. And after Leeuwenhoek's initial study, tardigrades were largely ignored for the next three centuries, in large part because of their lack of economic importance.

Answer to On Your Own

Architect Eugene Tsui was inspired by the sturdiness of the tardigrade to build what he calls "the world's safest house."

The shape of Ojo de Sol, Tsui's house in Berkeley, California, mimics that of the water bear. He says he designed the house to be oval because "nature doesn't build boxes. They're among the weakest forms because stress is concentrated in corners and along flat surfaces, vulnerable to collapse."

Tsui hoped to design a house to withstand the earthquakes and wildfires, disasters that Northern California is prone to. Fires skirt curved walls instead of penetrating them, and the arches on the upper floor are wood, steel, and concrete. The structure might be safe from some natural events, but in regard to water bears, the question would be, "Can it resist drought?"

WEIRD SCIENCE

WATER BEARS

You're alive and you know it, but how? Well, eating, breathing, and moving around are all pretty sure signs of life. And once something stops eating or breathing, the end is near. Or is it? Oddly enough, this doesn't seem to be the case for one group of invertebrates–the water bears.

Grin and Bear It

When conditions get really rough–too hot, too cold, but mostly too dry to survive–a water bear will shut down its body processes. It's similar to a bear going into hibernation, but it is even more extreme. When a water bear can't find water, it dries itself out and forms a sugar that coats its cells. Scientists think this may keep the water bear's cells from breaking down, and it may be the key to its survival.

During this hibernation-like state, called *cryptobiosis* (CRIP toh bie OH sis), the water bear doesn't eat, move, or breathe. And amazingly, it doesn't die either. Once you add water, the water bear will come right back to normal life!

Water Bear

Hard to Put a Finger On

Officially called tardigrades (TAHR di graydz), water bears have been difficult to classify. But the 700 different species of water bears are probably most closely related to arthropods. Most make their homes on wet mosses and lichens. Some water bears feed on nematodes (a tiny, unsegmented worm) and rotifers (a tiny wormlike or spherical animal). Most feed on the fluids from mosses found near their homes.

From the tropics to the Arctic, the world is full of water bears. None are much larger than a grain of sand, but all have a slow, stomping walk. Some tardigrades live as deep as the bottom of the ocean, more than 4,700 m below sea level. Other water bears live at elevations of 6,600 m above sea level, well above the tree line. It is a wonder how water bears can withstand the range of temperatures found in these places, from 151°C to –270°C.

On Your Own

▶ What do you think people can learn from an organism like the water bear? Write down at least one reason why it is worthwhile to study these special creatures.

56

EYE ON THE ENVIRONMENT

Sizable Squid

"Before my eyes was a horrible monster . . . It swam crossways in the direction of the *Nautilus* with great speed, watching us with its enormous staring green eyes. The monster's mouth, a horned beak like a parrot's, opened and shut vertically." So wrote Jules Verne in his science-fiction story *Twenty Thousand Leagues Under the Sea*. But what was this horrible monster that was about to attack the submarine *Nautilus*? Believe it or not, it was a creature that actually exists—a giant squid!

▲ *This giant squid was already dead when it was caught in a fishing net off the coast of New Zealand.*

Squid Facts

As the largest of all invertebrates, giant squids range from 8 m to 25 m long and weigh as much as 2,000 kg. It's hard to know for sure, though, because no one has ever studied a living giant squid. Scientists have studied only dead or dying giant squids that have washed ashore or have been trapped in fishing nets.

Giant squids are very similar to their much smaller relatives. They have a torpedo-shaped body, two tentacles, eight arms, a mantle, a funnel, and a beak. All their body parts are much larger, though! A giant squid's eyes, for instance, may be as large as a volleyball! And like adult squids of smaller species, giant squids feed not only on fish but also on smaller squids. Given the size of giant squids, it's hard to imagine that they have any enemies in the ocean, but they do.

A Hungry Enemy

Weighing in at 20 tons, toothed sperm whales eat giant squids. How do we know this? As many as 10,000 squid beaks have been found in the stomach of a single sperm whale. The hard beaks of giant squids are indigestible. It seems that giant squids are a regular meal for sperm whales. Yet this meal can result in some battle scars. Many whales bear ring marks on their forehead and fins that match the size of the suckers found on giant squids.

Fact or Fiction?

▶ Read Chapter 18 of Jules Verne's *Twenty Thousand Leagues Under the Sea,* and then try to find other stories about squids. Write your own story about a giant squid, and share it with the class.

57

Answer to Fact or Fiction?
Answers will vary.

Background

According to accounts, the giant squid can put up quite a fight against a whale.

Lighthouse keepers in South Africa claim to have seen a giant squid attack and subsequently drown a baby southern whale after an intense battle that lasted for more than an hour.

A Soviet whaler reported a deadly battle between an adult sperm whale and a giant squid. In that case, each did fatal damage to the other. The whale was finally strangled by the tentacles of the squid, but the squid's beak was found in the whale's stomach.

Researchers do know that squids have excellent eyesight—and some of the largest eyes in the animal kingdom—and one of the most highly developed brains of any invertebrate, two things that would contribute to making them difficult to catch.

They are also one of the most difficult mollusks to eat. Clyde Roper has a reputation for cooking and teaching courses on cephalopod cuisine; he was among the first to taste a portion of giant squid, but to his great dismay, the meat is bitter and has an ammonia flavor. It turns out that a profusion of ammonium ions, which are less dense than water, help the squid maneuver through the ocean.

Chapter Resources & Worksheets

Visual Resources

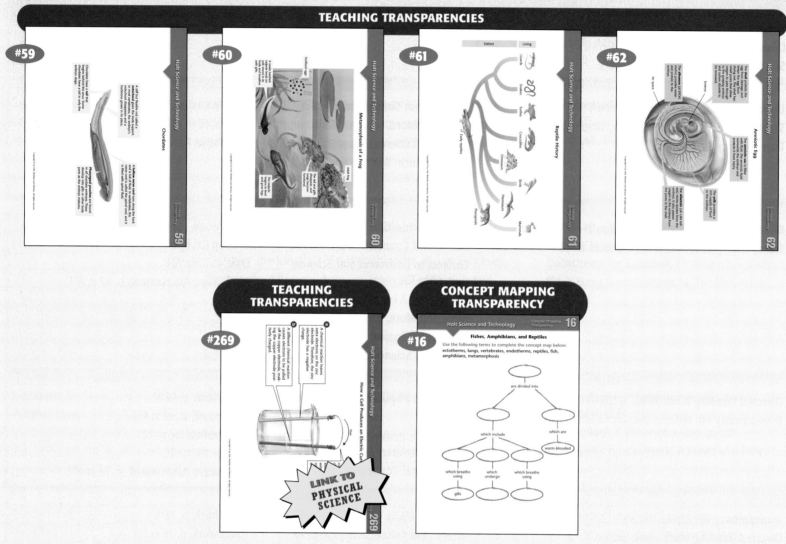

Chapter 3 • Fishes, Amphibians, and Reptiles

Review & Assessment

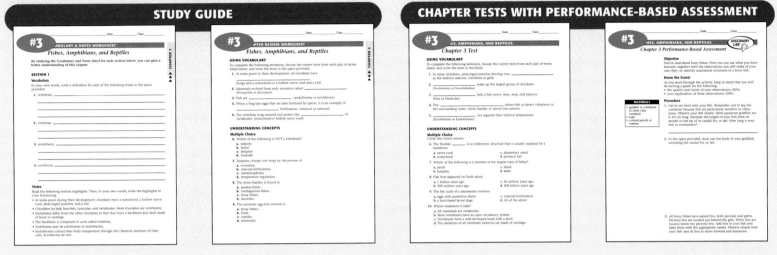

STUDY GUIDE

#3 ABULARY & NOTES WORKSHEET

Fishes, Amphibians, and Reptiles

By studying the Vocabulary and Notes listed for each section below, you can gain a better understanding of this chapter.

SECTION 1
Vocabulary
In your own words, write a definition for each of the following terms in the space provided.

1. vertebrate

2. vertebrae

3. endotherm

4. ectotherm

Notes
Read the following section highlights. Then, in your own words, write the highlights in your ScienceLog.
• At some point during their development, chordates have a notochord, a hollow nerve cord, pharyngeal pouches, and a tail.
• Chordates include lancelets, tunicates, and vertebrates. Most chordates are vertebrates.
• Vertebrates differ from the other chordates in that they have a backbone and skull made of bone or cartilage.
• The backbone is composed of units called vertebrae.
• Vertebrates may be ectotherms or endotherms.
• Endotherms control their body temperature through the chemical reactions of their cells. Ectotherms do not.

#3 APTER REVIEW WORKSHEET

Fishes, Amphibians, and Reptiles

USING VOCABULARY
To complete the following sentences, choose the correct term from each pair of terms listed below, and write the term in the space provided.

1. At some point in their development, all chordates have _____
(lungs and a notochord or a hollow nerve cord and a tail)

2. Mammals evolved from early ancestors called _____
(therapsids or dinosaurs)

3. Fish are _____ (endotherms or ectotherms)

4. When a frog lays eggs that are later fertilized by sperm, it is an example of _____ fertilization. (internal or external)

5. The vertebrae wrap around and protect the _____ of vertebrates. (notochord or hollow nerve cord)

UNDERSTANDING CONCEPTS
Multiple Choice

6. Which of the following is NOT a vertebrate?
a. tadpole
b. lizard
c. lamprey
d. tunicate

7. Tadpoles change into frogs by the process of
a. evolution.
b. internal fertilization.
c. metamorphosis.
d. temperature regulation.

8. The swim bladder is found in
a. jawless fishes.
b. cartilaginous fishes.
c. bony fishes.
d. lancelets.

9. The amniotic egg first evolved in
a. bony fishes.
b. birds.
c. reptiles.
d. mammals.

CHAPTER TESTS WITH PERFORMANCE-BASED ASSESSMENT

#3 HES, AMPHIBIANS, AND REPTILES

Chapter 3 Test

USING VOCABULARY
To complete the following sentences, choose the correct term from each pair of terms listed, and write the term in the blank.

1. In some chordates, pharyngeal pouches develop into _____ as the embryo matures. (vertebrae or gills)

2. _____ make up the largest group of chordates. (Vertebrates or Invertebrates)

3. _____ help a fish move, steer, stop, and balance. (Fins or Denticles)

4. The _____ allows fish to detect vibrations in the surrounding water. (swim bladder or lateral line system)

5. _____ can regulate their internal temperature. (Ectotherms or Endotherms)

UNDERSTANDING CONCEPTS
Multiple Choice
Circle the correct answer.

6. The flexible _____ is an embryonic structure that is usually replaced by a backbone.
a. nerve cord
b. notochord
c. alimentary canal
d. postanal tail

7. Which of the following is a member of the largest class of fishes?
a. perch
b. lamprey
c. shark
d. skate

8. Fish first appeared on Earth about
a. 1 billion years ago.
b. 500 million years ago.
c. 65 million years ago.
d. 400 billion years ago.

9. The life cycle of a salamander involves
a. eggs with protective shells.
b. a land-based larval stage.
c. internal fertilization.
d. All of the above

10. Which statement is false?
a. All mammals are vertebrates.
b. Most vertebrates have an open circulatory system.
c. Vertebrates have a well-developed head with a skull.
d. The skeletons of all vertebrate embryos are made of cartilage.

#3 HES, AMPHIBIANS, AND REPTILES   DISCOVERY LAB

Chapter 3 Performance-Based Assessment

Objective
You've read about bony fishes. Now you can use what you have learned—together with the observations you will make of your own fish—to identify anatomical structures of a bony fish.

Know the Score!
As you work through the activity, keep in mind that you will be earning a grade for the following:
• the quality and clarity of your observations (50%)
• your explanation of these observations (50%)

MATERIALS
• goldfish in a fishbowl or other clear container
• ruler
• colored pencils or markers

Procedure
1. Get at eye level with your fish. Remember not to tap the container because fish are particularly sensitive to vibrations. Observe your fish closely. Most aquarium goldfish are 5–10 cm long. Estimate the length of your fish from its mouth to the tip of its caudal fin, or tail. How long is your fish in centimeters?

2. In the space provided, draw just the body of your goldfish, including the caudal fin, or tail.

3. All bony fishes have paired fins, both pectoral and pelvic. Pectoral fins are located just behind the gills. Pelvic fins are located below the pectoral fins. Add fins to your fish and label them with the appropriate names. Observe closely how your fish uses its fins to move forward and maneuver.

Lab Worksheets

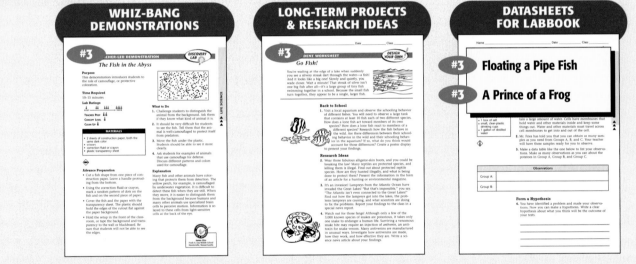

WHIZ-BANG DEMONSTRATIONS

#3 ACHER-LED DEMONSTRATION   DISCOVERY LAB

The Fish in the Abyss

Purpose
This demonstration introduces students to the role of camouflage, or protective coloration.

Time Required
10–15 minutes
Lab Ratings
EASY
TEACHER PREP
CONCEPT LEVEL
CLEAN UP

MATERIALS
• 2 sheets of construction paper, both the same dark color
• scissors
• correction fluid or crayon
• plastic transparency sheet

Advance Preparation
• Cut a fish shape from one piece of construction paper. Leave a handle protruding from the bottom.
• Using the correction fluid or crayon, mark a random pattern of dots on the fish and on the second piece of paper.
• Cover the fish and the paper with the transparency sheet. The plastic should hold the edges of the cutout flat against the paper background.
• Hold the cutout in the front of the classroom, or tape the background and transparency to the wall or blackboard. Be sure that students will not be able to see the edges.

What to Do
1. Challenge students to distinguish the animal from the background. Ask them if they know what kind of animal it is.

2. It should be very difficult for students to see the fish. Tell them that the animal is well-camouflaged to protect itself from predators.

3. Move the fish under the plastic. Students should be able to see it more clearly.

4. Ask students for examples of animals that use camouflage for defense. Discuss different patterns and colors used for camouflage.

Explanation
Many fish and other animals have coloring that protects them from detection. The yellow perch, for example, is camouflaged by underwater vegetation. It is difficult to detect these fish when they are still. When they move, it is easier to distinguish them from the background because humans and many other animals use specialized brain cells to perceive motion. Information is relayed to these cells from light-sensitive cells at the back of the eye.

LONG-TERM PROJECTS & RESEARCH IDEAS

#3 DENT WORKSHEET   DESIGN YOUR OWN

Go Fish!

You're wading at the edge of a lake when suddenly you see a silvery streak dart through the water—a fish! And it looks like a big one! Slowly and quietly, you wade closer. Wait a minute! That streak of silver isn't one big fish after all—it's a large group of tiny fish swimming together in a school. Because the small fish turn together, they appear to be a single, larger fish.

What to Do
1. Visit a local aquarium and observe the schooling behavior of different fishes. You will need to observe a large tank that contains at least 10 fish each of two different species. How does a lone fish act toward members of its own species? How does a lone fish react to members of a different species? Research how the fish behave in the wild. Are there differences between their schooling behavior in the wild and their schooling behavior in the aquarium? If so, what do you think would account for those differences? Create a poster display to present your findings.

Research Ideas
2. Wear those fabulous alligator-skin boots, and you could be breaking the law! Many reptiles are protected species, and killing them is illegal. Find out about protected reptile species. How are they hunted illegally, and what is being done to protect them? Present the information in the form of an article for a hunting or environmental magazine.

3. It's an invasion! Lampreys from the Atlantic Ocean have invaded the Great Lakes! "But that's impossible," you say. "The Atlantic isn't even connected to the Great Lakes!" Find out how the lampreys got into the lakes, the problems lampreys are causing, and what scientists are doing to fix the problems. Report your findings to the class in a special news report.

4. Watch out for those fangs! Although only a few of the 3,000 known species of snakes are poisonous, it takes only one snake to endanger a human life. Surviving a venomous snake bite may require an injection of antivenin, an antitoxin for snake venom. Many antivenins are manufactured in unusual ways. Investigate how antivenins are made, how they work, and how effective they are. Write a science news article about your findings.

DATASHEETS FOR LABBOOK

Name _____ Date _____ Class _____

#3 *Floating a Pipe Fish*

#3 *A Prince of a Frog*

• 1 box of salt
• small, clear-plastic drinking cups
• 1 gallon of distilled water

tain a large amount of water. Cells have membranes that hold water and other materials inside and keep some things out. Water and other materials must travel across cell membranes to get into and out of the cell.

2. Mr. Fries has told you that you can obtain as many samples as you need from Groups A, B, and C. Your teacher will have these samples ready for you to observe.

3. Make a data table like the one below to list your observations. Make as many observations as you can about the potatoes in Group A, Group B, and Group C.

Observations		
Group A:		
Group B:		

Form a Hypothesis
4. You have identified a problem and made your observations. Now you can make a hypothesis. Write a clear hypothesis about what you think will be the outcome of your tests.

Applications & Extensions

CRITICAL THINKING & PROBLEM SOLVING

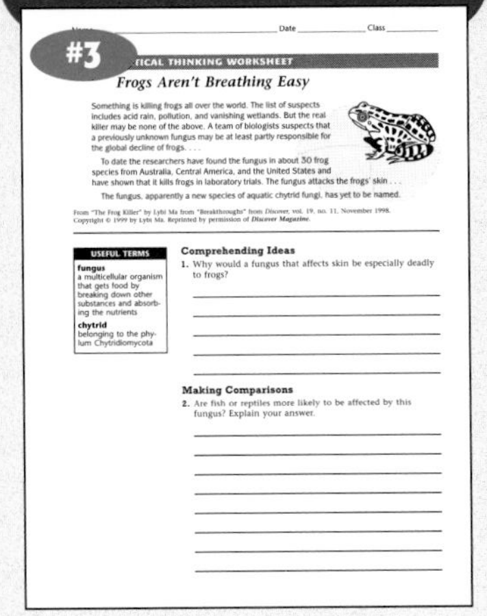

#3 TICAL THINKING WORKSHEET

Frogs Aren't Breathing Easy

Something is killing frogs all over the world. The list of suspects includes acid rain, pollution, and vanishing wetlands. But the real killer may be none of the above. A team of biologists suspects that a previously unknown fungus may be at least partly responsible for the global decline of frogs.

To date the researchers have found the fungus in about 30 frog species from Australia, Central America, and the United States and have shown that it kills frogs in laboratory tests. The fungus attacks the frogs' skin . . .

The fungus, apparently a new species of aquatic chytrid fungus, has yet to be named.

From "The Frog Killer" by Life Sciences "Breakthroughs" from *Discover*, vol. 19, no. 11, November 1998. Copyright © 1999 by Life Inc. Reprinted by permission of *Discover Magazine*.

USEFUL TERMS
fungus
a multicellular organism that gets food by breaking down other substances and absorbing the nutrients
chytrid
belonging to the phylum Chytridiomycota

Comprehending Ideas
1. Why would a fungus that affects skin be especially deadly to frogs?

Making Comparisons
2. Are fish or reptiles more likely to be affected by this fungus? Explain your answer.

SCIENCE TECHNOLOGY

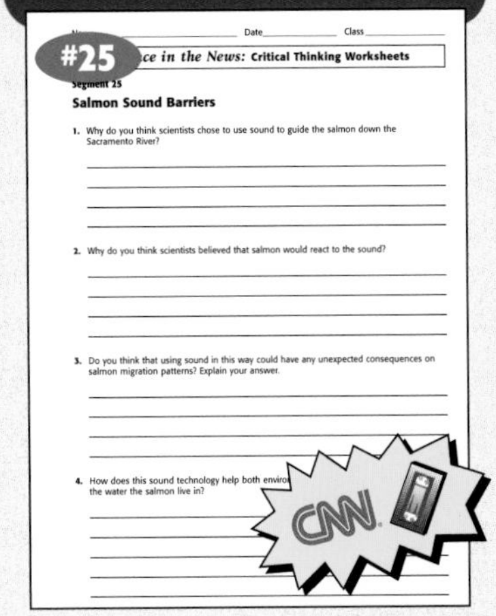

#25 nce in the News: Critical Thinking Worksheets

Segment 15
Salmon Sound Barriers

1. Why do you think scientists chose to use sound to guide the salmon down the Sacramento River?

2. Why do you think scientists believed that salmon would react to the sound?

3. Do you think that using sound in this way could have any unexpected consequences on salmon migration patterns? Explain your answer.

4. How does this sound technology help both the environment and the water the salmon live in?

EYE ON THE ENVIRONMENT

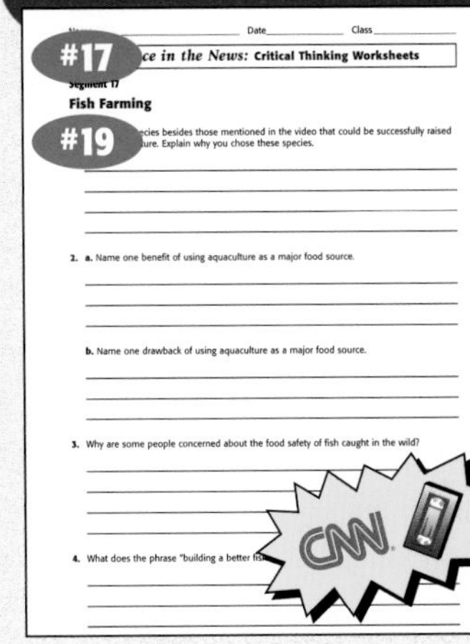

#17 nce in the News: Critical Thinking Worksheets

Segment 13
Fish Farming

#19

1. _____ species besides those mentioned in the video that could be successfully raised _____ ure. Explain why you chose these species.

2. a. Name one benefit of using aquaculture as a major food source.

b. Name one drawback of using aquaculture as a major food source.

3. Why are some people concerned about the food safety of fish caught in the wild?

4. What does the phrase "building a better _____

SECTION 1

What Are Vertebrates?

▶ **Chordates**

Chordate embryos have four basic features that distinguish them from other animals. The first is the notochord, a semiflexible rod that runs along the length of the body. They also have a hollow dorsal nerve cord, with nerve fibers that make contact with the muscles; pharyngeal slits, which are openings between the pharynx and the outside of the animal; and a postanal tail, which is an extension of the notochord and dorsal nerve cord.

IS THAT A FACT!

☞ Cephalochordates (lancelets) have more than 100 pharyngeal slits that are used to strain food particles from water.

▶ **Vertebrates**

Vertebrates, which belong to the phylum Chordata, first appeared on Earth during the late Cambrian period, more than 500 million years ago. The first vertebrates were jawless creatures; jaws appeared about 100 million years later. Vertebrates include fishes, amphibians, reptiles, birds, and mammals.

SECTION 2

Fishes

▶ **Ray-Finned Fishes**

The actinopterygians, or ray-finned fishes, are the largest class of fishes. There are about 20,000 species of ray-finned fishes, making them by far the largest group of aquatic vertebrates as well.

• The first ray-finned fish appeared during the Devonian period.

▶ **Cartilaginous Fishes**

Sharks, skates, and rays are all Chondrichthyes, or cartilaginous fishes. About 800 species of cartilaginous fishes exist, compared with about 20,000 species of bony fishes. Cartilaginous fishes are an amazingly diverse group both behaviorally and physically. For example, sharks range in size from the 14 m (40 ft) whale shark to the 0.6 m (2 ft) dogfish shark. Shark diets differ greatly too. Although most eat other fish, great white sharks have been known to eat seals and other marine mammals. Some sharks, such as the gentle basking shark, eat nothing but plankton.

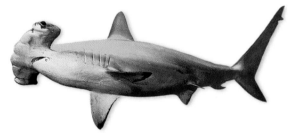

• Nurse sharks have special sensory organs beneath their nose called barbels that help them locate food on the bottom of the ocean.

IS THAT A FACT!

☞ Some ray-finned fishes have evolved special abilities. For example, Siamese fighting fish are capable of breathing air in addition to taking oxygen from water through their gills. Fish such as the walking catfish and mudskipper can even crawl on land!

☞ More people are killed in the United States each year by dogs than have been killed by great white sharks in the last century.

SECTION 3

Amphibians

▶ Frogs and Toads

What's the difference between toads and frogs? Toads are types of frogs that belong to the family Bufonidae. These "true toads" generally have stubby bodies, short hind legs, and dry and warty skin, and they tend to lay their eggs in long chains. "True frogs," which are members of the family Ranidae, generally have bulging eyes, strong and long webbed feet, and smooth skin, and they tend to lay their eggs in clusters. There are many exceptions to these rules, however; for example, there are some warty frogs and some smooth-skinned toads.

▶ Salamanders

Salamanders belong to the order Caudata. These carnivorous amphibians are distinguished from other amphibians by the presence of a tail, two pairs of legs of approximately the same size, ribs, teeth on both jaws, and other muscular and skeletal characteristics. Salamanders live in cool, moist habitats in almost all northern temperate areas of the world.

IS THAT A FACT!

- Some salamanders can extend their sticky, mucus-coated tongues as far as half their body length.

- Most salamanders can regenerate lost toes and even entire limbs. As a defense mechanism, they sometimes voluntarily shed their tail. Muscle contractions in the detached tail distract a predator long enough to enable the salamander to make a quick getaway.

SECTION 4

Reptiles

▶ Reptile Characteristics

Most of the 6,000 species of reptiles in existence today live in tropical areas. They include snakes, crocodiles, lizards, turtles, and tuatara, which are lizardlike animals that can be found only on some of the islets of New Zealand. Reptiles range in size from the tiny gecko lizard (3 cm) to the anaconda snake (up to 12 m).

▶ Crocodiles and Alligators

These two closely related carnivorous reptiles belong to the order Crocodylia. How do they differ from each other? Alligators have broader snouts than crocodiles. Also, the fourth tooth on either side of a crocodile's jaw protrudes when the crocodile's mouth is closed.

- Estuarine crocodiles can live to be over 100 years old.

IS THAT A FACT!

- The Chinese alligator, a relatively small animal found in China's Yangtze River region, is an endangered species and may indeed be extinct.

For background information about teaching strategies and issues, refer to the *Professional Reference for Teachers*.

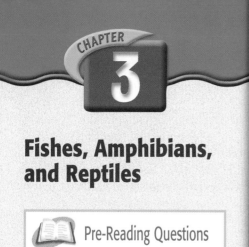

CHAPTER
3

Fishes, Amphibians, and Reptiles

Pre-Reading Questions

Students may not know the answers to these questions before reading the chapter, so accept any reasonable response.

Suggested Answers

1. Ectotherms are sometimes called cold-blooded. They do not control their body temperature through the chemical reactions of their cells. Their body temperature depends on the temperature of the environment.

2. A reptile has thick, dry skin and lays amniotic eggs. An amphibian has thin, moist skin that it can breathe through, and it must live in or near water.

Sections

Pre-Reading
Questions

1. What does it mean to say an animal is cold-blooded?

2. What is the difference between a reptile and an amphibian?

58

internet connect

go.hrw.com

HRW On-line Resources

For worksheets and other teaching aids, visit the HRW Web site and type in the keyword: **HSTVR1**

SCiLINKS
NSTA

www.scilinks.com

Use the *sci*LINKS numbers at the end of each chapter for additional resources on the **NSTA** Web site.

Smithsonian Institution®

www.si.edu/hrw

Visit the Smithsonian Institution Web site for related on-line resources.

CNNfyi.com

www.cnnfyi.com

Visit the CNN Web site for current events coverage and classroom resources.

OIL ON WATER

To stay afloat, sharks store a lot of oil in their liver. In this activity, you will build a model of an oily liver to see how an oily liver can keep a shark afloat.

Procedure

1. Use a **beaker** to measure out equal amounts of **water** and **cooking oil.**

2. Fill **one balloon** with the water.

3. Fill a **second balloon** with the cooking oil.

4. Tie the balloons so that no air remains inside. Float each balloon in a **bowl half full of water.** Observe what happens to the balloons.

Analysis

5. Compare how the two balloons floated.

6. The function of an oily liver is to keep the fish from sinking. How does the structure of the liver complement its function?

START-UP Activity

OIL ON WATER

MATERIALS
FOR EACH GROUP: • beaker • water • cooking oil • two balloons • bowl

Answers to START-UP Activity

5. The balloon filled with water will eventually settle about halfway to the bottom of the tank. The oil-filled balloon will float.

6. Sample answer: The oil in an oily liver is less dense than water. This property provides buoyancy to a cartilaginous fish and helps it stay afloat.

A BLAST FROM THE PAST!

In December 1938, Marjorie Courtenay Latimer made an amazing discovery. On a fishing dock in South Africa, she found a coelacanth (SEE luh kahnth). She sent a sketch of the fish to her friend J.L.B. Smith, an expert on fish. Smith recognized the fish right away. So what's so amazing about this giant fish? Scientists had thought that coelacanths became extinct about 70 million years ago! In this chapter, you will learn about other fishes as well as about amphibians and reptiles.

59

Focus

What Are Vertebrates?

This section introduces students to vertebrates and other chordates. Students will learn about the characteristics of vertebrates and the traits that set them apart from other chordates. They will also discover the differences between ectotherms and endotherms.

Bellringer

While you are taking attendance, ask students to ponder this question:

What are some of the physical characteristics shared by dinosaurs and people?

Have each student jot down two or three ideas. Then briefly discuss students' lists before beginning the section.

1) Motivate

DEMONSTRATION

Assembling Skeletons As an introduction to vertebrates, show students how to reassemble a small mammal skeleton. Obtain owl pellets (the bones of animals eaten by owls) from a nature center or biological supply company. Provide students with a simple illustration of a small mammal skeleton as a reference. In groups of two or three, have students break apart pellets and sort the bones, reconstructing an "exploded view" of whatever small mammal skeletons they find. Sheltered English

Directed Reading Worksheet Section 1

SECTION 1
READING WARM-UP

Terms to Learn

vertebrate
vertebrae
endotherm
ectotherm

What You'll Do

◆ List the four characteristics of chordates.
◆ Describe the main characteristics of vertebrates.
◆ Explain the difference between an ectotherm and an endotherm.

What Are Vertebrates?

Have you ever seen a dinosaur skeleton at a museum? Fossilized dinosaur bones were put back together to show what the animal looked like. Most dinosaur skeletons are huge compared with the skeletons of the humans who view them. But humans have many of the same kinds of bones that dinosaurs had; ours are just smaller. Your backbone is very much like the one in a dinosaur skeleton, as shown in **Figure 1**. Animals with a backbone are called **vertebrates**.

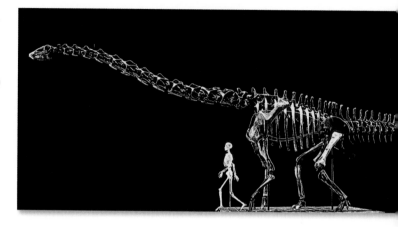

Figure 1 *Humans and dinosaurs are both vertebrates.*

Chordates

Vertebrates belong to the phylum Chordata. Members of this phylum are called *chordates*. Vertebrates make up the largest group of chordates, but there are two other groups of chordates—lancelets and tunicates. These are shown in **Figure 2**. These chordates do not have a backbone or a well-developed head. They are very simple compared with vertebrates. But all three groups share chordate characteristics.

At some point in their life, all chordates have four special body parts: a *notochord*, a *hollow nerve cord*, *pharyngeal* (fuh RIN jee uhl) *pouches*, and a *tail*. These are shown in **Figure 3** on the next page.

Figure 2 *Both tunicates, like the sea squirts at left, and the lancelet, shown above, are marine organisms.*

60

Multicultural
CONNECTION

In many parts of Asia, lancelets are commercially harvested and are an important food source. Have students research the use of lancelets as a food source, examining such things as taste, price per pound, and availability in the United States. Students could present their findings in an oral or written report or use the information they have gathered to develop recipes using lancelets.

A stiff but flexible rod called a **notochord** gives the body support. In most vertebrates, the embryo's notochord disappears and a backbone grows in its place.

A **hollow nerve cord** runs along the back and is full of fluid. In vertebrates, this nerve cord is called the *spinal cord,* and it is filled with *spinal fluid.*

Chordates have a **tail** that begins behind the anus. Some chordates have a tail in only the embryo stage.

Pharyngeal pouches are found in all chordate embryos. These develop into gills or other body parts as the embryo matures.

Figure 3 *The chordate characteristics in a lancelet are shown here. All chordates have these four characteristics at some point in their life.*

Getting a Backbone

Most chordates are vertebrates. Vertebrates have many traits that set them apart from the lancelets and tunicates. For example, vertebrates have a backbone. The backbone is a segmented column of bones. These bones are called **vertebrae** (VUHR tuh BRAY). You can see the vertebrae of a human in **Figure 4.** The vertebrae surround the nerve cord and protect it. Vertebrates also have a well-developed head protected by a skull. The skull and vertebrae are made of either cartilage or bone. *Cartilage* is the tough material that the flexible parts of our ears and nose are made of.

The skeletons of all vertebrate embryos are made of cartilage. But as most vertebrates grow, the cartilage is usually replaced by bone. Bone is much harder than cartilage.

Because bone is so hard, it can easily be fossilized. Many fossils of vertebrates have been discovered, and they have provided valuable information about relationships among organisms.

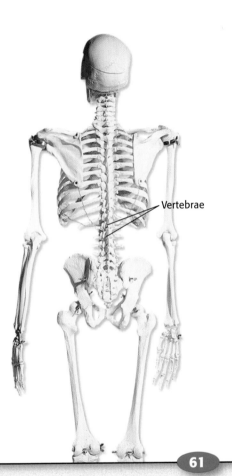

Vertebrae

Figure 4 *The vertebrae interlock to form a strong but flexible column of bone. The backbone protects the spinal cord and supports the rest of the body.*

61

2 Teach

MATH and **MORE**

Using the figures below, have students construct a pie graph to show the relative numbers of the species in the different classes of vertebrates.

Fish	25,000
Amphibians	4,600
Reptiles	6,000
Birds	9,000
Mammals	4,300

 **Science Skills Worksheet** "Grasping Graphing"

REAL-WORLD CONNECTION

Paleontology Have students research the field of paleontology and report their findings to the class. The report could be part of a special "career day" on which students present reports on a variety of scientific fields. Suggest that students answer questions such as the following: What do paleontologists do? What type of education do they need? What types of career opportunities exist for paleontologists?

 Teaching Transparency 59 "Chordates"

WEIRD SCIENCE

Tunicates are actually more well developed as young larvae than they are when they "mature" into adults! As larvae, tunicates have many chordate features, look much like tadpoles, and are able to swim. As they reach adulthood, however, they lose their tail (and therefore their ability to swim), and their nervous system disintegrates.

internet**connect**

SCI**LINKS** NSTA

TOPIC: Vertebrates
GO TO: www.scilinks.org
*sci***LINKS NUMBER:** HSTL380

3 Extend

QuickLab

MATERIALS

FOR EACH GROUP:
• fever thermometer

Answer to QuickLab

Human body temperature will not fluctuate more than a few tenths of a degree, even after exercise. An ectotherm's body temperature fluctuates more dramatically, depending on the temperature of its environment.

ACTIVITY

Invite a paleontologist or fossil enthusiast to speak with the class about fossil hunting in your area.

4 Close

Quiz

1. What is a segmented column of bones that supports the body of a vertebrate called? (backbone)

2. Of birds, fishes, mammals, reptiles, and amphibians, which are ectotherms and which are endotherms? (Birds and mammals are endotherms. Fishes, amphibians, and reptiles are ectotherms.)

ALTERNATIVE ASSESSMENT

Writing Have small groups of students compile lists of three or four questions related to the content in this section. Then have students use their questions to quiz each other.

Body Temperature

Use a nonglass **fever thermometer** for this experiment. Take your temperature every hour for at least 6 hours. Make a graph of your body temperature by placing the time of day on the *x*-axis and your temperature on the *y*-axis. Does your temperature change throughout the day? How much? Do you think your body temperature changes after exercise? How would your results be different if you were an ectotherm?

---

internet connect

SCI*LINKS*
NSTA

TOPIC: Vertebrates
GO TO: www.scilinks.org
*sci*LINKS NUMBER: HSTL380

Are Vertebrates Warm or Cold?

Most animals need to stay warm. The chemical reactions that take place in their body cells occur only at certain temperatures. An animal's body temperature cannot be too high or too low. But some animals control their body temperature more than others.

Staying Warm Birds and mammals warm their body by capturing the heat released by the chemical reactions in their cells. Their body temperature stays nearly constant even as the temperature of their environment changes. Animals that maintain a constant body temperature are called **endotherms.** Endotherms are sometimes called *warmblooded* animals. Because of their constant body temperature, endotherms can live in cold environments.

Cold Blood? On sunny days, lizards, like the one in **Figure 5,** bask in the sun. As they become warm, they also become more active. They are able to hunt for food and escape predators. But when the temperature drops, lizards slow down.

Lizards and other animals that do not control their body temperature through the chemical reactions of their cells are called **ectotherms.** Their body temperature fluctuates with the temperature of their environment. Nearly all fishes, amphibians, and reptiles are ectotherms. Ectotherms are sometimes called *coldblooded* animals.

Figure 5 *Lizards bask in the sun to absorb heat.*

SECTION REVIEW

1. How are vertebrates the same as other chordates? How are they different?

2. How are endotherms and ectotherms different?

3. **Applying Concepts** Your pet lizard is not moving very much. The veterinarian tells you to put a heat lamp in the cage. Why might this help?

▼ Answers to Section Review

1. Like other chordates, vertebrates have a notochord, a hollow nerve cord, pharyngeal pouches, and a tail at some point in their lives. Unlike other chordates, vertebrates have a backbone and a skull.

2. Endotherms regulate their body temperature by capturing the heat released by the chemical reactions in their cells. Ectotherms do not tightly control their body temperature through the chemical reactions of their cells. Their body temperature depends on the temperature of their environment.

3. A lizard is an ectotherm. The heat lamp will warm the cage and cause the body temperature of the lizard to rise. The lizard will become more active when its temperature rises.

Fishes

Find a body of water, and you'll probably find fish. Fishes live in almost every water environment, from shallow ponds and streams to the depths of the oceans. You can find fishes in cold arctic waters and in warm tropical seas. Fishes can be found in rivers, lakes, marshes, and even in water-filled caves.

Fish were the first vertebrates on Earth. Fossil evidence indicates that fish appeared about 500 million years ago. Today Earth's marine and freshwater fishes make up more species than all other vertebrates combined. There are more than 25,000 species of fishes, and more are being discovered. A few are shown in **Figure 6.**

Figure 6 *These are just some of the many species of fishes. Do any look familiar?*

Angelfish

Surgeonfish

Sea horse

Catfish

Wolf eel

Fish Characteristics

Although the fishes on this page look very different from each other, they share many characteristics that help them live in water.

Many fishes are predators of other animals. Others are herbivores. Because they must actively search for food, they need a strong body, well-developed senses, and a brain.

63

Terms to Learn

fins   gills
scales   denticles
lateral line swim bladder
  system

What You'll Do

◆ Describe the three classes of living fishes, and give an example of each.
◆ Describe the function of a swim bladder and an oily liver.
◆ Explain the difference between internal fertilization and external fertilization.

Homework

Writing **Researching Fishes** Have students visit the supermarket and write down each type of canned fish for sale and each type of frozen and/or fresh fish for sale. Students should then choose one of the fish and write a brief, half-page paper describing the size and appearance of the fish in its natural habitat, areas where it can be found, and the amount of the fish harvested each year.

SECTION 2

Focus

Fishes

This section introduces students to fish, the first vertebrates. Students will explore the characteristics of fish, including their swimming ability and their complex senses of vision, smell, and hearing. Students will also learn about the three classes of fishes.

Bellringer

Have students write a book-title pun on the subject of fish. Write a few titles on the board to get students' creative juices flowing, such as the following:

I Like Fish, by Ann Chovie
Life on a Limb, by Anna Perch
Fish Story, by Rod Enreel

1 Motivate

GROUP ACTIVITY

Have students turn the classroom or hallway into a fantasy sea world. Using books, magazines, and other media, students should draw, accurately color, and cut out two or three different fish each. Before posting the fish around the room, have students make a card with the name of the fish, its range, and its size. Sheltered English

Directed Reading Worksheet Section 2

READING 📖 STRATEGY

Prediction Guide Before students read the passage about fishes, ask them whether the following statements are true or false.

1. Sharks are considered fish. (true)

2. Some fish will suffocate if they stop swimming. (true)

3. All fish need to swim to stay alive. (false)

Students will discover the answers as they explore Section 2.

DISCUSSION

Aquarium Presentations
Encourage students who have aquariums to share information about their fish with the class. Discuss the importance of providing oxygen-rich water and other care requirements.

REAL-WORLD CONNECTION

Minnows and carp make up the largest family of fishes, with 1,600 species. They are usually the most abundant freshwater fish in North America, Europe, Asia, and Africa. You may even have one in your own home; goldfish and tetras are carp, and in a large enough setting, they can grow to several inches in length. Under ideal conditions, fish continue to grow for their entire lives.

MISCONCEPTION ALERT

Fish remove oxygen gas that is dissolved in the water. They *do not* use the oxygen that is part of the water molecule itself. Each molecule of water contains one atom of oxygen, but it is unavailable to the fish.

Born to Swim Fishes have many body parts that help them swim. Strong muscles attached to the backbone allow fishes to swim vigorously after their prey. Fishes swim through the water by moving their fins. **Fins** are fanlike structures that help fish move, steer, stop, and balance. Many fishes have bodies covered by **scales,** which protect the body and reduce friction as they swim through the water. **Figure 7** shows some of the external features of a typical fish.

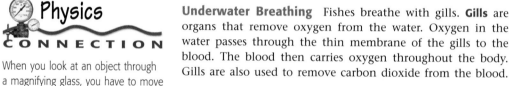
Dorsal fin
Lateral line
Pelvic fin
Anal fin
Tail fin
Eye
Gills
Gill cover
Pectoral fins

Figure 7 *Fishes come in a variety of shapes and sizes, but all have gills, fins, and a tail.*

Physics CONNECTION

When you look at an object through a magnifying glass, you have to move the lens back and forth in front of your eye to bring the object into focus. The same thing happens in fish eyes. Fish have special muscles to change the position of the lenses of their eyes. By moving the eye lenses, fish can bring objects into focus.

Making Sense of the World Fishes have well-developed vision, hearing, and sense of smell. Most fishes also have a lateral line system. The **lateral line system** is a row or rows of tiny sense organs along each side of the body that often extend onto the head. This system detects water vibrations, such as those caused by another fish swimming by. Fishes have a brain that keeps track of all the information coming in from these senses. A tough skull protects the brain.

Underwater Breathing Fishes breathe with gills. **Gills** are organs that remove oxygen from the water. Oxygen in the water passes through the thin membrane of the gills to the blood. The blood then carries oxygen throughout the body. Gills are also used to remove carbon dioxide from the blood.

Making More Fish Most fishes reproduce by *external fertilization.* The female lays unfertilized eggs in the water, and the male drops sperm on them. But some species of fish reproduce by internal fertilization. In *internal fertilization,* the male deposits sperm inside the female. In most cases the female then lays eggs that contain the developing embryos. Baby fish hatch from the eggs. But in some species, the embryos develop inside the mother, and the baby fish are born live.

🖅 **internetconnect**

SCI**LINKS** NSTA
TOPIC: Fishes
GO TO: www.scilinks.org
*sci***LINKS NUMBER:** HSTL385

IS THAT A FACT!

Air has 26 times more oxygen than water at the same temperature. Consequently, fish expend much more energy breathing than most mammals do.

Types of Fishes

Fishes include five very different classes of animals. Two classes are now extinct. We know about them only because of fossils. The three classes of fishes living today are *jawless fishes, cartilaginous fishes,* and *bony fishes.*

Jawless Fishes The first fishes did not have jaws. You might think that having no jaws would make it hard to eat and would lead to extinction. But the jawless fishes have thrived for half a billion years. Today there are about 60 species of jawless fishes.

Modern jawless fishes include lampreys, as shown in **Figure 8,** and hagfish. These fishes are eel-like, and they have smooth, slimy skin and a round, jawless mouth. Their skeleton is made of cartilage, and they have a notochord but no backbone. These fishes have a skull, a brain, and eyes.

Figure 8 *Lampreys are parasites that live by attaching themselves to other fishes.*

Cartilaginous Fishes Did you know that a shark is a fish? Sharks, like the one in **Figure 9,** belong to a class of fishes called cartilaginous (KART'l AJ uh nuhs) fishes. In most vertebrates, soft cartilage in the embryo is gradually replaced by bone. In sharks, skates, and rays, however, the skeleton never changes from cartilage to bone. That is why they are called cartilaginous fishes.

Sharks are the most well-known cartilaginous fishes, but they are not the only ones. Another group includes skates and rays. A sting ray is shown in **Figure 10.**

As any shark lover knows, cartilaginous fishes have fully functional jaws. These fishes are strong swimmers and expert predators. Like most predators, they have keen senses. Many have excellent senses of sight and smell, and they have a lateral line system.

Figure 9 *Sharks, like this hammerhead, rarely prey on humans. They prefer to eat their regular food, which is fish.*

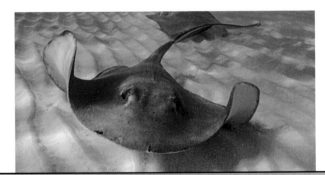

Figure 10 *Rays, like this sting ray, usually feed on shellfish and worms on the sea floor.*

65

Homework

Have students indicate which class (or classes) of fishes have the following characteristics; *J* for jawless, *C* for cartilaginous, and *B* for bony.

gills (J, C, B)
denticles (C)
cartilage skeleton (J, C)
swim bladder (B)
scales (B)

Prediction Guide Ask students: What are the three types of fishes alive in the world today?

(jawless, cartilaginous, and bony)

BRAIN FOOD

Sharks lack some of the features of bony fishes, such as a swim bladder. They also lack movable side fins. In bony fishes, the side fins behind the head can be swiveled so the fish can move backward and forward. Sharks can't do this. How would this affect the shark's movement through the water?

It is difficult or impossible for the shark to stop or to swim backward.

CONNECT TO
ENVIRONMENTAL SCIENCE

Once home to 200–500 species of fishes, Lake Victoria, in East Africa, is now home to the Nile perch and little else. Most of the native fishes were small cichlids, with each species unique in appearance and habit. But they were relatively difficult to fish commercially. The Nile perch was being tested in a nearby lake for introduction into Lake Victoria for commercial fishing when it mysteriously appeared in the lake on its own. It has since nearly wiped out the native fishes in this huge lake, to the point that the Nile perch is now largely feeding on its own young and shrimp. As a commercial fishery, the introduction is considered a success. Ecologically, it is a disaster.

MATH and MORE

Carcharodon megalodon shark teeth are as much as 17.5 cm long. Based on its tooth length, scientists estimate the Miocene-era shark was probably 12 m long, which is about twice as long as today's great white shark. Have students imagine that they discovered some shark teeth with the following lengths: 35 cm, 70 cm, and 8.75 cm. Have them use ratios to estimate the sizes of the sharks these teeth came from. (24 m, 48 m, and 6 m)

Answer to MATHBREAK

There are 23,750 species of bony fishes (25,000 × 0.95 = 23,750).

CONNECT TO PHYSICAL SCIENCE

The electric eel is truly electric—more than half of its body is made up of electricity-producing cells. Found in shallow fresh-water rivers in South America, it can reach 3 m in length and produces a prey-killing jolt of 600 V—enough to kill a person.

You can illustrate an electric current with the following Teaching Transparency.

Teaching Transparency 269
"How a Cell Produces an Electric Current"

LINK TO PHYSICAL SCIENCE

Figure 11 *A shark's denticles and human teeth are made of the same materials.*

The skin of cartilaginous fishes is covered with small tooth-like **denticles** that give it the feel of sandpaper. If you rub your hand on a shark's skin from head to tail, it feels smooth. But if you rub your hand from tail to head, you can get cut! Look at the magnified denticles in **Figure 11**.

To stay afloat, cartilaginous fishes store a lot of oil in their liver. Even with oily livers, these fishes are heavier than water. They have to keep moving in order to stay afloat. Once they stop swimming, they gradually glide to the bottom.

Cartilaginous fishes do not swim just to keep from sinking, however. Some must swim to maintain the flow of water over their gills. If these fishes stop swimming, they will suffocate. Others do not have to swim. They can lie on the ocean floor and pump water across their gills.

Bony Fishes When you think of a fish, you probably think of something like the fish shown in **Figure 12**. Goldfish, tuna, trout, catfish, and cod are all bony fishes, the largest class of fishes. Ninety-five percent of all fishes are bony fishes. They range in size from 1 cm long to more than 6 m long.

As their name implies, bony fishes have a skeleton made of bone instead of cartilage. The body of a bony fish is covered by bony scales.

Unlike cartilaginous fishes, bony fishes can float in one place without swimming. This is because they have a swim bladder that keeps them from sinking. The **swim bladder** is a balloonlike organ that is filled with oxygen and other gases from the bloodstream. It gives fish *buoyancy,* or the ability to float in water. The swim bladder and other body parts of bony fishes are shown in **Figure 13**.

Figure 12 *A goldfish is a bony fish.*

MATH BREAK

A Lot of Bones

If there are 25,000 species of fishes and 95 percent of all fishes are bony fishes, how many species of bony fishes are there?

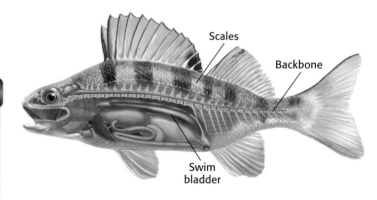

Scales

Backbone

Swim bladder

Figure 13 *Bony fishes have a swim bladder, a bony skeleton, and scales.*

IS THAT A FACT!

Basking sharks, which are the second largest fish, are hunted for the squalene oil in their liver. Although basking-shark livers are extremely large, the Basking Shark Society reports that 2,500–3,000 livers are needed to produce just 1 ton (0.91 metric tons) of squalene oil. Between 1987 and 1994, South Korea alone imported an average of 52 tons (47 metric tons) of the oil from Japan. Squalene oil is used as cooking oil, a skin moisturizer, and a lubricant.

There are two main groups of bony fishes. Almost all bony fishes are *ray-finned fishes*. Ray-finned fishes have paired fins supported by thin rays of bone. Ray-finned fishes include many familiar fishes, such as eels, herrings, trout, minnows, and perch. **Figure 14** shows a ray-finned fish.

Lobe-finned fishes and *lungfishes* make up a second group of bony fishes. Lobe-finned fishes have fins that are muscular and thick. There are six known species of modern lungfishes. You can see a lungfish in **Figure 15**. Scientists think that ancient fishes from this group were the ancestors of amphibians.

Figure 14 *Ray-finned fishes are some of the fastest swimmers in the world. A pike, like this one, can swim as fast as the fastest human runners can run, about 48 km/h.*

Figure 15 *Lungfishes have air sacs, or lungs, and can gulp air. They are found in Africa, Australia, and South America and live in shallow waters that often dry up in the summer.*

SECTION REVIEW

1. What are the three types of fishes? Which type are the coelacanths?

2. Most bony fishes reproduce by external fertilization. What does this mean?

3. What is the lateral line system, and what is its function?

4. **Analyzing Relationships** Compare the ways that cartilaginous fishes and bony fishes maintain buoyancy.

67

▼ **Answers to Section Review**

1. The three types of fishes are jawless fishes, cartilaginous fishes, and bony fishes. The coelacanth is a bony fish.

2. In external fertilization, the female lays unfertilized eggs, and sperm fertilize the egg outside the female's body.

3. The lateral line system is a row of sense organs along the side of a fish's body that detect water vibrations caused by other objects in the water.

4. Cartilaginous fishes have oily livers to help them stay afloat. Bony fishes have a swim bladder that helps them remain buoyant.

4) Close

Quiz

1. Of the 25,000 species of fishes, about what percentage of them are bony fishes? (95 percent)

2. Sharks are a member of what class of fishes? (cartilaginous)

ALTERNATIVE ASSESSMENT

Concept Mapping Create a concept map using the following terms (students must also supply the connecting words linking the terms):

vertebrate, chordate, notochord, tail, hollow nerve-chord, pharyngeal pouches

QuickLab

MATERIALS

FOR EACH GROUP:
• water
• cooking oil
• balloon
• bowl

Safety Caution: Students should be cautious when working with cooking oil, water, and any other liquids. Oil can stain clothing. Spills should be cleaned up immediately.

Answers to QuickLab

The balloon filled with oil will float, and the balloon with the water will sink. This occurs because the density of oil is lower than that of water. The oily liver of a cartilaginous fish provides buoyancy to a fish and helps it stay afloat.

Focus

Amphibians

In this section, students will discover when and how the first amphibians evolved from fishes. They will find out how amphibians breathe, reproduce, and develop through the process of metamorphosis. Students will also explore the three major groups of amphibians.

 **Bellringer**

On the board or overhead projector, instruct the students to answer the following questions in their ScienceLog:

What is an advantage to the thin, moist skin of amphibians? What is the primary disadvantage to such skin? (They can absorb oxygen and water right through their skin, but they also lose moisture through skin.)

1 Motivate

DEMONSTRATION

Illustrating Fossilization Fill a small bucket halfway with sand. Place a kitchen sponge on top of the sand. Pour sand on top of the sponge until the bucket is nearly filled. Next, pour table salt in a small bucket of warm water, and stir until the salt no longer dissolves. Pour the solution over sand in the bucket, and leave overnight. On the next day, uncover the sponge. The water should have evaporated or drained to the bottom of the sand, and the salt should have hardened the sponge. Explain to students that fossils are formed in a similar manner. (Dissolved minerals enter openings or spaces in plant or animal material and harden.) Sheltered English

Terms to Learn

lung   metamorphosis
tadpole

What You'll Do

◆ Describe the importance of amphibians in evolution.
◆ Explain how amphibians breathe.
◆ Describe metamorphosis in amphibians.

Amphibians

By the end of the Devonian period, 350 million years ago, fishes lived wherever there was water. But none of these vertebrates could live on land. And the land was a wonderful place for a vertebrate. It had lush green forests, many tasty insects, and few predators. But for vertebrates to adapt to life on land, they needed lungs for breathing and legs for walking. How did these changes occur?

Moving to Land

Most of the amphibians living on Earth today are frogs or salamanders, like those in **Figure 16.** But the early amphibians looked much different. Fossil evidence indicates that the first amphibians evolved from ancient ancestors of modern lungfishes. These fishes developed lungs to get oxygen from the air. A **lung** is a saclike organ that takes oxygen from the air and delivers it to the blood. The fins of these ancient fishes became strong enough to support the fishes' body weight and eventually became legs.

Fossils show that the first amphibians looked like a cross between a fish and a salamander, as shown in **Figure 17.** The early amphibians were the first vertebrates to live most of their life on land, and they were very successful. Many were very large—up to 10 m long—and could stay on dry land longer than today's amphibians can. But early amphibians still had to return to the water to keep from drying out, to avoid overheating, and to lay their eggs.

Figure 16 Modern amphibians include frogs and salamanders.

Barred leaf frog

Sierra Nevada salamander

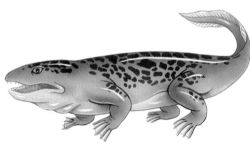

Figure 17 Ancient amphibians probably looked something like this.

IS THAT A FACT!

• A group of frogs is called an army.
• A group of toads is called a knot.
• Fear of frogs is called ranidaphobia.
• Fear of toads is called bufonophobia.

Characteristics of Amphibians

Amphibian means "double life." Most amphibians have two parts to their life. Because amphibian eggs do not have a shell and a special membrane to prevent water loss, the embryos must develop in a very wet environment. After amphibians emerge from an egg, they live in the water, like fishes do. Later they develop into animals that can live on land. But even adult amphibians are only partly adapted to life on land, and they must always live near water.

Amphibians are ectotherms. Like the body of a fish, the body of an amphibian changes temperature according to the temperature of its environment.

Thin-Skinned Most amphibians do not have scales. Their skin is thin, smooth, and moist. They do not drink water. Instead, they absorb it through their skin. Amphibians can breathe by gulping air into their lungs. But many also absorb oxygen through their skin, which is full of blood vessels. Some salamanders, like the one in **Figure 18,** breathe only through their skin. Because amphibian skin is so thin and moist, these animals can lose water through their skin and become dehydrated. For this reason, most amphibians live in water or in damp habitats.

The skin of many amphibians is brilliantly colored. The colors are often a warning to predators because the skin of many amphibians contains poison glands. These poisons may simply be irritating or they may be deadly. The skin of the dart-poison frog, shown in **Figure 19,** contains one of the most deadly toxins known.

Figure 18 *The four-toed salamander has no lungs. It gets all of its oxygen through its skin.*

Figure 19 *The skin of this dart-poison frog is full of poison glands. In South America, hunters rub the tips of their arrows in the deadly toxin.*

Self-Check

How is amphibian skin like a lung? *(See page 152 to check your answers.)*

69

READING STRATEGY

Prediction Guide Before reading this section, ask students to answer the following question in their ScienceLog. *Amphibian* means "double life." Why would we give this class of animals such a name? After reading this section, ask students to evaluate their answers.

CONNECT TO PHYSICAL SCIENCE

One of the loudest of all animals, the Puerto Rican coqui frog, can belt out at an amazing 120 decibels (db). (Noise is classified as physically painful above 130 db.) Just 5 cm (2 in.) long, the frog is disappearing from the rain forest, an alarming trend seen among many of the world's amphibian species.

Homework

Research Cloning Tell students that amphibians were the first vertebrates to be successfully cloned. Have students use library or Internet resources to locate information about the history of cloning and report their findings to the class.

Answers to Self-Check

Amphibians use their skin to absorb oxygen from the air. Their skin is thin and moist and full of blood vessels, just like a lung.

Directed Reading Worksheet Section 3

ACTIVITY

Observing Development

Obtain frog or salamander eggs either locally or from a biological supply company. Set up an aquarium, and allow students to observe the metamorphosis that follows. Students should sketch the process each step of the way. Note: if the animals were not collected locally, they cannot be released into the wild.
Sheltered English

RETEACHING

Poster Project Have students create a poster PORTFOLIO with captions showing how a tadpole changes into a frog. Sheltered English

Some students may have the mistaken impression that they can get warts from touching frogs and toads. Tell them that warts are caused by human viruses.

Teaching Transparency 60
"Metamorphosis of a Frog"

Leading a Double Life   The amphibian embryo usually develops into an aquatic larva called a **tadpole**. The tadpole can live only in wet environments. It obtains oxygen through gills and uses its long tail to swim. Later the tadpole loses its gills and develops lungs and limbs. This change from a larval form to an adult form is called **metamorphosis** and is shown in **Figure 20**. Adult amphibians are capable of surviving on land.

Figure 20
Most frogs and salamanders go through metamorphosis.

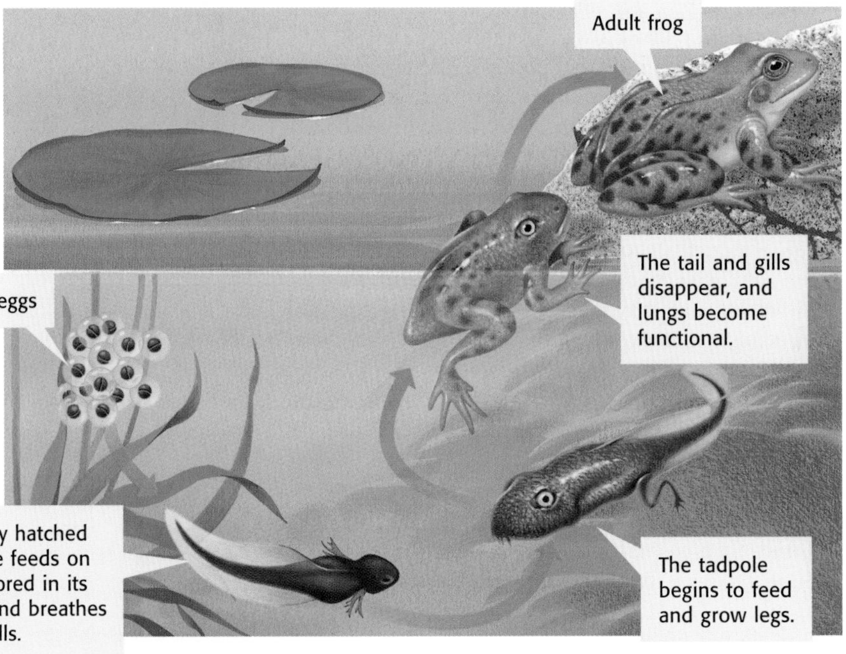

Adult frog

The tail and gills disappear, and lungs become functional.

Fertilized eggs

A newly hatched tadpole feeds on yolk stored in its body and breathes with gills.

The tadpole begins to feed and grow legs.

A few amphibians skip the aquatic stage and develop directly into adult frogs or salamanders. For example, one species of frog lays eggs on moist ground. Male adults guard the developing embryos. When an embryo begins to move, a male frog quickly takes it into its mouth and protects it inside its vocal sacs. When the embryo finishes developing, the adult frog opens its mouth, and a tiny frog jumps out. You can see this frog in **Figure 21**.

Figure 21   *Darwin frogs live in Chile and Argentina. A male frog may carry 5 to 15 embryos in its vocal sacs until the young are about 1.5 cm in length.*

⚛ WEIRD SCIENCE

Coast foam-nest tree frogs mate in trees that overhang ponds and streams. Then the females lay their eggs in large foamy, cocoonlike masses that cake over for protection from the sun. After a week or so of development, the tadpoles are ready to emerge, but only after a rain comes and moistens the foam. Once moistened, the foam drips into the water below, carrying with it the young tadpoles!

Kinds of Amphibians

It is estimated that there are 4,600 species of amphibians alive today. These belong to three groups: caecilians (see SIL yuhns), salamanders, and frogs and toads.

Caecilians Most people are not familiar with caecilians. These amphibians do not have legs and are shaped like worms or snakes, as shown in **Figure 22.** But they have the thin, moist skin of amphibians. Unlike other amphibians, some caecilians have bony scales. Many caecilians have very small eyes underneath their skin and are blind. Caecilians live in the tropical areas of Asia, Africa, and South America. About 160 species are known.

Salamanders Of modern amphibians, salamanders are the most like prehistoric amphibians. Although salamanders are much smaller than their ancient ancestors, they have a similar body shape, a long tail, and four strong legs. They range in size from a few centimeters long to 1.5 m long.

There are about 390 known species of salamanders. Most of them live under stones and logs in the damp woods of North America. They eat small invertebrates. A few, such as the axolotl (AK suh LAHT ′l), shown in **Figure 23,** do not go through metamorphosis. They live their entire life in the water.

Figure 22 *Caecilians are legless amphibians that live in damp soil in the tropics. Caecilians eat small invertebrates in the soil.*

Figure 23 *This axolotl is an unusual salamander. It retains its gills and never leaves the water.*

Ecological Indicators

Amphibians are often called ecological indicators. When large numbers of amphibians begin to die or show deformities, this may indicate a problem with the environment.

Sometimes deformities are caused by parasites, but amphibians are also extremely sensitive to chemical changes in their environment. Based on what you know about amphibians, why do you think they are sensitive to water pollution and air pollution?

71

Answers to APPLY

Because amphibians' skin is responsible for gas and water exchange, amphibians are highly sensitive to changes in air and water quality.

RESEARCH

Writing ✏ Have interested students conduct research about the field of herpetology, the branch of zoology that deals with amphibians and reptiles. Students could prepare reports and present them to the class. As an alternative, invite a herpetologist or other zoologist from the area to speak with the class about herpetology.

4 **Close**

Quiz

1. Where do most amphibians start their lives? (in water)
2. What is the meaning of amphibian? (double life)
3. What is the largest group of amphibians? (frogs and toads)

ALTERNATIVE ASSESSMENT

Writing ✏ Have students compose a song or poem accurately describing the life cycle of an amphibian of their choice.

 **PG 128**

A Prince of a Frog

Frogs and Toads Ninety percent of all amphibians are frogs or toads. They are found all over the world, from deserts to rain forests. Frogs and toads are very similar to each other, as you can see in **Figure 24.** In fact, toads are a type of frog.

Frog

Toad

Figure 24 *Frogs have smooth, moist skin. Toads spend less time in water than frogs do, and their skin is drier and bumpier.*

Frogs and toads are highly adapted for life on land. Adults have powerful leg muscles for jumping. They have well-developed ears for hearing, and they have vocal cords for calling. They also have extendible, sticky tongues. The tongue is attached to the front of the mouth so that it can be flipped out quickly to catch insects.

Singing Frogs Frogs are well known for their nighttime choruses, but many frogs sing in the daytime too. Like humans, they force air from their lungs across vocal cords in the throat. But frogs have something we lack. Surrounding their vocal cords is a thin sac of skin called the *vocal sac*. When frogs vocalize, the sac inflates with air, like a balloon does, and vibrates. You can see this in **Figure 25.** The vibrations of the sac increase the volume of the song so that it can be heard over long distances.

Figure 25 *Most frogs that sing are males, and their songs have different meanings.*

Examine the princely characteristics of a friendly frog on page 128 of your LabBook.

SECTION REVIEW

1. Describe metamorphosis in amphibians.
2. Why do amphibians have to be near water or in a very wet habitat?
3. What adaptations allow amphibians to live on land?
4. Name the three types of amphibians. How are they similar? How are they different?
5. **Analyzing Relationships** Describe the relationship between lungfishes and amphibians. What characteristics do they share? How do they differ?

72

▼ *Answers to Section Review*

1. After fertilization of an egg, the embryo develops into a tadpole that lives in water. The tadpole loses its gills and develops lungs and legs to become an adult.

2. Amphibians must live near water because they have very thin, moist skin and they can easily dehydrate.

3. lungs (instead of gills) and legs

4. Frogs and toads, salamanders, and caecilians all have a thin, moist skin; salamanders and frogs and toads have legs, but caecilians do not; caecilians have scales.

5. Both have lungs and can breathe air; amphibians have stronger legs and skin that absorbs oxygen; amphibians go through metamorphosis, but lungfish do not.

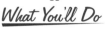

Terms to Learn

therapsid
amniotic egg

What You'll Do

- Explain the adaptations that allow reptiles to live on land.
- Name the three main groups of vertebrates that evolved from reptiles.
- Describe the characteristics of an amniotic egg.
- Name the three orders of modern reptiles.

Reptiles

About 35 million years after the first amphibians colonized the land, some of them evolved special traits that prepared them for life in an even drier environment. These animals developed thick, dry skin that protected them from water loss. Their legs became stronger and more vertical, so they were better able to walk. And they evolved a special egg that could be laid on dry land. These animals were reptiles, the first animals to live completely out of the water.

Reptile History

Fossils show that soon after the first reptiles appeared, they split into groups. This can be shown in a family tree of the reptiles, as illustrated in **Figure 26.**

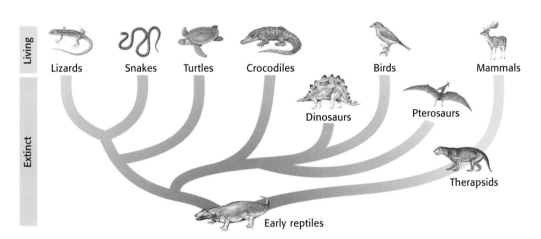

Figure 26 *Early reptiles were the ancestors of modern reptiles, birds, and mammals.*

Many of the most fascinating reptiles are now extinct. When we think of extinct reptiles, we usually think of dinosaurs. But only a fraction of the reptiles living in prehistoric times were land-dwelling dinosaurs. Many were swimming reptiles. A few were flying pterosaurs. And there were turtles, lizards, snakes, and crocodiles. In addition, there was a group of mammal-like reptiles called therapsids. As you can see in Figure 26, **therapsids** (thuh RAP sidz) were the ancestors of mammals.

73

IS THAT A FACT!

The pteranodon, a particularly large type of pterosaur, had a wingspan of more than 6.5 m (20 ft).

Teaching Transparency 61 "Reptile History"

Directed Reading Worksheet Section 4

Focus

Reptiles

This section introduces students to reptiles. Students will learn how reptiles evolved and split into three major groups: turtles and tortoises, crocodiles and alligators, and lizards and snakes. They will also learn about reptiles' physical characteristics and behaviors.

Bellringer

Have students list three adjectives they associate with reptiles. They should record their responses in their ScienceLog under the heading *First impressions.* After they read the section, have them record three more adjectives under the heading *Second impressions.*

1 Motivate

DISCUSSION

Exploring Fears Ask students to list the five most fearsome creatures on Earth. Likely, many of the named animals will be reptiles, especially snakes. Ask students:

- Why is this so? Is their reputation deserved? (While many reptiles are capable of killing humans—about 400 of the 1,600 species of snakes are poisonous—more people die from insect bites each year than from reptile bites. In the United States, only 5 to 15 deaths per year result from snake bites. However, worldwide, snakes are the second deadliest animals, killing as many as 30,000–40,000 people each year.)

ACTIVITY

Organizing Reptiles Before reading about the types of reptiles, take a moment to try to put the following reptiles into their three orders. Match the animal on the left with its closest relative on the right. Check your answers after reading.

turtle   crocodile
snake   tortoise
alligator   lizard

(turtle, tortoise; snake, lizard; alligator, crocodile)

USING THE FIGURE

Encourage students to make comparisons between reptile eggs and amphibian eggs. (Amphibian eggs don't have shells and must be laid in water or moist ground. Reptile eggs do have a shell and can be laid in the dry earth.)

- Ask: How might these facts favor reptile reproduction over amphibian reproduction during a drought? (Dehydration would kill off amphibian embryos, but reptile embryos would be more likely to survive.)
  Sheltered English

GUIDED PRACTICE

Writing Have students make a list of reasons why animals that internally regulate their temperatures have advantages over those that do not. Provide several examples to help students get started.

Teaching Transparency 62
"Amniotic Egg"

Figure 27 *Many people think snakes are slimy, but the skin of snakes and other reptiles is scaly and dry.*

Characteristics of Reptiles

Reptiles are adapted for life on land. Although crocodiles, turtles, and a few species of snakes live in the water, all of these animals are descended from reptiles that lived on land. All reptiles use lungs to breathe air, just as you do.

Thick-Skinned A very important adaptation for life on land is thick, dry skin, which forms a watertight layer. This thick skin keeps cells from losing water by evaporation. Most reptiles cannot breathe through their skin the way amphibians can. Most depend entirely on their lungs for oxygen and carbon dioxide exchange. Check out the snake's skin in **Figure 27.**

Coldblooded? Like fishes and amphibians, reptiles are ectotherms. That means that they usually cannot maintain a constant body temperature. Reptiles are active when their environment is warm, and they slow down when their environment is cool.

A few reptiles can generate some heat from their own body. For example, some lizards in the southwestern United States can keep their body temperature at about 34°C, even when the air temperature is cool. Still, modern reptiles are limited to mild climates. They cannot tolerate the cold polar regions, where many mammals and birds thrive.

The Amazing Amniotic Egg Among reptiles' many adaptations to land life, the most critical is the amniotic (AM nee AH tik) egg. The **amniotic egg** is surrounded by a shell, as shown in **Figure 28.** The shell protects the developing embryo and keeps the egg from drying out. An amniotic egg can be laid under rocks, in the ground, in forests, or even in the desert. The amniotic egg is so well adapted to a dry environment that even crocodiles and turtles return to land to lay their eggs.

Figure 28 *Compare the amphibian eggs at left with the reptile eggs at right. What differences can you see?*

WEIRD SCIENCE

The Texas horned toad of southwestern North America is actually a lizard with a bizarre defense mechanism. When threatened, the lizard puffs itself up, increasing its blood pressure until the capillaries around its eyes burst. The predator is stunned when it is then squirted with blood from up to 2.4 m (7 ft) away.

Parts of an Amniotic Egg The shell is just one important part of an amniotic egg. The other parts of an amniotic egg are illustrated in **Figure 29.** The egg protects the developing embryo from predators, bacterial infections, and dehydration.

Figure 29 An Amniotic Egg

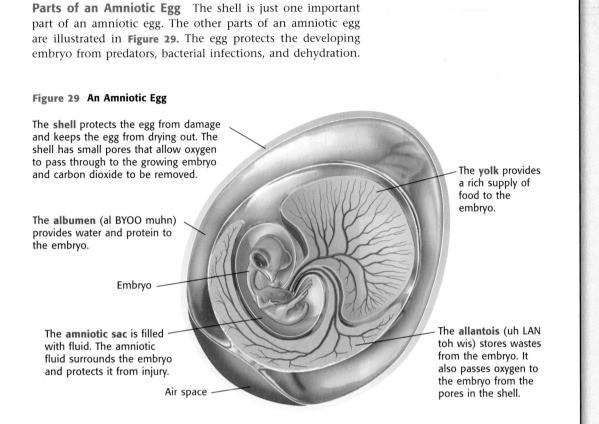

The **shell** protects the egg from damage and keeps the egg from drying out. The shell has small pores that allow oxygen to pass through to the growing embryo and carbon dioxide to be removed.

The **albumen** (al BYOO muhn) provides water and protein to the embryo.

Embryo

The **amniotic sac** is filled with fluid. The amniotic fluid surrounds the embryo and protects it from injury.

Air space

The **yolk** provides a rich supply of food to the embryo.

The **allantois** (uh LAN toh wis) stores wastes from the embryo. It also passes oxygen to the embryo from the pores in the shell.

Reptile Reproduction The amniotic egg is fertilized inside the female. A shell then forms around the egg, and the female lays the egg. Because of the shell, reptiles can reproduce only by internal fertilization.

Most reptiles lay their eggs in soil or sand. A few do not lay eggs. Instead the embryos develop inside the mother's reproductive passages, and the young are born live. In either case, the embryo develops into a tiny young reptile. Reptiles do not have a larval stage and do not undergo metamorphosis.

Types of Reptiles

In the age of the dinosaurs, from 300 million years ago until about 65 million years ago, most land vertebrates were reptiles. Today the 6,000 species of living reptiles represent only a handful of the many species of reptiles that once lived.

Modern reptiles include turtles and tortoises, crocodiles and alligators, and lizards and snakes.

> ✓ **Self-Check**
>
> 1. What adaptations of reptiles are important for living on dry land?
> 2. Why must animals that lay eggs with shells reproduce by internal fertilization?
>
> *(See page 152 to check your answers.)*

75

ACROSS THE SCIENCES

Background

Fish can reverse their direction without slowing down at all. They can also turn with a turning radius as small as 10 to 30 percent of the length of their bodies. Yellowfin tuna have been reported to swim as fast as 73 km/h. Compare all of this with a typical human-made ship. A ship cruises at about 37 km/h, it must reduce its speed by about 50 percent to turn around, and it requires a circle with a radius of 10 times its hull length!

The mobility of a fish and a ship differ in other ways as well. A ship's motion is limited by the rigidity of its hull, while a fish's body is very smooth and flexible. Robotics technology is still too simple to accurately reproduce the flapping of a fish's tail. For this reason, fish-inspired mechanisms had performed rather poorly until the creation of RoboTuna.

Teaching Strategy

Lead a classroom discussion about swimming styles. Ask the students to comment on their own swimming technique. Do they swim more like a fish or a rowboat? How do they turn around? What kinds of swimming techniques have other animals adopted? You might also discuss the swimming methods of dogs, jellyfish, frogs, and whales.

Robot Fish

When is a fish tail not a fish tail? When it's the tail of RoboTuna, a robotic fish designed by scientists at the Massachusetts Institute of Technology.

Something Fishy Going On

There's no doubt about it—fish are quicker and much more maneuverable than most ships and submarines. So why aren't ships and submarines built more like fish—with tails that flap back and forth? This question caught the imagination of some scientists at MIT and inspired them to build RoboTuna, a model of a bluefin tuna. This robot fish is 124 cm long and is composed of six motors, a skin of foam and Lycra™, and a skeleton of aluminum ribs and hinges connected by pulleys and strings.

A Tail of Force and Motion

The MIT scientists propose that if ships were designed to more closely resemble fish, the ships would use much less energy and thus save money. A ship moving through water leaves a trail of little whirlpools called *vortices* behind it. These vortices increase the friction between the ship and the water. A fish, however, senses the vortices and responds by flapping its tail, creating vortices of its own. The fish's vortices counteract the effects of the original vortices, and the fish is propelled forward with much less effort.

RoboTuna has special sensors that measure changes in water pressure in much the same way that a living tuna senses vortices. Then the robot fish flaps its vortex-producing tail, allowing it to swim like a living fish. As strange as it may seem, RoboTuna may represent the beginning of a new era in nautical design.

Viewing Vortices

▶ Fill a roasting pan three-quarters full with water. Wait long enough for the water to stop moving. Then tie a 6 cm piece of yarn or ribbon to the end of a pencil. Drag the pencil through the water with the yarn or ribbon trailing behind it. How does the yarn or ribbon respond? Where are the vortices?

▶ *Inner Workings of MIT's RoboTuna*

1. A strut supports the robot, encloses the tendons, and conveys control and sensor information.

2. Ribs and flexible beams hold the skin in place while allowing the body to flex continuously.

3. A skin of foam and Lycra is smooth enough to eliminate wrinkles or bulges and prevent the stray turbulence they cause.

Answers to Viewing Vortices

The end of the ribbon or yarn should wiggle back and forth. This is caused in part by the creation of vortices, which trail behind the ribbon or yarn. You might want to put some sand on the bottom of the pan and have students observe how the sand grains move as the pencil passes over them.

WEIRD SCIENCE

WARM BRAINS IN COLD WATER

Of the world's 30,000 kinds of fish, only a few carry around their own brain heaters. *Brain heaters?* Why would a fish need a special heater just for its brain? Before you can answer that question, you have to think about how fish keep warm in the cold water of the ocean.

A Question of Temperature

Most fish and marine organisms are ectotherms. An ectotherm's body temperature closely matches the temperature of its surroundings. Endotherms, on the other hand, maintain a steady body temperature regardless of the temperature of their surroundings. Humans are endotherms. Other mammals, such as dogs, elephants, whales, and birds, are also endotherms. But only a few kinds of fish—tuna, for example— are endotherms. These fish are still coldblooded, but they can heat certain parts of their bodies. Endothermic fish can hunt for prey in extremely chilly water. Yet these fish pay a high price for their ability to inhabit very cold areas—they use a lot of energy.

Being endothermic requires far more energy than being ectothermic. Some fish, such as swordfish, marlin, and sailfish, have adaptations that let them heat only part of their body. Instead of using large amounts of energy to warm the entire body, they warm only their eyes and brain. That's right—they have special brain heaters!

▶ *Why do you think it is important to protect the brain and eyes from extreme cold?*

Warming the Brain

In a "brain-warming" fish, a small mass of muscle attached to each eye acts as a thermostat. It adjusts the temperature of the brain and eyes as the fish swims through different temperature zones. These "heater muscles" help maintain delicate nerve functions that are important to finding prey.

Heater muscles allow the swordfish, for example, to swim in both warm surface waters of the ocean and depths of 485 m, where the temperature drops to near freezing. This adaptation has an obvious advantage: It gives the fish a large range of places to look for food.

Ectotherms in Action

▶ Contact a local pet store that sells various kinds of fish. Find out what water temperature is best for different fish from different regions of the Earth. For example, compare the ideal water temperatures for goldfish, discus fish, and angelfish. Why do you think fish-tank temperatures must be carefully controlled?

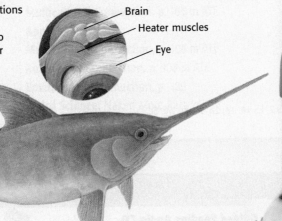

- Brain
- Heater muscles
- Eye

85

Answer to Ectotherms in Action

Student answers will vary, depending on the fish they select. For instance, a Japanese goldfish is best suited for cool temperatures near 18°C (64°F), a South American discus requires warm temperatures of about 28°C (82°F), and a South American angelfish fares best in a temperature range of 24–26°C (75–79°F). The temperature in fish tanks must be controlled to ensure the fish's survival.

Background

The body temperature of an ectothermic animal, commonly called "coldblooded," is about the same temperature as its surroundings. Amphibians, reptiles, and most fish are ectothermic. When the sun warms the body of an ectothermic animal, its body temperature can rise above that of an endothermic, or "warmblooded" animal.

Endothermic animals include all birds and mammals. The body of an endothermic animal produces most of its heat by metabolizing food. In many endothermic animals, a layer of fat beneath the skin and a covering of feathers, fur, or hair also help the animal maintain a constant body temperature. The principal means of reducing body heat are panting and sweating.

Many ectothermic animals partially control their body temperature through their behavior. For example, ectothermic land animals may bask in the sunlight to become warmer or move to the shade to cool down. Fish may swim closer to the surface of the water to warm themselves. If they become too warm, they may swim to deeper, cooler water.

Chapter Resources & Worksheets

Visual Resources

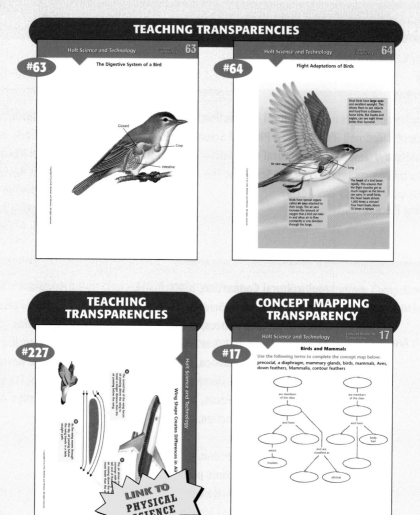

TEACHING TRANSPARENCIES

#63 — The Digestive System of a Bird

#64 — Flight Adaptations of Birds

TEACHING TRANSPARENCIES

#227 — Wing Shape Creates Differences in Air

LINK TO PHYSICAL SCIENCE

CONCEPT MAPPING TRANSPARENCY

#17 — Birds and Mammals

Use the following terms to complete the concept map below: precocial, a diaphragm, mammary glands, birds, mammals, Aves, down feathers, Mammalia, contour feathers

Meeting Individual Needs

DIRECTED READING

#4 — DIRECTED READING WORKSHEET — Birds and Mammals

REINFORCEMENT & VOCABULARY REVIEW

#4 — REINFORCEMENT WORKSHEET — Mammals Are Us

#4 — VOCABULARY REVIEW WORKSHEET — Is It a Bird or a Mammal?

SCIENCE PUZZLERS, TWISTERS & TEASERS

#4 — SCIENCE PUZZLERS, TWISTERS & TEASERS — Birds and Mammals

Chapter 4 • Birds and Mammals

Review & Assessment

STUDY GUIDE

CHAPTER TESTS WITH PERFORMANCE-BASED ASSESSMENT

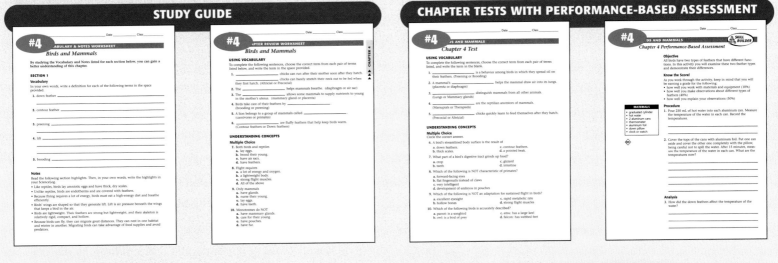

Lab Worksheets

LABS YOU CAN EAT

LONG-TERM PROJECTS & RESEARCH IDEAS

DATASHEETS FOR LABBOOK

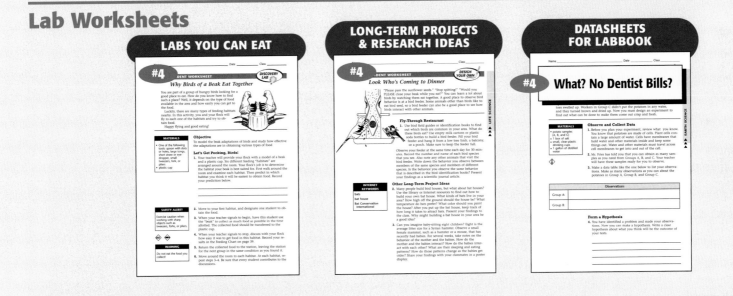

Applications & Extensions

CRITICAL THINKING & PROBLEM SOLVING

EYE ON THE ENVIRONMENT

Birds

▶ Birds of a Feather

Ornithologists classify feathers based on their function and location on the bird's body. Contour feathers have a stiff shaft and firm barbs on the inner and outer vanes, although the base often is downy. Contour feathers include those on the outer surface of the body and the flight feathers of the wings (remiges) and the tail (rectrices). The auriculars, which cover the ears, are small, modified contour feathers.

- Semiplumes are small but have a relatively large shaft with downy vanes. They are hidden beneath the body feathers. Semiplumes fill in the spaces between the larger contour feathers, provide insulation, and increase buoyancy in water birds.

- Down feathers are tiny, completely fluffy, and have no shaft. In adult birds, down feathers remain hidden beneath contour feathers, but they are the sole body covering for many newly hatched birds. Down is important for insulation and is most abundant in water birds.

IS THAT A FACT!

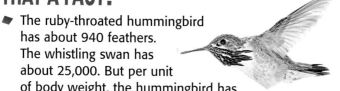

- The ruby-throated hummingbird has about 940 feathers. The whistling swan has about 25,000. But per unit of body weight, the hummingbird has more feathers than the swan. This is because small birds have a greater need for efficient heat retention.

▶ Stick Together

Branching out from the shaft of a typical contour feather are thin, rather stiff barbs. On either side of the barbs grow even smaller barbules. There are several hundred on each barb. Each barbule has tiny hooks that wrap around the barbules of the adjacent barb so that all the parts of the feather are tightly attached to each other. This construction is what provides firmness to the feathers and increases their ability to insulate and waterproof a bird.

IS THAT A FACT!

- Cormorants and anhingas are fish-eating birds that must dive to catch their food. To decrease their buoyancy and enhance their ability to dive deep, they have unusually heavy bones (for a bird), reduced air sacs, and nonwaterproof plumage. After a dive, they must find a perch and spread their wings to dry off.

▶ Forms of Flight

During flapping flight, a bird's inner wing functions as an anchor for the outer portion and helps provide speed and power. At the bottom of the downstroke, which propels the bird, the "wrist" flexes and begins the upstroke.

- Soaring flight allows a bird to gain and maintain altitude without flapping its wings. Instead, the birds "ride" on warm air currents called thermals. Vultures, hawks, and eagles can use soaring flight because they fulfill the requirements of large size, maneuverability, and light wing load (the ratio of a bird's wing surface area to its weight).

- Kingfishers, kestrels, and some hawks are able to hover, but none match the hummingbird's ability to maintain a position in midair. Hummingbirds move their wings only from the shoulder, which provides unusual flexibility and maneuverability.

IS THAT A FACT!

- Hummingbirds are the only birds that can fly backward.

- A chimney swift that lived 9 years was estimated to have flown 2,000,000 km during its lifetime.

SECTION 2

Mammals

▶ Fur

All mammals have hair, but not all "fur-bearing" mammals have true fur. True fur consists of two layers: a dense undergrowth of short ground hairs, which provide insulation, and longer guard hairs, which protect the skin and the ground hairs by repelling rain or snow.

▶ Rodent Teeth

Rodents, which include rats, mice, beavers, squirrels, guinea pigs, and capybaras, have evolved a unique jaw articulation to compensate for the huge incisors that grow throughout the animal's life. Both the upper and the lower pair are separated from the cheek teeth by a large gap. When the cheek teeth are engaged in chewing, the lower jaw is pulled back and the incisors do not meet. When the animal is gnawing with its incisors, the lower jaw is pulled forward and downward so the incisors can meet. Rodents spend a lot of time gnawing with their incisors to keep them worn down to a manageable level.

▶ Beneficial Bats

The insectivorous Mexican free-tailed bats in Texas eat an estimated 20,000 tons of insects each year. They provide a vital, chemical-free system of insect control.

- Guano from insectivorous bats is a valuable fertilizer in many countries because of its high nitrogen and phosphorous content. In some caves, the guano covers and helps preserve archaeologically valuable artifacts and fossils.

- Although some fruit-eating bats can reduce a farmer's harvest, many of them are essential to dispersing seeds that are responsible for new plant growth. Other bats eat only pollen and nectar and are the primary or exclusive pollinators of various plants.

IS THAT A FACT!

- Shrews and other small mammals have a high metabolic rate to compensate for large amounts of heat loss resulting from their large ratio of body surface to volume. A captive shrew (genus *Sorex*) consumed 3.3 times its body weight in a 24-hour period.

- From mid-April to mid-October, hundreds of thousands of Mexican free-tailed bats and thousands of several other species live in Carlsbad Caverns, in New Mexico. At night, the bats fly from the cave in great swarms that resemble clouds of smoke when seen from a distance. It is believed that early explorers of the southwest followed the "smoke" and discovered the cave.

- A three-toed sloth has nine cervical vertebrae and can turn its head 270°. Two-toed sloths and most mammals have seven neck vertebrae.

For background information about teaching strategies and issues, refer to the *Professional Reference for Teachers.*

CHAPTER

4

Birds and Mammals

Pre-Reading Questions

Students may not know the answers to these questions before reading the chapter, so accept any reasonable response.

Suggested Answers

1. Planes and birds stay aloft because air traveling over the top of a wing moves faster than air traveling below it. This generates higher pressure beneath the wing than above it, causing lift.

2. Kangaroos are marsupial. Most mammals are placental.

3. Yes: monotremes are mammals that lay eggs. Bats are mammals that can fly.

Sections

Pre-Reading Questions

1. What holds a bird or plane up when it flies?

2. How do kangaroos differ from most other mammals?

3. Can mammals lay eggs? Can they fly?

86

PEST CONTROL FOR GIRAFFES!

Why is this bird riding on this giraffe? Well, this tickbird is more than a passenger. In fact, the tickbird and the giraffe, a mammal, have a special relationship. The tickbird eats ticks and other pests off the giraffe. The tickbird also warns the giraffe if danger is near. In this chapter, you will learn what makes birds and mammals unique and about different kinds of birds and mammals.

---

internet connect

go.hrw.com	**www.scilinks.com**	**www.si.edu/hrw**	**www.cnnfyi.com**
HRW On-line Resources	*sci*LINKS NSTA	Smithsonian Institution	CNNfyi.com
For worksheets and other teaching aids, visit the HRW Web site and type in the keyword: **HSTVR2**	Use the *sci*LINKS numbers at the end of each chapter for additional resources on the **NSTA** Web site.	Visit the Smithsonian Institution Web site for related on-line resources.	Visit the CNN Web site for current events coverage and classroom resources.

LET'S FLY!

How do birds and airplanes fly? This activity will give you a few hints.

Procedure

1. Carefully fold a **piece of paper** to make a paper airplane. Make the folds even and the creases sharp.

2. Throw the plane very gently. What happened?

3. Take the same plane, and throw it more forcefully. Did anything change?

4. Reduce the size of the wings by folding them inward, toward the center crease. Make sure the two wings are the same size and shape.

5. Throw the airplane again, first gently and with more force. What happened each time?

Analysis

6. Analyze what effect the force of your throw has on the paper airplane's flight. Do you think this is true of bird flight? Explain.

7. What happened when the wings were made smaller? Why do you think this happened? Do you think wing size affects the way a bird flies?

8. Based on your results, how would you design and throw the perfect paper airplane? Explain your answer.

87

LET'S FLY!

MATERIALS
FOR EACH STUDENT: • piece of paper

Safety Caution

Remind students to review all safety cautions and icons before beginning this lab activity. Instruct them to throw their planes only into areas where other students are not present.

Answers to START-UP Activity

2. Answers will vary.

3. Answers will vary, but forcefully thrown planes probably went farther.

5. Answers will vary.

6. Answers will vary. Speed helps keep planes aloft. The same is true for birds.

7. Answers will vary. Smaller wings make the plane more maneuverable but less able to glide; longer wings offer more surface area to keep the plane or bird in the air.

8. Answers will vary, but good design will depend on what kind of flight is desired.

Focus

Birds

In this section, students learn which characteristics make birds unique and which characteristics they share with reptiles. Students also learn how birds are adapted for flight. Finally, students learn about bird migration and about how birds raise their young.

🔔 Bellringer

Pose the following question to students on the board or an overhead projector:

What are some ways that birds are beneficial to people? (provide meat, eggs, and feathers; offer natural insect and rodent control; serve as pets; pollinate plants; spread plant seeds; consume and eliminate decaying animals)

1 Motivate

ACTIVITY

Light as a Feather Divide the class into small groups. Provide each group with a feather (preferably a wing feather), a paper clip, a small scale, and a meterstick. Tell students to weigh the feather and the paper clip. Next tell the class to let group members take turns dropping the feather and the paper clip from a height of 1 m. Challenge groups to brainstorm about the differences they observe and about the role of feather shape in bird flight.
Sheltered English

Directed Reading Worksheet Section 1

Terms to Learn

down feather   lift
contour feather   brooding
preening

What You'll Do

◆ Name two characteristics that birds share with reptiles.
◆ Describe the characteristics of birds that make them well suited for flight.
◆ Explain *lift*.
◆ List some advantages of migration.

Birds

Great blue heron

Have you ever fed pigeons in a city park or watched a hawk fly in circles in the sky? Humans have always been birdwatchers, perhaps because birds are easier to recognize than almost any other animal. Unlike other animals, all birds have feathers. Birds are also well known for their ability to fly. Birds belong to the class Aves. The word *aves* comes from the Latin word for bird. In fact, the word *aviation*—the science of flying airplanes—comes from the same word.

Figure 1 *There are almost 9,000 species of birds on Earth today.*

Toucan

Hummingbird

Figure 2 *Birds have light, fluffy down feathers and leaf-shaped contour feathers.*

Bird Characteristics

The first birds appeared on Earth about 150 million years ago. Birds are thought to be descendants of dinosaurs.

Even today birds share some characteristics with reptiles. Like reptiles, birds are vertebrates. The legs and feet of birds are covered by thick, dry scales, like those of reptiles. Even the skin around their beaks is scaly. Like reptiles, birds have *amniotic eggs,* that is, eggs with an amniotic sac and a shell. However, the shells of bird eggs are generally harder than the leathery shells of turtles and lizards.

Birds also have many characteristics that set them apart from the rest of the animal kingdom. They have beaks instead of teeth and jaws, and they have feathers, wings, and many other adaptations for flight.

Birds of a Feather Birds have two main types of feathers— down feathers and contour feathers. Examples of each are shown in **Figure 2.** Because feathers wear out, birds shed their worn feathers and grow new ones.

88

Homework

Writing | **Researching Bird Breeding** Tell students that biologists have used their understanding of parent-offspring relationships in birds to breed birds in captivity. Tell students to research how scientists mimic parent birds in order to feed and otherwise support chicks. Encourage them to research the success of these captive-breeding efforts.

PORTFOLIO

Down feathers are fluffy, insulating feathers that lie next to a bird's body. To keep from losing heat, birds fluff up their down feathers to form a layer of insulation. Air trapped in the feathers helps keep birds warm. **Contour feathers** are made of a stiff central *shaft* with many side branches, called *barbs*. The barbs link together to form a smooth surface, as can be seen in **Figure 3**. Contour feathers cover the body and wings of birds to form a streamlined flying surface.

Birds take good care of their feathers. They use their beaks to spread oil on their feathers in a process called **preening**. The oil is secreted by a gland near the bird's tail. The oil helps make the feathers water repellent and keeps them clean.

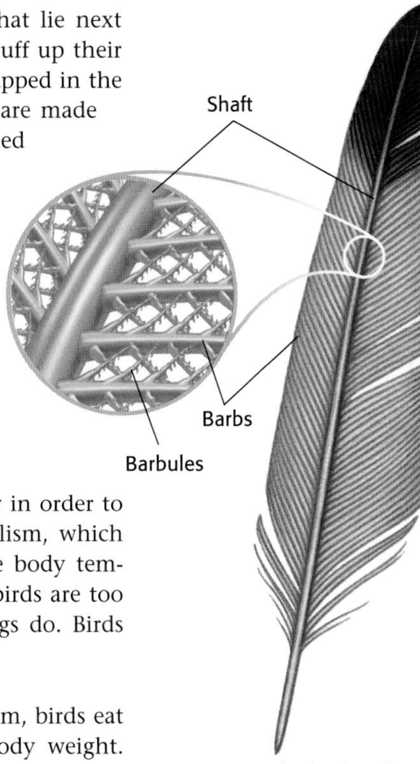

Shaft

Barbs

Barbules

High-Energy Animals Birds need a lot of energy in order to fly. To get this energy, they have a high metabolism, which generates a lot of body heat. In fact, the average body temperature of a bird is 40°C, warmer than yours! If birds are too hot, they lay their feathers flat and pant like dogs do. Birds cannot sweat to cool their bodies.

Eat Like a Bird? Because of their high metabolism, birds eat large amounts of food in proportion to their body weight. Some small birds eat almost constantly to maintain their energy! Most birds eat a high-protein, high-fat diet of insects, nuts, seeds, or meat. This kind of diet requires only a small digestive tract. A few birds, such as geese, eat the leaves of plants.

Birds don't have teeth, so they can't chew their food. Instead, food goes directly from the mouth to the *crop,* where it is stored. Birds also have an organ called a *gizzard,* which often contains small stones. The stones in the gizzard grind up the food so that it can be easily digested by the intestine. A bird's digestive system is shown in **Figure 4**.

Figure 3 *The barbs of a contour feather have cross branches called barbules. Barbs and barbules give the feather strength and shape.*

Figure 4 *The digestive system of a bird allows food to be rapidly converted into usable energy.*

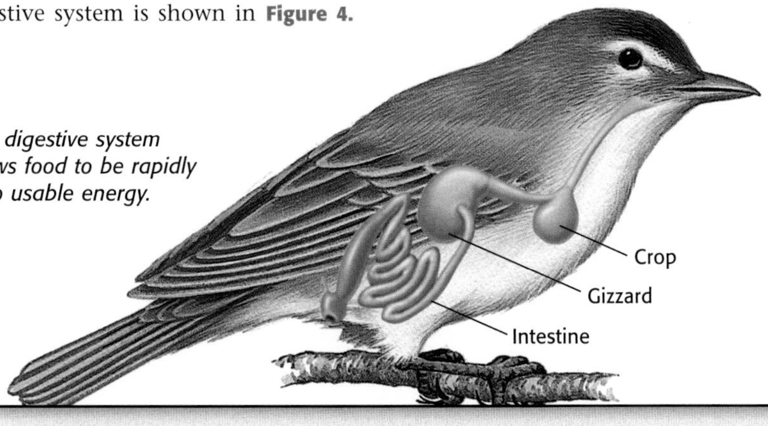

Crop

Gizzard

Intestine

89

2 Teach

GUIDED PRACTICE
Making Models

MATERIALS
FOR EACH GROUP:
• pipe cleaners
• straws

Use the board to illustrate how a contour feather is constructed of a main shaft, projecting barbs, barbules, and barbule hooks.

Tell students to insert one or two pipe cleaners into a straw to make it stiff. Then tell them to follow the illustration to construct a model of a feather with at least three barbs and accompanying barbules and hooks.
Sheltered English

Multicultural CONNECTION

Bird myths and mythical birds are common cultural themes around the world. In the Hindu religion, the king of birds is a winged monster called Garuda that feeds on snakes. The fifteenth-century collection of stories *The Thousand and One Nights* presented the mythic roc, or *rukh,* that was so enormous it fed on elephants. And the folklore of the Athapascans, Inuit, and Hopi—three Native American cultures—features a huge eaglelike creature called a thunderbird.

Teaching Transparency 63 "The Digestive System of a Bird"

Answers to Self-Check

1. Down feathers are not stiff and smooth and could not give structure to the wings. They are adapted to keep the bird warm.

2. Birds need tremendous amounts of food for fuel because it takes a lot of energy to fly.

READING STRATEGY

Prediction Guide Before students read these pages, ask them:

Why are birds such successful flyers? (Birds possess feathers, a high metabolism, wings, lightweight bones, and air sacs.)

Have them review their answers after they read the text.

USING THE FIGURE

Remind students that several bird species, including ostriches, kiwis, and emus, are flightless. Tell students to research the body and wing structure of flightless birds and to write another paragraph for each caption that explains any differences between the characteristics of flightless birds and birds that fly. Sheltered English

Teaching Transparency 64 "Flight Adaptations of Birds"

Self-Check

1. Why don't birds have wings made of down feathers?

2. Why do birds eat large quantities of food?

(See page 152 to check your answers.)

Up, Up, and Away

Most birds are flyers. Even flightless birds, such as ostriches, are descended from ancestors that could fly.

Birds have a long list of adaptations for flight. Birds must take in a large amount of energy from the food they eat and a large amount of oxygen from the air they breathe in order to fly. Feathers and wings are also important, as are strong muscles. Birds have lightweight bodies so that they can get off the ground. **Figure 5** on these two pages explains many of the bird characteristics that are important for flight.

Figure 5 Flight Adaptations of Birds

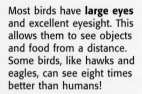

Most birds have **large eyes** and excellent eyesight. This allows them to see objects and food from a distance. Some birds, like hawks and eagles, can see eight times better than humans!

Air sacs

Lung

The **heart** of a bird beats rapidly. This ensures that the flight muscles get as much oxygen as the blood can carry. In small birds, the heart beats almost 1,000 times a minute! Your heart beats about 70 times a minute.

Birds have special organs called **air sacs** attached to their lungs. The air sacs increase the amount of oxygen that a bird can take in and allow air to flow constantly in one direction through the lungs.

90

Loons are heavy-bodied water birds. Their legs are set far back on their bodies for maximum streamlining while swimming. As a consequence, loons can barely walk on land. And because the ratio of their wing surface area to their body weight is so low, they have difficulty getting airborne. For comparison, think of a big-bodied plane with small wings. To get airborne, loons must "run" on the water while flapping their wings. They may have to taxi for half a kilometer to get aloft!

The shape of a bird's **wings** is related to the kind of flying it does. Short, rounded wings allow rapid maneuvers, like the movements of a fighter plane. Long narrow wings are best for soaring, like the movement of a glider.

Bird skeletons are compact and strong. Some of the vertebrae, ribs, and hip bones are fused together. This makes the skeleton of birds more rigid than that of other vertebrates. The **rigid skeleton** lets a bird move its wings powerfully and efficiently.

Science CONNECTION

These characteristics help birds fly, but how do airplanes fly? Find out on page 118.

Birds that fly have powerful **flight muscles** attached to a large breastbone called a **keel.** These muscles move the wings.

Keel

Bone is a heavy material, but birds have much **lighter skeletons** than those of other vertebrates because their bones are hollow. But bird bones are still very strong because they have thin cross-supports that provide strength, much like the trusses of a bridge do.

91

Observing Bird Bones Obtain several bones from a chicken or a turkey, such as the lower leg bones (drumsticks) and thigh bones, that have been cooked and thoroughly cleaned. Carefully break open the bones so that students can examine the air spaces inside. Sheltered English

Homework

Writing **Researching Falconry**
Falconry is an ancient sport that may date back to the eighth century B.C. in Assyria. It was immensely popular among the European upper classes in the Middle Ages. Today, the sport is tightly regulated by the United States Fish and Wildlife Service, which issues permits that allow individuals to trap and train hawks, falcons, and occasionally eagles. Have students research and write a report about the history of falconry. Their report should include information about the role of falconry in raptor conservation.

internetconnect

SCILINKS
NSTA
TOPIC: Bird Characteristics
GO TO: www.scilinks.org
*sci***LINKS NUMBER:** HSTL405

Science BIOopers

The common name of a bird may be an accurate description of what it looks like, but it does not always accurately reflect what kind of bird it actually is. For example, the common nighthawk is not a hawk at all, although it appears hawklike in flight. The nighthawk belongs to the Caprimulgidae family, which are mostly insect eaters. Members of this family were called goatsuckers because Caprimulgidae comes from the Latin *caper,* "goat," and *mulgeo,* "to milk." According to legend, the birds sucked milk from goats at night!

2 Teach, continued

MEETING INDIVIDUAL NEEDS

Writing | Advanced Learners

Have students research and prepare a report on the parts and functions of an airplane's wing, comparing the information to the parts and functions of a bird's wing. For example, a bird spreads its primary wing feathers to slow down. Is there a movable piece on the plane's wing that helps slow down the plane when it is approaching the airstrip for a landing?

QuickLab

MATERIALS

FOR EACH STUDENT:
• drinking straw
• push or straight pin
• tissue paper (3 × 0.5 cm)

Safety Caution: Remind students to review all safety cautions and icons before beginning this lab activity. Students should be especially careful not to stick themselves with the pin when making the hole. They should not use any straw that another student has already used.

CONNECT TO PHYSICAL SCIENCE

For both birds and aircraft, the shape of the wing creates differences in maneuverability and air speed. Designing an airplane wing requires taking into account what kind of flying the plane will need to do. Selective pressures have generated a vast array of wing shapes in birds, enabling different species to fly in very different ways. Use Teaching Transparency 227 to illustrate the effect of wing shape on air speed and lift.

QuickLab

Bernoulli Effect

Is it true that fast-moving air creates low pressure? You bet. You can see this effect easily with a straw and a piece of paper. First find a partner. Use a **pin** to make a hole in one side of a **drinking straw.** Cut or tear a small strip of **paper** about 3 cm long and 0.5 cm wide. Hold the strip of paper as close to the hole as you can without letting the paper touch the straw. Ask your partner to blow into the straw. The fast-moving air will create low pressure in the straw. The higher air pressure in the room will push the paper against the hole. Try it!

Getting off the Ground

How do birds overcome gravity and fly? Birds flap their wings to get into the air and to push themselves through the air. Wings provide lift. **Lift** is the upward pressure on the wing that keeps a bird in the air.

When air flows past a wing, some of the air is forced over the top of the wing, and some is forced underneath. A bird's wing is curved on top. As shown in **Figure 6,** the air on top has to move *farther* than the air underneath. As a result, the air on top moves *faster* than the air underneath. The fast-moving air on top creates low pressure in the air. This is called the *Bernoulli effect.* The air pressure under the wing is higher and pushes the wing up.

Figure 6 *A bird's wing is shaped to produce lift. Air moving over the top of the wing moves faster than air moving underneath the wing. This creates a difference in air pressure that keeps a bird in the air.*

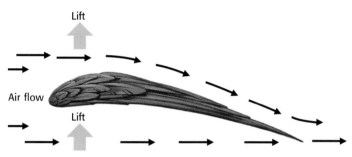

Lift

Air flow

Lift

Birds generate extra lift by flapping their wings. The faster a bird flies, the greater the lift. Another factor that affects lift is wing size. The larger the wing, the greater the lift. This is why birds with large wings can soar long distances without flapping their wings. An albatross, like the one in **Figure 7,** can glide over the ocean for many hours without flapping its wings.

Figure 7 *The wandering albatross has a wingspan of 3.5 m, the largest of any living bird. Its large wings allow the albatross to glide for very long periods of time. An albatross comes ashore only to lay its eggs.*

 Teaching Transparency 227
"Wing Shape Creates Differences in Air Speed"
LINK TO PHYSICAL SCIENCE

IS THAT A FACT!

The wandering albatross's wings are 3–3.5 m long but are barely 23 cm wide. The wings are inefficient for flapping flight, but their unusual shape enables albatrosses to soar for months at a time, alighting only to nest and feed and when winds are too calm for soaring.

Fly Away

It is sometimes said that when the going gets tough, the tough get going. If that's true, birds must be some of the toughest animals in the world. For when times are hard, some birds get going faster and farther than any other animal. Because they are able to fly great distances, birds are able to migrate great distances.

Some birds have good reasons to migrate. By migrating, they can find better territories with more food. For example, in the far north in the summer, the Arctic sun is up nearly 24 hours a day. Plants, insects, and other organisms increase explosively, providing lots of food. It's a great place for birds to raise their young. However, the winters are long and harsh, and there is little to eat. So when winter comes, birds fly south to find better feeding grounds.

Bringing Up Baby

Like reptiles, birds reproduce by internal fertilization and lay amniotic eggs with the developing embryo inside. But unlike most reptiles, birds must keep their eggs warm for the embryo to develop.

Most birds build elaborate nests and lay their eggs inside them. **Figure 8** shows a few of the many different kinds of bird nests. Birds sit on their eggs until the eggs hatch, using their body heat to keep the eggs warm. This is called **brooding.** Some birds, such as gulls, share brooding duties equally between males and females. But among songbirds, the female is in charge of brooding the eggs, and the male brings her food.

Raising young birds is hard work. Some birds, such as cuckoos and cowbirds, have found a way to make other birds do their work for them. A cuckoo lays its eggs in the nest of another species of bird. When the cuckoo egg hatches, the young cuckoo is fed and protected by the foster parents.

Figure 8 *There are many different types of bird nests. Birds use grass, branches, mud, hair, feathers, and many other building materials.*

Homework

Migration Mapping Migratory birds fly over almost every part of North America. However, they generally follow one of four main migration routes. Have students research the primary migration corridors, or flyways, in North America (Pacific, Mississippi, Central, and Atlantic) and illustrate them on a map. Also have students list at least three species of birds that travel along each flyway, along with the time of year the birds travel.
Sheltered English

COOPERATIVE LEARNING

Explain to students that many birds have elaborate courtship behaviors, or displays. Have students work in small groups to research the courtship behavior of a species of their choosing. Possibilities include golden eagles, mockingbirds, emperor penguins, and whooping cranes. Tell groups that they will be presenting their findings to the class. Have them divide tasks among group members; one person can do research, another can write the presentation, another can present the material, and another can make a poster.

93

IS THAT A FACT!

Migrating takes a lot of energy. Small birds may lose as much as 40 percent of their body weight on a long migratory flight. Even though the costs are high, birds that migrate experience a payoff when they reach areas with good weather and abundant food.

SCIENCE HUMOR

A hen is the only one who can lay down on the job and still get results.

MEETING INDIVIDUAL NEEDS

Konrad Lorenz (1903–1989), the man in **Figure 9,** was one of the founders of modern ethology, the study of animal behavior by comparative methods. Many of Lorenz's studies involved birds. In 1935, Lorenz observed behavior in young ducks and geese that we now know as *imprinting.* During a critical stage after hatching, young birds will follow the first moving object they see, even if it's not their biological parents. Have students research imprinting and summarize the results of Lorenz's classic bird studies. Have them compose their findings in a short report.

PORTFOLIO

DISCUSSION

Precocial Versus Altricial After students have read this page, ask them to name the advantages and disadvantages of being a precocial chick. (Advantages are that precocial chicks can help find their own food and are not as vulnerable to the elements because their down protects them. A disadvantage is that they are especially vulnerable to predators.)

Ask them to name the advantages and disadvantages of being altricial chicks. (An advantage is that chicks are often safer in a nest. Disadvantages are that parents need to cover the chicks constantly to keep them warm until their feathers grow in, and parents must leave the chicks to find food for themselves and the chicks.)

Figure 9 *Precocial chicks learn to recognize their parents right after they hatch. But if their parents are not there, the chicks will follow the first moving thing they see, even a person.*

Figure 10 *Both parents of altricial chicks leave the nest in search of food. They return to the nest with food every few minutes, sometimes making 1,000 trips a day between the two of them!*

Ready to Go Some baby birds hatch from the egg ready to run around and eat bugs. Chicks that hatch fully active are *precocial* (pree KOH shuhl). Chickens, ducks, and shorebirds all hatch precocial chicks. Precocial chicks are covered with downy feathers and follow their parents as soon as they can stand up. You can see some precocial chicks following a stand-in parent in **Figure 9.** Precocial chicks depend on their mother for warmth and protection, but they can walk, swim, and feed themselves.

Help Wanted The chicks of hawks, songbirds, and many other birds hatch weak, naked, and helpless. These chicks are *altricial* (al TRISH uhl). Their eyes are closed when they are born. Newly hatched altricial chicks cannot walk or fly. Their parents must keep them warm and feed them for several weeks. **Figure 10** shows altricial chicks being fed by a parent.

When altricial chicks grow their first flight feathers, they begin learning to fly. This takes days, however, and the chicks often end up walking around on the ground. The parents must work feverishly to distract cats, weasels, and other predators and protect their young.

SECTION REVIEW

1. List three ways birds are similar to reptiles and three ways they are different.

2. Explain the difference between precocial chicks and altricial chicks.

3. People use the phrase "eats like a bird" to describe someone who eats very little. Is this saying appropriate? Why or why not?

4. Name some of the adaptations that make bird bodies lightweight.

5. **Understanding Technology** Would an airplane wing that is not curved on top generate lift? Draw a picture to illustrate your explanation.

▼ **Answers to Section Review**

1. Answers may vary. Both birds and reptiles have scales and amniotic eggs, and both are vertebrates. Unlike reptiles, birds are endotherms, have feathers, and have air sacs.

2. Precocial chicks are fully active after hatching and are covered with downy feathers. Newly hatched altricial chicks cannot walk or fly and do not have feathers.

3. No; birds eat a tremendous amount of food in relation to their mass.

4. Birds' skeletons are compact. Their bones are hollow. Their feathers are light. They even have less DNA than other vertebrates.

5. No; air must move faster over the top of the wing to create lift. A flat wing would cause air to move at the same speed above and below and would not generate lift.

Kinds of Birds

There are almost 9,000 species of birds on Earth. Birds range in size from the 1.6 g bee hummingbird to the 125 kg North African ostrich. The bodies of birds have different characteristics too, depending on where they live and what they eat. Because of their great diversity, birds are classified into 29 different orders. That can be confusing, so birds are often grouped into four nonscientific categories: flightless birds, water birds, birds of prey, and perching birds. These categories don't include all birds, but they do show how different birds can be.

BRAIN FOOD

An ostrich egg has a mass of about 1.4 kg. A single ostrich egg is big enough to provide scrambled eggs for a family of four every morning for several days.

Flightless Birds

Ostriches, kiwis, emus, and other flightless birds do not have a large keel for flight. Though they cannot fly, many flightless birds are fast runners.

▲ The **kiwi,** of New Zealand, is a forest bird about the size of a chicken. Its feathers are soft and hair-like. Kiwis sleep during the day. At night, they hunt for worms, caterpillars, and berries.

◄ The **ostrich** is the largest living bird. Ostriches can reach a height of 2.5 m and a mass of 125 kg. An ostrich's two-toed feet look almost like hoofs, and these birds can run up to 64 km/h (40 mi/h).

▲ **Penguins** are unique flightless birds. They have a large keel and very strong flight muscles, but their wings have been modified into flippers. They flap these wings to swim underwater. Although penguins are graceful swimmers, they walk clumsily on land.

95

3) Extend

GOING FURTHER

Birds of prey such as eagles, owls, falcons and hawks are called *raptors*. There are raptor centers throughout the United States, many of which specialize in the care and rehabilitation of injured birds. The centers frequently serve as wildlife education centers, too. Many house and display for educational purposes birds that are too wounded or too accustomed to people to survive on their own. Have students research and contact these centers for more information about raptors and their care (remind them to include a stamped, self-addressed envelope if they expect a response by mail). If a raptor center is nearby, encourage students to work with the school administration to arrange a visit by a naturalist and a bird or two.

DEBATE

Destroy Wildlife to Save It?

The artist John James Audubon (1785–1851) painted pictures of birds that he shot. This was the only way he could get close enough to see the level of detail he needed in his paintings. Although modern cameras and binoculars provide researchers with excellent detail, scientists still sometimes kill birds for study and museum collections. This allows them to place the birds in proper evolutionary context. The results allow scientists to confirm the discovery of new species and develop specific conservation measures. Ask students to debate the pros and cons of this scientific technique.

Water Birds

Water birds are sometimes called *waterfowl*. These include cranes, ducks, geese, swans, pelicans, loons, and many other species. These birds usually have webbed feet for swimming, but they are also strong flyers.

Male **wood ducks** have beautiful ▶ plumage to attract females. Like all ducks, they are strong swimmers and flyers.

◀ The **blue-footed booby** is a tropical water bird. These birds have an elaborate courtship dance that includes raising their feet one at a time.

The **common loon** is the ▶ most primitive of modern birds. It can remain underwater for several minutes while searching for fish.

Birds of Prey

Eagles, hawks, falcons, and other birds of prey are meat eaters. They may eat mammals, fish, reptiles, birds, or other animals. The sharp claws on their feet and their sharp, curved beaks help these birds catch and eat their prey. They also have very good vision. Most birds of prey hunt during the day.

◀ Owls, like this **northern spotted owl,** are the only birds of prey that hunt at night. They have a keen sense of hearing to help them find their prey.

▲ **Ospreys** are fish eaters. They fly over the water and catch fish with their feet.

WEIRD SCIENCE

Some oceanic birds can eject a smelly oil from their stomachs. Fulmars can spew the foul-smelling liquid about 1 m as a defensive weapon. Elimination of the oil can also reduce a bird's weight before flight. The behavior is instinctive; newly hatched fulmars have been observed regurgitating the fluid while still emerging from the shell. The oil is also exchanged by adult fulmars during courtship. Eliminating the rich oil may help birds keep their metabolisms at the proper level.

Perching Birds

Songbirds, like robins, wrens, warblers, and sparrows, are perching birds. These birds have special adaptations for perching on a branch. When a perching bird lands on a branch, its feet automatically close around the branch. So even if the bird falls asleep, it will not fall off.

▲ **Parrots** are not songbirds, but they have special feet for perching and climbing. Their strong, hooked beak allows them to open seeds and slice fruit.

▲ **Chickadees** are lively little birds that frequently flock to garden feeders. They often dangle underneath a branch while hunting for insects, seeds, or fruits.

Most tanagers are tropical birds, ▶ but the **scarlet tanager** spends the summer in North America. The male is red, but the female is a yellow-green color that blends into the trees.

SECTION REVIEW

1. How did perching birds get their name?

2. Birds of prey have extremely good eyesight. Why is good vision important for these birds?

3. **Interpreting Illustrations** Look at the illustrations of bird feet at right. Which foot belongs to a water bird? a perching bird? Explain your answers.

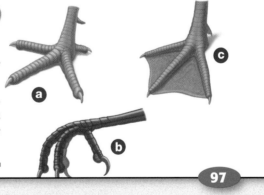

▼ *Answers to Section Review*

1. Perching birds have special feet that allow them to perch easily on branches.

2. As birds of prey, they are flying high above the ground; they need to be able to spot their prey from great distances.

3. The foot in figure (c) belongs to a water bird. The foot in figure (b) belongs to a perching bird. The water bird has webbed feet. The perching bird has a foot adapted to grasping. (The foot in figure (a) belongs to a pheasant.)

Focus

Mammals

This section introduces the mammals and describes their common characteristics. Students will learn the differences between monotremes, marsupials, and placental mammals and will provide examples of different kinds of mammals.

Bellringer

Write the following on the board or overhead transparency:

In the next 5 minutes, list as many characteristics of mammals as you can think of.

After the 5 minutes are up, ask students what characteristics they have listed, and put their answers on the board. Use their answers as a springboard for discussion about what mammals are and where they live.

1) Motivate

DISCUSSION

Domestication of Animals
Ask students to describe how humans have interacted with wild mammals over time.
(Humans have hunted mammals and used their meat for food, their hides for clothing and shelter, and their bones for tools.)

Then ask students how the domestication of mammals, such as horses, cattle, pigs, and dogs, changed the lives of early humans. It became easier to obtain food (eggs, milk), to cultivate crops (oxen pulling plows), to catch wild game (hunting dogs), and to control pests (cats).

Terms to Learn

mammary glands   placental
diaphragm   mammal
monotreme   gestation period
marsupial

What You'll Do

◆ Describe common characteristics of mammals.
◆ Explain the differences between monotremes, marsupials, and placental mammals.
◆ Give some examples of each type of mammal.

Mandrill baboon

Figure 12 *Therapsids had characteristics of both reptiles and mammals and may have looked something like this.*

98

internetconnect

SCI
LINKS
NSTA

TOPIC: The Origin of Mammals
GO TO: www.scilinks.org
*sci***LINKS NUMBER:** HSTL415

Mammals

Of all the vertebrates, we seem most interested in mammals. Maybe that's because we are mammals ourselves. But with about 4,500 species, mammals are actually a small class of animals. Mollusks, for example, include more than 90,000 species.

Mammals come in many different forms—from the tiniest bats, which weigh less than a cracker, to the largest whales. The blue whale, with a mass of more than 90,000 kg, is the largest animal—vertebrate or invertebrate—that has ever lived. You can find mammals in the coldest oceans, in the hottest deserts, and in every climate in between. You can see some of the variety of mammals in **Figure 11**.

Rhinoceros

Figure 11 *Even though they look very different, all of these animals are mammals.*

Beluga whale

The Origin of Mammals

Fossil evidence suggests that about 280 million years ago, mammal-like reptiles called therapsids appeared. *Therapsids* (thuh RAP sidz) were the early ancestors of mammals. An artist's rendition of a therapsid is shown in **Figure 12**.

About 200 million years ago, the first mammals appeared in the fossil record. These mammals were about the size of mice. The early mammals were endotherms. Because they did not depend on their surroundings for heat, they could forage at night and avoid their dinosaur predators during the day.

When the dinosaurs became extinct, there was more land and food available for the mammals. Mammals began to diversify and live in many different environments.

WEIRD SCIENCE

The world's smallest mammal is the Kitti's hog-nosed bat, which weighs only 2 g and is 33 mm long. This tiny bat lives in limestone caves in southwest Thailand.

Characteristics of Mammals

Dolphins and elephants are mammals, and so are monkeys, horses, and rabbits. You are a mammal, too! These animals are very different, but all mammals share many distinctive traits.

Mamma! All mammals have mammary glands; this sets them apart from other animals. **Mammary glands** secrete a nutritious fluid called milk. All female mammals supply milk to their young. Female mammals usually bear live young and care for their offspring, as illustrated in **Figure 13.** Although only mature female mammals make milk, male mammals also have small inactive mammary glands.

Figure 13 *Like all mammals, this calf gets its first meals from its mother's milk.*

All milk is made of water, protein, fat, and sugar. But the milk from different mammals has varying amounts of each nutrient. For example, human milk has half as much fat as cow's milk but twice as much sugar. The milk of seals may be more than one-half fat. At birth, elephant seals have a mass of 45 kg. After drinking this rich milk for just 3 weeks, their mass is 180 kg!

Cozy and Warm If you've ever had a dog fall asleep in your lap, you already know that mammals are really warm! All mammals are endotherms. Like birds, mammals require a lot of energy from the food they eat. Mammals quickly break down food in their bodies and use the energy released from their cells to keep their bodies warm. Usually a mammal keeps its body temperature constant. Only when a mammal is hibernating, estivating, or running a fever does its body temperature change.

Figure 14 *Mammals feel warm to the touch because they are endotherms.*

IS THAT A FACT!

Milk is more than food; it also contains antibodies that help the mother's offspring fight off infection.

2) Teach

ACTIVITY

Offspring Number Divide the class into small groups. Tell students to check references to determine the average number of offspring and frequency of births for a field mouse, a pig, a horse, a chimpanzee, and a human. Then tell them to find out how long the babies are dependent on their parents and what the average life span is of each of these mammals. Have students discuss whether they see any pattern. (Short-lived animals tend to have more offspring and give birth more frequently. Their offspring tend to have a short period of dependence on their parents.)

The groups should present their findings to the class and compare what they have learned.

Homework

Create a Timeline Have students use library references to create a timeline of mammalian evolution from their first appearance in the Triassic period (Mesozoic era) some 230 million years ago through the Cenozoic era to the present. Encourage students to illustrate their timelines with original drawings or pictures from books or magazines.
Sheltered English

 Directed Reading Worksheet Section 2

MEETING INDIVIDUAL NEEDS

Writing | Advanced Learners
Explain to students that males and females of the same species often vary in size and coloration. Tell them this sex-related difference is called *sexual dimorphism*. Examples in mammals are the male lion's mane, the male deer's antlers, different facial coloration in mandrills (a species of baboon), and larger canine teeth in male baboons. Have students research and write a brief report on possible reasons for sexual dimorphism in mammals.

PORTFOLIO

DEMONSTRATION

Comparing Skulls Display the skulls of several species for students to study. Ideally, include several mammal skulls, a reptile skull, a bird skull, and an amphibian skull. Tell students to carefully examine the skulls, paying close attention to the similarities and differences between classes (major groups) and within the mammal class. Ask them to describe differences in dentition (tooth structure and arrangement) and speculate about advantages and disadvantages of the arrangements they observe.
Sheltered English

---

internetconnect

SCiLINKS
NSTA

TOPIC: Characteristics of Mammals
GO TO: www.scilinks.org
*sci*LINKS NUMBER: HSTL420

Figure 15 *The thick fur of this arctic fox keeps its body warm in even the coldest winters.*

Figure 16
Mountain lions have sharp canine teeth for grabbing their prey. Donkeys have sharp incisors in front for cutting plants and flat grinding teeth in the back of their mouth.

Staying Warm Mammals have adaptations to help them keep warm. One way they stay warm is by having a thick coat, and many mammals have luxurious coats of fur. All mammals, even whales, have hair somewhere on their body. This is another trait that sets mammals apart from other animals. Mammals that live in cold climates usually have thick coats of hair, such as the fox in **Figure 15**. But large mammals that live in warm climates, like elephants, have less hair. Gorillas and humans have similar amounts of hair on their bodies, but human hair is finer and shorter.

Most mammals also have a layer of fat under the skin that acts as insulation. Whales and other mammals that live in cold oceans depend on a layer of fat called *blubber* to keep them warm.

Crunch! Another trait that sets mammals apart from other animals is their teeth. Birds don't even have teeth! And although fish and reptiles have teeth, their teeth tend to be all alike. In contrast, most mammals' teeth are specialized. They have different shapes and sizes for different functions.

Let's look at your teeth, for example. The teeth in the front of your mouth are cutting teeth, called *incisors*. Most people have four on top and four on the bottom. The next teeth are stabbing teeth, called *canines*. Canines help you grab food and hold onto it. Farther back in your mouth are flat teeth called *molars* that help grind up food.

The kinds of teeth a mammal has reflect its diet. Dogs, cats, wolves, foxes, and other meat-eating mammals have large canines. Molars are better developed in animals that eat plants. **Figure 16** shows the teeth of different mammals.

Unlike other vertebrates, mammals have two sets of teeth. A young mammal's first small teeth are called *milk teeth*. These are replaced by a set of permanent adult teeth after the mammal begins eating solid food and its jaw grows larger.

Multicultural CONNECTION

Native peoples of the Arctic region, such as the Inuit, have traditionally hunted marine mammals, such as seals, whales, and walruses. They use the seal's fur for water-repellent clothing and boots. They use seal blubber and whale blubber for lamp oil and for making soaps and lubricants. They even use marine mammal intestines to make waterproof outerwear.

Getting Oxygen Just as a fire needs oxygen in order to burn, all animals need oxygen to efficiently "burn," or break down, the food they eat. Like birds and reptiles, mammals use lungs to get oxygen from the air. But mammals also have a large muscle to help bring air into their lungs. This muscle is called the **diaphragm,** and it lies at the bottom of the rib cage.

Large Brains The brain of a mammal is much larger than the brain of another animal the same size. This allows mammals to learn, move, and think quickly. A mammal's highly developed brain also helps it keep track of what is going on in its environment and respond quickly.

Mammals depend on five major senses to provide them with information about their environment: vision, hearing, smell, touch, and taste. The importance of each sense for any given mammal often depends on the mammal's environment. For example, mammals that are active at night rely more heavily on their ability to hear than on their ability to see.

Mammal Parents All mammals reproduce sexually. Like birds and reptiles, mammals reproduce by internal fertilization. Most mammals give birth to live young, and all mammals nurse their young. Mammal parents are very protective, with one or both parents caring for their young until they are grown. **Figure 17** shows a brown bear caring for its young.

Figure 17 *A mother bear will attack anything that threatens her cubs.*

Activity

Like all mammals, you have a diaphragm. Place your hand underneath your rib cage. What happens as you breathe in and out? You are feeling the motion of your abdominal muscles, which are connected to your diaphragm. Contract and relax your abdominal muscles. What happens?

TRY at HOME

Answer to Explore
Contracting the abdominal muscles causes the diaphragm to contract and draw air into the lungs. Relaxing them allows air to leave the lungs.

CONNECT TO
PHYSICAL SCIENCE

MATERIALS
• 60 cc syringe (without needle)
• beaker of colored water

The diaphragm is a muscle that enables mammals to breathe. The diaphragm regulates the air pressure in the lungs. Tell students that in this simple model, the plunger of the syringe represents the diaphragm of a mammal. The barrel of the syringe represents the lungs. The colored water represents the air outside the body. Push the plunger all the way into the barrel. Place the tip of the syringe in the colored water. Pull the plunger back and fill the barrel with water. As you do this, explain that the barrel is filling because the pressure inside the barrel is decreasing as the space inside the barrel is increasing. Water is entering the barrel to equalize the pressure. This same principle enables the diaphragm to pull air into the lungs. Sheltered English

SECTION REVIEW

1. Name three characteristics that are unique to mammals.

2. What is the purpose of a diaphragm?

3. **Making Inferences** Suppose you found a mammal skull on an archaeological dig. How would the teeth give you clues about the mammal's diet?

101

▼ *Answers to Section Review*

1. Mammals have mammary glands, fur, and specialized teeth.

2. A diaphragm helps draw air into the lungs.

3. Large canine teeth would indicate that the animal was a meat eater. Flat molars, grinding teeth, and sharp incisors would suggest a plant eater.

Prediction Guide Before students read about marsupials, ask them to respond true or false to the following statement:

> Marsupials are native only to Australia. (false)

Have them check their answer after they read the page.

CROSS-DISCIPLINARY FOCUS

Anthropology The artwork of Australia's Aborigines, an indigenous people, often depicts the country's unique and varied wildlife. Have students research the history of the tribes and the symbolism of the animals in their paintings. Students should bring their information to class to share their findings with their classmates.

Homework

Researching Mammals The platypus is an amphibious mammal. Tell students to find the word *amphibious* in a dictionary if they do not already know what it means. Then have them list examples of other amphibious mammals in their ScienceLog. (Examples include river otters, hippopotamuses, beavers, and muskrats.)

Kinds of Mammals

Mammals are divided into three groups based on the way their young develop. These groups are monotremes, marsupials, and placental mammals.

Monotremes Mammals that lay eggs are called **monotremes**. Monotremes are the only mammals that lay eggs, and early scientists called them "furred reptiles." But monotremes are not reptiles; they have all the mammal traits. They have mammary glands and a thick fur coat, and they are endotherms.

A female monotreme lays eggs with thick, leathery shells. Like bird and reptile eggs, monotreme eggs have a yolk and albumen to feed the developing embryo. The female incubates the eggs with her body heat. Newly hatched young are not fully developed. The mother protects her young and feeds them milk. Unlike other mammals, monotremes do not have nipples, and the babies cannot suck. Instead, the tiny monotremes nurse by licking milk from the skin and hair around their mother's mammary glands.

Figure 18 *Echidnas are about the size of a house cat. They have large claws and long snouts that help them dig ants and termites out of their nests.*

Two Kinds of Monotremes Monotremes are found only in Australia and New Guinea, and just three species of monotremes are alive today. Two are echidnas (ee KID nuhs), spine-covered animals with long snouts. Echidnas have long sticky tongues for catching ants and termites. You can see an echidna in **Figure 18**.

The third monotreme is the duckbilled platypus, shown in **Figure 19**. The duckbilled platypus is a swimming mammal that lives and feeds in rivers and ponds. It has webbed feet and a flat tail to help it move through the water. It also has a flat, rubbery bill that it uses to dig for food and to dig long tunnels in riverbanks to lay its eggs.

Figure 19 *When underwater, a duckbilled platypus closes its eyes and ears. It uses its sensitive bill to find food.*

102

IS THAT A FACT!

The platypus is one of the very few poisonous mammals.

WEIRD SCIENCE

Monotremes lack the glands that produce hydrochloric acid and peptic enzymes that help mammals digest protein. Scientists think that digestion in the echidnas is aided by the grinding action of the dirt they eat.

Marsupials You probably know that kangaroos, like those in **Figure 20,** have pouches. Kangaroos are **marsupials,** mammals with pouches. Like all mammals, marsupials are endotherms. They have mammary glands, fur, and teeth. Unlike the monotremes, marsupials do not lay eggs. They give birth to live young.

Like newly hatched monotremes, marsupial infants are not fully developed. At birth, the tiny embryos of a kangaroo are no larger than bumblebees. Shortly after birth, they drag themselves through their mother's fur until they reach a pouch on her abdomen. Inside the pouch are mammary glands. The young kangaroo climbs in, latches onto a nipple, and drinks milk until it is able to move around by itself and leave the pouch for short periods. Young kangaroos are called joeys.

There are about 280 species of marsupials. The only marsupial in North America north of Mexico is the opossum (uh PAHS suhm), shown in **Figure 21.** Other marsupials include koalas, shown in **Figure 22,** Tasmanian devils, and wallabies. Most marsupials live in Australia, New Guinea, and South America.

Figure 20 *After birth, a kangaroo continues to develop in its mother's pouch. Older joeys leave the pouch but return if there is any sign of danger.*

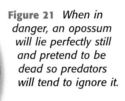

Figure 21 *When in danger, an opossum will lie perfectly still and pretend to be dead so predators will tend to ignore it.*

Figure 22 *Koalas sleep in trees during the day and are active at night. They eat nothing but eucalyptus leaves.*

BRAIN FOOD

When a kangaroo first climbs into its mother's pouch, the mother's milk is nonfat. Later, the milk is about 20 percent fat. A mother kangaroo with two babies that are different ages supplies nonfat milk to the baby and fat milk to the older one. Each youngster nurses from a different nipple.

103

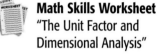
CONNECT TO EARTH SCIENCE

About 50 million years ago, Australia and New Guinea began to separate from a larger continent into distinct land masses of their own. Placental mammals apparently did not reach Australia and New Guinea before the land masses separated from the other continents, although marsupials and monotremes were present then. Placental mammals found in Australia and New Guinea today are descendants of placental mammals that came to these regions only recently.

Answer to MATHBREAK

First calculate the number of ants per day, as follows:

$$\frac{50 \text{ ants}}{1 \text{ Calorie}} = \frac{x \text{ ants}}{1{,}800 \text{ Calories/day}}$$

$x = 90{,}000$ ants per day

at a rate of two ants per lick:
45,000 licks

The time will vary, but if the rate is 60 licks per minute, then

$$\frac{45{,}000 \text{ licks}}{60 \text{ licks/min}} = 750 \text{ minutes}$$

$$\frac{750 \text{ min}}{60 \text{ min/hour}} = 12.5 \text{ hours per day}$$

Answer to Self-Check

Monotremes are mammals that lay eggs. Marsupials bear live young but carry them in pouches or skin folds before they are able to live independently. Placentals develop inside the mother's body and are nourished through a placenta before birth.

CROSS-DISCIPLINARY FOCUS

Archaeology When archaeologists study the homes of prehistoric people, they usually look for traces of structures or fire circles, and they investigate caves. But scientists studying early South American Indians have learned that they used the shells of early armadillos to build roofs for their homes. These ancestors of modern armadillos had shells up to 3 m long.

INDEPENDENT PRACTICE

Concept Mapping Have students create a concept map that compares the development and life histories of monotremes, marsupials, and placental mammals. Some terms and concepts students can use include:

> type of egg with a shell, incubation, gestation, nest, uterus, mammary glands, method of nursing

---

÷ 5 ÷ Ω ≤ ∞ + Ω √ 9 ∞ ≤ Σ 2

MATH**BREAK**

Ants for Dinner!

The giant anteater can stick its tongue out 150 times a minute. Count how many times you can stick out your tongue in a minute. Imagine that you are an anteater and you need 1,800 Calories a day. If you need to eat 50 ants to get 1 Calorie, how many ants would you have to eat per day? If you could catch two ants every time you stuck your tongue out, how many times a day would you have to stick out your tongue? How many hours a day would you have to eat?

104

Placental Mammals Most mammals are placental mammals. In **placental mammals,** the embryos stay inside the mother's body and develop in an organ called the *uterus.* Placental embryos form a special attachment to the uterus of their mother called a *placenta.* The placenta supplies food and oxygen from the mother's blood to the growing embryo. The placenta also removes wastes from the embryo.

The time during which an embryo develops within the mother is called the **gestation period.** Gestation (jeh STAY shuhn) periods in placental animals range from a few weeks in mice to as long as 23 months in elephants. Humans have a gestation period of about 9 months.

> ### ✓ Self-Check
>
> Explain the difference between a monotreme, a marsupial, and a placental mammal. *(See page 152 to check your answer.)*

Kinds of Placental Mammals

Over 90 percent of all the mammals on Earth are placental mammals. Living placental mammals are classified into 18 orders. The characteristics of the most common orders are given on the following pages.

Toothless Mammals

This group includes anteaters, armadillos, aardvarks, pangolins, and sloths. Although these mammals are called "toothless," only the anteaters are completely toothless. The others have small teeth. Most toothless mammals feed on insects they catch with their long sticky tongues.

Armadillos eat ▶ insects, frogs, mushrooms, and roots. When threatened, an armadillo rolls up into a ball and is protected by its tough plates.

▲ The largest anteater is the 40 kg **giant anteater** of South America. Anteaters never destroy the nests of their prey. They open the nests, eat a few ants or termites, and then move on to another nest.

IS THAT A FACT!

Both placental mammals and marsupials have a placenta. So why do we call one group placental? The difference is that in marsupials, the placenta does not play a major role in nourishing the fetus, while in placental mammals, it does.

Insect Eaters

Insect eaters, or *insectivores,* live on every continent except Australia and Antarctica. Most insectivores are small, and most have long pointed noses to dig into the soil for food. Compared with other mammals, they have a very small brain and few specialized teeth. Insectivores include moles, shrews, and hedgehogs.

◀ The **star-nosed mole** has sensitive feelers on its nose to help it find insects and feel its way while burrowing underground. Although they have tiny eyes, moles cannot see.

▲ **Hedgehogs** live throughout Europe, Asia, and Africa. Their spines keep them safe from most predators.

Rodents

More than one-third of all mammalian species are rodents, and they can be found on every continent except Antarctica. Rodents include squirrels, mice, rats, guinea pigs, porcupines, and chinchillas. Most rodents are small animals with long, sensitive whiskers. Rodents are chewers and gnawers. All rodents have sharp front teeth for gnawing. Because rodents chew so much, their teeth wear down. So a rodent's incisors grow continuously, just like your fingernails do.

▲ The **capybaras** (KAP i BAH ruhs) of South America are the largest rodents in the world. A female can have a mass of 70 kg—as much as a grown man.

▲ Like all rodents, **beavers** have gnawing teeth. They use these teeth to cut down trees.

Science Bloopers

Tree shrews are tiny animals that look like squirrels with long, cone-shaped noses. Though they are insectivores and have shrewlike noses, tree shrews are not actually shrews. Until late in the twentieth century, zoologists thought tree shrews were primates. Recently, taxonomists recognized their uniqueness and placed them in their own order, Scandentia.

BRAIN FOOD

Tell students that if they were tracking lagomorphs in the snow, they would probably find all four footprints aligned or even prints from the back feet in front of those from the front feet! When moving quickly, lagomorphs rely on their powerful back legs to propel them forward. Their jump distance is increased when they swing their back legs forward until they touch down nearly in line with their front feet and then push off. Lagomorphs are one of the most efficient animals with this type of locomotion. Cheetahs can also do this.

DISCUSSION

Bat Fact and Fiction Ask students if the following statements are true or false:

1. Some bats have wing spans of more than 1.5 m. (True; the flying foxes of Indonesia are the largest bats.)

2. A single little brown bat can catch 1,200 mosquito-size insects in 1 hour. (true)

3. Bats present a serious disease threat to humans. (False; less than one-half of 1 percent of bats carry rabies. Most bite only when threatened.)

Lagomorphs

Rabbits, hares, and pikas belong to a group of placental mammals called lagomorphs. Like rodents, they have sharp gnawing teeth. But unlike rodents, they have two sets of incisors in their upper jaw and short tails. Rabbits and hares have long, powerful hind legs for jumping. To detect their many predators, they have sensitive noses and large ears and eyes.

◀ **Pikas** are small animals that live high in the mountains. Pikas gather plants and mound them in "haystacks" to dry. In the winter, they use the dry plants for food and insulation.

▲ The large ears of this **black-tailed jack rabbit** help it hear well.

Flying Mammals

Bats are the only mammals that can fly. Bats are active at night and sleep in sheltered areas during the day. Most bats eat insects. But some bats eat fruit, and three species of vampire bats drink the blood of other animals.

Most bats hunt for insects at night. They find their way using echolocation. Bats make clicking noises when they fly. Trees, rocks, insects, and other objects reflect the sound back to the bat, making an echo.

Echoes from a big, hard tree sound very different from those reflecting off a soft, tasty moth. Bats that echolocate often have enormous ears to help them hear the echoes of their own clicks.

In many Asian countries, **bats** ▶ are symbols of good luck, long life, and happiness.

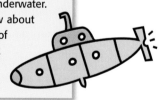

APPLY

Bats and Submarines

What do bats have in common with submarines? Submarines use a form of echolocation called sonar to find and avoid objects underwater. Based on what you know about echolocation, what kind of instruments do you think are needed to navigate a submarine with sonar?

106

Answer to APPLY

A submarine would need instruments to send signals and receive echoes and would need instruments to calculate distances using that information.

IS THAT A FACT!

Of the known mammal species, 25 percent are bats.

Carnivores

Carnivores are a group of mammals that have large canines and special teeth for slicing meat. The name *carnivore* means "meat eater"—the mammals in this group primarily eat meat. Carnivorous mammals include lions, wolves, weasels, otters, bears, raccoons, and hyenas. Carnivores also include a group of fish-eating marine mammals called *pinnipeds.* The pinnipeds include seals, sea lions, and walruses. Some carnivores also eat plants. For example, black bears eat grass, nuts, and berries and only rarely eat meat. But many carnivores eat nothing but other animals.

▼ **Raccoons** have handlike paws that help them catch fish and hold their food. They can handle objects almost as well as monkeys can.

▲ **Coyotes** are members of the dog family. They live throughout North America and in parts of Central America.

▲ Cats are divided into two groups, big cats and small cats. All the big cats can roar. The largest of the big cats is the **Siberian tiger,** with a mass of up to 300 kg.

◀ **Walruses** are pinnipeds. Unlike other carnivores, walruses do not use their canines for tearing food. Instead, they use them to defend themselves, to dig for food, and to climb on ice.

107

SCIENCE HUMOR

Q: Why did the lion cross the savanna?

A: to get to the other pride

ACTIVITY

Comparing Footprints Have students compare footprints or foot casts of two common carnivores, the domestic dog and the domestic cat. Students can make footprints by having a pet step on damp, claylike soil. They can make casts by pouring plaster of paris in a dried footprint. Have them study the casts and hypothesize about the reasons for the features and differences they notice. **Sheltered English**

DEBATE

Carnivore Conservation
Explain to students that many carnivores are endangered because of habitat loss, hunting, and poaching. Historically, it has been difficult to persuade people to preserve animals that they considered dangerous to themselves and to livestock. Some carnivores are endangered because people hunt them for their fur or for body parts believed to have medicinal qualities. Have students debate the extent to which we should preserve large carnivores, such as wolves and tigers, and the steps that we should take to do so.

MISCONCEPTION /// ALERT \\\

Not all Carnivora are strict carnivores. For example, pandas feed primarily on bamboo, and coatis eat mostly fruit. Tell students that, in this case, animals are classified according to ancestral relationships, not their actual diet.

🌐 Multicultural CONNECTION

Hernando Cortéz reintroduced the horse into North America during the 1500s. Before then, Native Americans had to walk long distances on foot, carrying heavy loads on their backs. The arrival of the horse changed their lives forever. They were able to travel long distances more easily and were able to expand their trade routes. They were also able to hunt bison and other animals more efficiently. For plains tribes, such as the Kiowa, the horse became an important part of practical life and a key part of their culture.

REAL-WORLD CONNECTION

Water Buffaloes Many kinds of hoofed mammals are used for draft work. In the United States, thousands of farms still rely on horses or mules to pull some farm equipment. Oxen, llamas, goats, and camels are used in various parts of the world for pulling or carrying. But perhaps no animal is as widely used as the water buffalo. Water buffaloes are large, strong, and relatively docile animals. They are hardy and can survive eating rough, native vegetation. They were originally domesticated in Asia thousands of years ago and are still vital to the farms of southern China and Southeast Asia. The water buffalo was introduced to Africa about 1,400 years ago and is still used for draft work there. More recently, the water buffalo was introduced to Central and South America. Have interested students research and present to the class an oral report on the importance of water buffaloes or other draft animals to farmers around the world.

Hoofed Mammals

Horses, pigs, deer, and rhinoceroses are just a few of the many mammals that have thick hoofs. Most hoofed mammals are adapted for swift running. Because they are plant eaters, they have large, flat molars to help them grind plant material.

Hoofed mammals are divided into groups based on the number of toes they have. Odd-toed hoofed mammals have one or three toes. Horses and zebras have a single large hoof, or toe. Other odd-toed hoofed mammals include rhinoceroses and tapirs. Even-toed hoofed mammals have two or four toes. These mammals include pigs, cows, camels, deer, hippopotamuses, and giraffes.

▲ **Giraffes** are the tallest living mammals. They have long necks, long legs, and an even number of toes.

▲ **Tapirs** are large, three-toed mammals that live in forests. Tapirs can be found in Central America, South America, and Southeast Asia.

Camels are even-toed mammals. The hump of a camel is a large lump of fat that provides energy for the camel when food is scarce. ▶

108

IS THAT A FACT!

The limbs of hoofed mammals are adapted for running and walking long distances over open terrain. These animals have between one and four toes and very long foot bones. In human terms, they are balancing on the tips of their toes.

Trunk-Nosed Mammals

Elephants are the only mammals with a trunk. The trunk is an elongated and muscular combination of the upper lip and nose. Elephants use their trunk the same way we use our hands, lips, and nose. The trunk is powerful enough to lift a tree yet agile enough to pick small fruits one at a time. Elephants use their trunk to place food in their mouth and to spray their back with water to cool off.

There are two species of elephants, African elephants and Asian elephants. African elephants are larger and have bigger ears and tusks than Asian elephants. Both species eat plants. Because they are so large, elephants eat up to 18 hours a day to get enough food.

Elephants are the largest land animals. Male African elephants can reach a mass of 7,500 kg! Elephants are very intelligent and may live more than 60 years.

▼ **Elephants** are social animals. They live in herds of related females and their offspring. The whole family helps take care of young.

Self-Check

1. Why are bats classified as mammals and not as birds?
2. How are rodents and lagomorphs similar? How are they different?

(See page 152 to check your answers.)

Environment
CONNECTION

Both species of elephants are endangered. For centuries, humans have hunted elephants for their long teeth, called tusks. Elephant tusks are made of ivory, a hard material used for carving. Because of the high demand for ivory, much of the elephant population has been wiped out. Today elephant hunting is illegal.

SCIENCE HUMOR

Q: How do you make an elephant float?

A: Pour a glass of root beer, and add two elephants.

Answers to Self-Check

1. Bats bear live young, have fur, and do not have feathers.
2. Rodents and lagomorphs are small mammals with long, sensitive whiskers and gnawing teeth. Unlike rodents, lagomorphs have two sets of incisors and a short tail.

3 Extend

DEBATE

Elephants and People: Room for Both? As the human population in Africa has expanded, villages and ranches have spread into former elephant habitat. Fences prevent elephants from traveling traditional routes to forage and find water. In some areas elephants have raided crops, killed farmers who tried to defend their fields, and even destroyed their natural food sources because too many elephants were trying to live in too small an area. So although elephant populations have declined, current conditions have caused overcrowding among the ones that remain. Should "excess" elephants be killed? The meat from killed elephants is given to the local people, many of whom are in dire need of food. Have students debate the management of elephant populations.

GOING FURTHER

The ears of African and Asian elephants are the most noticeable difference between the two species. Have students explain the evolutionary significance of this difference by exploring how the ears differ and researching the environments in which the animals live. (The larger surface area of the African elephant's ears contains more blood vessels that can be exposed to a cooling breeze passing over the thin skin of the ears; the larger ears serve as "fans" for the animals in the searing African heat. Asian elephants spend a lot of time in the forest, shielded from the sun.)

RESEARCH

Writing Have students research and write a short report about one aspect of whale biology. Possibilities include whale behavior, feeding habits, anatomy, and communication. Encourage interested students to do preliminary research to find an interesting subject to study. Have students present their findings to the class.

PORTFOLIO

DEBATE

Whaling Have students research and debate the practice of hunting whales. Questions that they should be aware of include:

What is the history of whaling? What products do people obtain from whales? Are there other sources of these products? Why have some countries signed a treaty to cease commercial whaling? Why don't all countries sign the treaty? Are there any whale species with a population large enough to support an ongoing whaling industry?

Students should make a distinction between commercial whaling and small-scale whaling as it is practiced by people such as the Makah of Washington State.

Cetaceans

Whales, dolphins, and porpoises make up a group of water-dwelling mammals called cetaceans (see TAY shuhns). At first glance, whales and their relatives may look more like fish than mammals. But like all mammals, cetaceans are endotherms, have lungs, and nurse their young. Most of the largest whales are toothless whales that strain tiny, shrimp-like animals from sea water. But dolphins, porpoises, sperm whales, and killer whales have teeth, which they use to eat fish and other animals.

▲ **Spinner dolphins** spin like a football when they leap from the water. Like all dolphins, they are intelligent and highly social.

◀ Like bats, cetaceans use echolocation to "see" their surroundings. **Sperm whales,** like this one, use loud blasts of sound to stun fish, making them easier to catch.

Sirenia

The smallest group of water-dwelling mammals is called sirenia (sie REE nee uh). It includes just four species—three kinds of manatees and the dugong. These mammals are completely aquatic; they live along coasts and in large rivers. They are quiet animals that eat seaweed and water plants.

Manatees are also ▶ called sea cows.

110

WEIRD SCIENCE

Humpback whales have a fascinating fishing strategy. They make their own fishing nets out of bubbles! The bubble net can be up to 30 m (98 ft) in diameter, which is large enough for the whale to get inside. The whale creates this net by swimming around in a spiral directly underneath a school of fish. As the whale swims, it blows air out of its blowhole. This forms a bubble net entirely around the fish, trapping them. The whale then swims up through the net with its mouth wide open, scooping in fish as it goes.

Primates

Prosimians, monkeys, apes, and humans all belong to a group of mammals called *primates.* There are about 160 species of primates. All primates have the eyes facing forward, enabling both eyes to focus on a single point. Most primates have five fingers on each hand and five toes on each foot, with flat fingernails instead of claws. Primates' fingers and opposable thumbs are able to make complicated movements, like grasping objects. Primates have a large brain in proportion to their body size and are considered some of the most intelligent mammals.

Many primates live in trees. Their flexible shoulder joints and grasping hands and feet enable them to climb trees and swing from branch to branch. Most primates eat a diet of leaves and fruits, but some also eat animals.

◀ **Spider monkeys,** like most monkeys, have grasping tails. Their long arms, legs, and tails help them move among the trees.

▲ **Orangutans** and other apes frequently walk upright. Apes usually have larger brains and bodies than monkeys.

SECTION REVIEW

1. If you saw only the feet of a hippopotamus and a rhinoceros, could you tell the difference between the two animals? Explain your answer.

2. How are monotremes different from all other mammals? How are they similar?

3. To what group of placental mammals do dogs belong? How do you know?

4. **Making Inferences** What is a gestation period? Why do elephants have a longer gestation period than do mice?

internet connect

SC_**LINKS**_
NSTA

TOPIC: The Origin of Mammals, Characteristics of Mammals
GO TO: www.scilinks.org
*sci***LINKS NUMBER:** HSTL415, HSTL420

▼ *Answers to Section Review*

1. Yes; the hippopotamus would be the one with two toes, and the rhinoceros would be the one with three toes.

2. Monotremes are the only mammals that lay eggs. Like other mammals, they have fur and nurse their young.

3. Dogs are carnivores, related to wolves. They have large canine teeth and hunt prey in the wild.

4. A gestation period is the length of time a developing fetus remains inside the mother. Elephants have larger bodies and need more time to develop.

4) Close

Quiz

1. Why did the mammal population increase when the dinosaurs became extinct? (There was more land and food available for the mammals.)

2. Where do mammals get the energy they need to keep their bodies warm? (Mammals quickly break down food in their bodies and use the energy released from their cells to keep their bodies warm.)

3. What are three characteristics of primates? (Possible answers: eyes that face forward, five fingers on each hand and five toes on each foot, flat fingernails and toenails instead of claws, fingers and thumbs that can make complicated movements, and a large brain)

ALTERNATIVE ASSESSMENT

Have students create a poster that visually summarizes the physiological information they have learned about birds and mammals and that provides examples of each of the animal categories discussed in the chapter. For example, a picture of a bird of prey catching its food would illustrate the grasping talons of raptors.
Sheltered English

Reinforcement Worksheet
"Mammals Are Us"

Making Models Lab

What? No Dentist Bills?
Teacher's Notes

Time Required

Two 45-minute class periods

Lab Ratings

EASY ————————→ HARD

TEACHER PREP 🧪🧪
STUDENT SET-UP 🧪🧪
CONCEPT LEVEL 🧪🧪
CLEAN UP 🧪🧪

MATERIALS

Pea gravel is an acceptable substitute for aquarium gravel. It can be obtained from a local hardware store and is much less expensive. A 4:1 gravel to birdseed ratio works best.

Safety Caution

Remind students to review all safety cautions and icons before beginning this lab activity.

Randy Christian
Stovall Junior High School
Houston, Texas

What? No Dentist Bills?

When you eat, you must chew your food well. Chewing food into small bits is the first part of digestion. But birds don't have teeth. How do birds make big chunks of food small enough to begin digestion? In this activity, you will develop a hypothesis about how birds digest their food. Then you will build a model of a bird's digestive system to test your hypothesis.

Ask a Question

1. How are birds able to begin digestion without having any teeth?

Form a Hypothesis

2. Look at the diagram below of a bird's digestive system. Form a hypothesis that answers the question above. Write your hypothesis in your ScienceLog.

MATERIALS

- several resealable plastic bags of various sizes
- birdseed
- aquarium gravel
- water
- string
- drinking straw
- transparent tape
- scissors or other materials as needed

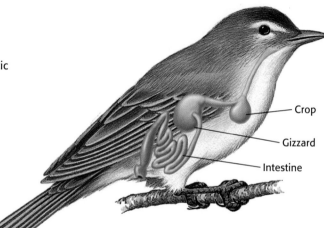

Crop

Gizzard

Intestine

112

Test the Hypothesis

3 Design a model of a bird's digestive system using the materials listed on page 112. Include in your design as many of these parts as possible: esophagus, crop, gizzard, intestine, and cloaca.

4 Using the materials you selected, build your model.

5 Test your model with the birdseed. Record your observations.

Analyze the Results

6 Did your "gizzard" grind the food?

7 What do you think *gizzard stones* are? How do you think they help a bird?

8 Does the amount of material added to your model gizzard change its ability to work effectively? Explain your answer.

9 Birds can break down food particles without teeth. What conclusions can you draw about how they do this?

Draw Conclusions

10 Analyze the strengths and weaknesses of your hypothesis based on your results. Was your hypothesis correct? Explain your answer.

11 What are some limitations of your model? How do you think you could improve it?

Going Further

Did you know that scientists have found "gizzard stones" with fossilized dinosaur skeletons? Look in the library or on the Internet for information about the evolutionary relationship between dinosaurs and birds. List the similarities and differences you find between these two types of animals.

Answers

1. A bird uses a gizzard instead of teeth.
6. Students should be able to demonstrate how their model gizzard grinds birdseed.
7. Gizzard stones are small pebbles that birds sometimes swallow. They settle in the gizzard and aid in digestion.
8. Model gizzards, no more than three-fourths full, will probably be most effective.
9. The gizzard stones help the birds break down the food.
11. Answers may include reducing the amount of food, adding gizzard stones, or adding more liquid to the food.

Datasheets for LabBook

Going Further

Scientists have long recognized similarities between birds and some dinosaurs, including an S-shaped neck, a unique ankle joint, and hollow bones.

Chapter Highlights

Chapter Highlights

VOCABULARY DEFINITIONS

SECTION 1

down feather a fluffy insulating feather that lies next to a bird's body

contour feather a feather made of a stiff central shaft with many side branches` called barbs

preening activity in which a bird uses its beak to spread oil on its feathers

lift an upward force on an object (such as a wing) caused by differences in pressure above and below the object; opposes the downward pull of gravity

brooding when a bird sits on its eggs until they hatch

SECTION 1

Vocabulary

down feather *(p. 89)*

contour feather *(p. 89)*

preening *(p. 89)*

lift *(p. 92)*

brooding *(p. 93)*

Section Notes

- Like reptiles, birds lay amniotic eggs and have thick, dry scales.

- Unlike reptiles, birds are endotherms and are covered with feathers.

- Because flying requires a lot of energy, birds must eat a high-energy diet and breathe efficiently.

- Birds' wings are shaped so that they generate lift. Lift is air pressure beneath the wings that keeps a bird in the air.

- Birds are lightweight. Their feathers are strong but lightweight, and their skeleton is relatively rigid, compact, and hollow.

- Because birds can fly, they can migrate great distances. They can nest in one habitat and winter in another. Migrating birds can take advantage of food supplies and avoid predators.

☑ Skills Check

Visual Understanding

LIFT The diagram on page 92 helps explain the concept of lift. Looking at this illustration, you can see that air must travel a greater distance over a curved wing than under a curved wing. The air above the wing must move faster than the air underneath in order to cover the greater distance in the same amount of time. Faster-moving air creates lower pressure above the wing. The higher pressure under the wing forces it up, creating lift.

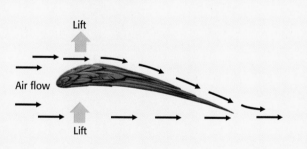

Lab and Activity Highlights

What? No Dentist Bills? **PG 112**

Datasheets for LabBook
(blackline masters for this lab)

SECTION 2

Vocabulary

mammary glands *(p. 99)*

diaphragm *(p. 101)*

monotreme *(p. 102)*

marsupial *(p. 103)*

placental mammal *(p. 104)*

gestation period *(p. 104)*

Section Notes

- All mammals have mammary glands; in females, mammary glands produce milk. Milk is a highly nutritious fluid fed to the young.

- Like birds, mammals are endotherms.

- Mammals maintain their high metabolism by eating a lot of food and breathing efficiently.

- Mammals have a diaphragm that helps them draw air into their lungs.

- Mammals have highly specialized teeth for chewing different kinds of food. Mammals that eat plants have incisors and molars for cutting and grinding plants. Carnivores have canines for seizing and tearing their prey.

- Mammals are the only vertebrates that have mammary glands, fur, and two sets of teeth.

- Mammals are divided into three groups: monotremes, marsupials, and placental mammals.

- Monotremes lay eggs instead of bearing live young. Monotremes produce milk but do not have nipples or a placenta.

- Marsupials give birth to live young, but the young are born as embryos. The embryos climb into their mother's pouch, where they drink milk until they are more developed.

- Placental mammals develop inside of the mother for a period of time called a gestation period. Placental mothers nurse their young after birth.

VOCABULARY DEFINITIONS, continued

SECTION 2

mammary glands glands that secrete a nutritious fluid called milk

diaphragm the sheet of muscle underneath the lungs of mammals that helps draw air into the lungs

monotreme a mammal that lays eggs

marsupial a mammal that gives birth to live, partially developed young that continue to develop inside the mother's pouch or skin fold

placental mammal a mammal that nourishes unborn offspring with a placenta inside the uterus

gestation period the time during which an embryo develops within the mother

Vocabulary Review Worksheet

Blackline masters of these Chapter Highlights can be found in the **Study Guide**.

---

internet**connect**

go.hrw.com

GO TO: go.hrw.com

Visit the **HRW** Web site for a variety of learning tools related to this chapter. Just type in the keyword:

KEYWORD: HSTVR2

SCILINKS.
N S T A

GO TO: www.scilinks.org

Visit the **National Science Teachers Association** on-line Web site for Internet resources related to this chapter. Just type in the sciLINKS number for more information about the topic:

TOPIC:	Bird Characteristics	*sci*LINKS NUMBER:	HSTL405
TOPIC:	Kinds of Birds	*sci*LINKS NUMBER:	HSTL410
TOPIC:	The Origin of Mammals	*sci*LINKS NUMBER:	HSTL415
TOPIC:	Characteristics of Mammals	*sci*LINKS NUMBER:	HSTL420

115

Lab and Activity Highlights

LabBank

Labs You Can Eat, Why Birds of a Beak Eat Together

Long-Term Projects & Research Ideas, Look Who's Coming to Dinner

Chapter Review

USING VOCABULARY

To complete the following sentences, choose the correct term from each pair of terms listed below:

1. ___?___ chicks can run after their mother soon after they hatch. ___?___ chicks can barely stretch their neck out to be fed when they first hatch. (*Altricial* or *Precocial*)

2. The ___?___ helps mammals breathe. (*diaphragm* or *air sac*)

3. The ___?___ allows some mammals to supply nutrients to young in the mother's uterus. (*mammary gland* or *placenta*)

4. Birds take care of their feathers by ___?___. (*brooding* or *preening*)

5. A lion belongs to a group of mammals called ___?___. (*carnivores* or *primates*)

6. ___?___ are fluffy feathers that help keep birds warm. (*Contour feathers* or *Down feathers*)

UNDERSTANDING CONCEPTS

Multiple Choice

7. Both birds and reptiles
   a. lay eggs.
   b. brood their young.
   c. have air sacs.
   d. have feathers.

8. Flight requires
   a. a lot of energy and oxygen.
   b. a lightweight body.
   c. strong flight muscles.
   d. All of the above

9. Only mammals
   a. have glands.
   b. nurse their young.
   c. lay eggs.
   d. have teeth.

10. Monotremes do not
    a. have mammary glands.
    b. care for their young.
    c. have pouches.
    d. have fur.

11. Lift
    a. is air that travels over the top of a wing.
    b. is provided by air sacs.
    c. is the upward force on a wing that keeps a bird in the air.
    d. is created by pressure from the diaphragm.

12. Which of the following is not a primate?
    a. a lemur   c. a pika
    b. a human   d. a chimpanzee

Short Answer

13. How are marsupials different from other mammals? How are they similar?

14. Both birds and mammals are endotherms. How do they stay warm?

15. What is the Bernoulli effect?

16. Why do some bats have large ears?

Concept Mapping

17. Use the following terms to create a concept map: monotremes, endotherms, birds, mammals, mammary glands, placental mammals, marsupials, feathers, hair.

CRITICAL THINKING AND PROBLEM SOLVING

Write one or two sentences to answer the following questions:

18. Unlike bird and monotreme eggs, the eggs of placental mammals and marsupials do not have a yolk. How do developing embryos of marsupials and placental mammals get the nutrition they need?

19. Most bats and cetaceans use echolocation. Why don't these mammals rely solely on sight to find their prey and examine their surroundings?

20. Suppose you are working at a museum and are making a display of bird skeletons. Unfortunately, the skeletons have lost their labels. How can you separate the skeletons of flightless birds from those of birds that fly? Will you be able to tell which birds flew rapidly and which birds could soar? Explain your answer.

MATH IN SCIENCE

21. A bird is flying at a speed of 35 km/h. At this speed, its body consumes 60 Calories per gram of body mass per hour. If the bird has a mass of 50 g, how many Calories will it use if it flies for 30 minutes at this speed?

INTERPRETING GRAPHICS

Endotherms use a lot of energy when they run or fly. The graph below shows how many Calories a small dog uses while running at different speeds. Use this graph to answer the questions below.

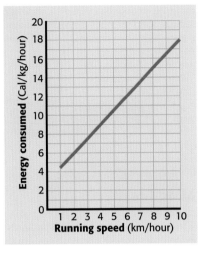

22. As the dog runs faster, how does the amount of energy it consumes per hour change?

23. How much energy per hour will this dog consume if it is running at 4 km/h? at 9 km/h?

24. Energy consumed is given in Calories per kilogram of body mass per hour. If the dog has a mass of 6 kg and is running at 7 km/h, how many Calories per hour will it use?

Reading Check-up

Take a minute to review your answers to the Pre-Reading Questions found at the bottom of page 86. Have your answers changed? If necessary, revise your answers based on what you have learned since you began this chapter.

117

Concept Mapping

17. An answer to this exercise can be found at the front of this book.

CRITICAL THINKING AND PROBLEM SOLVING

18. Marsupials get their nutrition from their mother's milk. Placental mammals get their nutrition from their mother's body through the placenta.

19. Bats and cetaceans are both active in dark environments, where sound is more helpful than sight.

20. Birds that fly will have a large keel and larger wings. The birds with longer wings probably soared because longer wings are necessary to provide enough surface area for greater lift.

MATH IN SCIENCE

21. 1,500 Cal

INTERPRETING GRAPHICS

22. The faster the dog goes, the more energy it uses.

23. At 4 km/h, the dog consumes 9 Cal/kg/h. At 9 km/h, the dog consumes 16.5 Cal/kg/h.

24. At 7 km/h, the dog consumes 13.5 Cal/kg/h.
13.5 Cal/kg/h × 6 kg = 81 Cal/h.

Concept Mapping Transparency 17

Blackline masters of this Chapter Review can be found in the **Study Guide.**

Background

The four aerodynamic forces described in this feature—lift, gravity, drag, and thrust—permit birds and humans to fly. Airplanes are designed differently to take advantage of these forces. Similarly, birds have particular adaptations that make them fast flyers or excellent gliders. Students should recognize how the physical features of airplanes and birds contribute to their ability to fly.

ACROSS THE SCIENCES

LIFE SCIENCE • PHYSICAL SCIENCE

The Aerodynamics of Flight

For centuries people have tried to imitate a spectacular feat that birds perfected millions of years ago—flight! It was not until 1903 that the Wright brothers were able to fly in a heavier-than-air flying machine. Their first flight lasted only 12 seconds, and they only traveled 37 m. Although modern airplanes are much more sophisticated, they still rely on the same principles of flight.

Fighting Gravity

The sleek body of a jet is shaped to battle drag, while the wings are shaped to battle Earth's gravity. In order to take off, airplanes must pull upward with a force greater than gravitational force. This upward force is called *lift*. Where does an airplane get lift? The top of an airplane wing is curved, and the bottom is flat. As the wing moves through the air, air must travel farther and faster above the wing than below it. This difference causes the pressure above the wing to be less than the pressure below the wing. This difference pulls the airplane upward.

Push and Pull

The shape of its wing is not enough to get an airplane off the ground. Wings require air to flow past them in order to create lift. Airplanes also rely on *thrust*, the force that gives an airplane forward motion. Powerful engines and propellers provide airplanes with thrust. As airplanes move faster, more air rushes past the wings, and lift increases.

Airplanes usually take off into a head wind, which pushes against the airplane as it travels. Any force that pushes against an airplane's motion, like a head wind, is called *drag* and

can slow an airplane down. The body of an airplane has smooth curves to minimize drag. A tail wind is an airflow that pushes the airplane from the rear and shortens travel time. In order to increase speed, engineers design airplanes with streamlined bodies to reduce drag. Wings can also be designed to increase lift. A rounded and longer wing provides greater lift, but it also produces more drag. Engineers must consider such trade-offs when they design airplanes. Athletes also consider drag when they choose equipment. For example, runners and cyclists wear tight-fitting clothing to reduce drag.

Think About It!

▶ Airplanes have a variety of shapes and sizes and are designed for many purposes, including transport, travel, and combat. Some planes are designed to fly fast, and others are designed to carry heavy loads. Do some research, and then describe how the aerodynamics differ.

▲ *The design of airplanes got a boost from our feathered friends.*

Answer to Think About It!

Heavy cargo airplanes travel at much slower speeds than fighter jets. Cargo airplanes generally have thick wings to provide enough lift to get their massive contents off the ground. Fighter jets are much lighter and do not require as much lift. They often have thinner wings. Many fighter jets have powerful engines to give them more thrust and speed. The fastest fighter jets can travel over 2,000 mph! Fighter jets also have smooth, aerodynamic surfaces to minimize drag, which would slow them down. Short-distance flyers, such as many personal airplanes, do not have expensive, powerful engines but rely on propellers to provide thrust.

WEIRD SCIENCE

NAKED MOLE-RATS

What do you call a nearly blind rodent that is 7 cm long and looks like a hot dog that has been left in the microwave too long? A naked mole-rat. For more than 150 years, this mammal—which is native to hot, dry regions of Kenya, Ethiopia, and Somalia—has puzzled scientists by its strange appearance and peculiar habits.

What's Hair Got to Do with It?

Naked mole-rats have such strange characteristics that you might wonder whether they are really mammals at all. Their grayish pink skin hangs loosely, allowing them to maneuver through the narrow underground tunnel systems they call home. At first glance, the naked mole-rats appear to be hairless, and hair is a key characteristic of mammals. However, naked mole-rats are not hairless, but they do lack fur. In fact, they have whiskers to guide them through the dark passages and hair between their toes to sweep up loose dirt like tiny brooms. Believe it or not, they also have hair on their lips to prevent dirt from entering their mouth as their massive teeth dig new passages through the dirt!

Naked mole-rats are so unique that they have become a popular attraction at zoos.

Is It Cold in Here?

Naked mole-rats have the poorest endothermic capacity of any mammal. Their body temperature remains close to the temperature of the air in their tunnels—a cool 31°C (more than 5°C cooler than the body temperature of humans). At night these animals minimize heat loss by huddling close together. Fortunately, the temperature does not change very much in their native habitat.

Who's in Charge?

Naked mole-rats are the only mammals known to form communities similar to those formed by social insects, such as honey bees. A community of naked mole-rats is made up of between 20 and 300 individuals that divide up tasks much like bees, wasps, and termites do. Each community has one breeding female, called the queen, and up to three breeding males. All females are biologically capable of reproducing, but only one does. When a female becomes a queen, she actually grows longer!

Think About It!

▶ At first glance, naked mole-rats appear to be missing several key characteristics of mammals. Do further research to find out what characteristics they have that classifies them as mammals.

WEIRD SCIENCE
Naked Mole-Rats

Answers to Think About It!

At first glance, the naked mole-rat (*Heterocephalus glaber*) may seem to not have all of the key characteristics of mammals. Encourage students to further investigate the naked mole-rat and discuss what features it has that qualify it as a mammal.

1. **Hair.** Although naked mole-rats appear hairless, closer inspection reveals that they do have specialized hairs on their face, feet, and lips.

2. **Mammary glands.** By definition, mammals feed their young with milk produced in the mammary glands. The queen has mammary glands, which she uses to feed her litter of 10 to 27 pups for about 4 weeks. All females are capable of reproducing and producing milk; however, only the queen does these activities.

3. **Placenta.** The young of all mammals except marsupials and monotremes develop in placentas. Naked mole-rat pups develop inside a placenta in the queen for 70 to 80 days.

4. **Endotherm.** Mammals have highly variable body temperatures. Despite their poor capacity to regulate internal body temperature, naked mole-rats are in fact endothermic.

119

SAFETY FIRST!

Exploring, inventing, and investigating are essential to the study of science. However, these activities can also be dangerous. To make sure that your experiments and explorations are safe, you must be aware of a variety of safety guidelines.

You have probably heard of the saying, "It is better to be safe than sorry." This is particularly true in a science classroom where experiments and explorations are being performed. Being uninformed and careless can result in serious injuries. Don't take chances with your own safety or with anyone else's.

Following are important guidelines for staying safe in the science classroom. Your teacher may also have safety guidelines and tips that are specific to your classroom and laboratory. Take the time to be safe.

Safety Rules!

Start Out Right

Always get your teacher's permission before attempting any laboratory exploration. Read the procedures carefully, and pay particular attention to safety information and caution statements. If you are unsure about what a safety symbol means, look it up or ask your teacher. You cannot be too careful when it comes to safety. If an accident does occur, inform your teacher immediately, regardless of how minor you think the accident is.

Safety Symbols

All of the experiments and investigations in this book and their related worksheets include important safety symbols to alert you to particular safety concerns. Become familiar with these symbols so that when you see them, you will know what they mean and what to do. It is important that you read this entire safety section to learn about specific dangers in the laboratory.

If you are instructed to note the odor of a substance, wave the fumes toward your nose with your hand. Never put your nose close to the source.

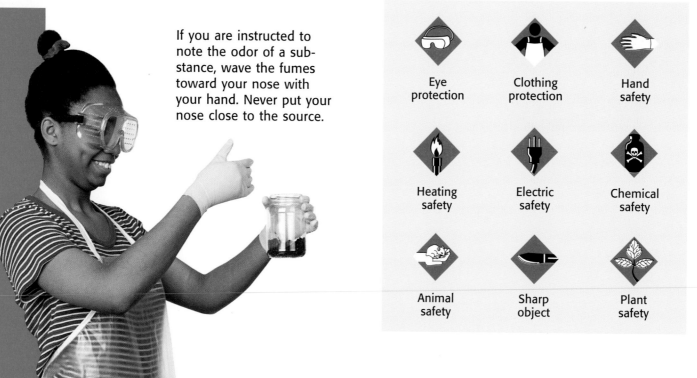

Eye protection	Clothing protection	Hand safety
Heating safety	Electric safety	Chemical safety
Animal safety	Sharp object	Plant safety

Eye Safety

Wear safety goggles when working around chemicals, acids, bases, or any type of flame or heating device. Wear safety goggles any time there is even the slightest chance that harm could come to your eyes. If any substance gets into your eyes, notify your teacher immediately, and flush your eyes with running water for at least 15 minutes. Treat any unknown chemical as if it were a dangerous chemical. Never look directly into the sun. Doing so could cause permanent blindness.

Avoid wearing contact lenses in a laboratory situation. Even if you are wearing safety goggles, chemicals can get between the contact lenses and your eyes. If your doctor requires that you wear contact lenses instead of glasses, wear eye-cup safety goggles in the lab.

Safety Equipment

Know the locations of the nearest fire alarms and any other safety equipment, such as fire blankets and eyewash fountains, as identified by your teacher, and know the procedures for using them.

Be extra careful when using any glassware. When adding a heavy object to a graduated cylinder, tilt the cylinder so the object slides slowly to the bottom.

Neatness

Keep your work area free of all unnecessary books and papers. Tie back long hair, and secure loose sleeves or other loose articles of clothing, such as ties and bows. Remove dangling jewelry. Don't wear open-toed shoes or sandals in the laboratory. Never eat, drink, or apply cosmetics in a laboratory setting. Food, drink, and cosmetics can easily become contaminated with dangerous materials.

Certain hair products (such as aerosol hair spray) are flammable and should not be worn while working near an open flame. Avoid wearing hair spray or hair gel on lab days.

Sharp/Pointed Objects

Use knives and other sharp instruments with extreme care. Never cut objects while holding them in your hands. Place objects on a suitable work surface for cutting.

Heat

Wear safety goggles when using a heating device or a flame. Whenever possible, use an electric hot plate as a heat source instead of an open flame. When heating materials in a test tube, always angle the test tube away from yourself and others. In order to avoid burns, wear heat-resistant gloves whenever instructed to do so.

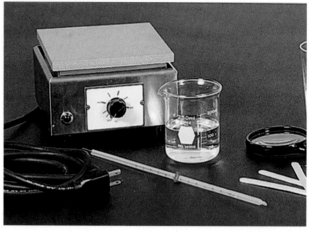

Electricity

Be careful with electrical cords. When using a microscope with a lamp, do not place the cord where it could trip someone. Do not let cords hang over a table edge in a way that could cause equipment to fall if the cord is accidentally pulled. Do not use equipment with damaged cords. Be sure your hands are dry and that the electrical equipment is in the "off" position before plugging it in. Turn off and unplug electrical equipment when you are finished.

Chemicals

Wear safety goggles when handling any potentially dangerous chemicals, acids, or bases. If a chemical is unknown, handle it as you would a dangerous chemical. Wear an apron and safety gloves when working with acids or bases or whenever you are told to do so. If a spill gets on your skin or clothing, rinse it off immediately with water for at least 5 minutes while calling to your teacher.

Never mix chemicals unless your teacher tells you to do so. Never taste, touch, or smell chemicals unless you are specifically directed to do so. Before working with a flammable liquid or gas, check for the presence of any source of flame, spark, or heat.

Animal Safety

Always obtain your teacher's permission before bringing any animal into the school building. Handle animals only as your teacher directs. Always treat animals carefully and with respect. Wash your hands thoroughly after handling any animal.

Plant Safety

Do not eat any part of a plant or plant seed used in the laboratory. Wash hands thoroughly after handling any part of a plant. When in nature, do not pick any wild plants unless your teacher instructs you to do so.

Glassware

Examine all glassware before use. Be sure that glassware is clean and free of chips and cracks. Report damaged glassware to your teacher. Glass containers used for heating should be made of heat-resistant glass.

DESIGN YOUR OWN

Aunt Flossie and the Bumblebee
Teacher's Notes

Time Required

One to three 45-minute class periods

Lab Ratings

EASY ———————————→ HARD

TEACHER PREP
STUDENT SET-UP
CONCEPT LEVEL
CLEAN UP

MATERIALS

The materials listed on the student page are enough for a group of 4–5 students. Materials students may need are construction paper in several bright colors, shoe boxes, scents, honey or some other sweet spread, twine, and binoculars or a hand lens. Encourage students to use recycled materials and to bring in their own supplies.

Safety Caution

Remind students to review all safety cautions and icons before beginning this lab activity.

Tell students to avoid wearing bright floral clothing and perfume or cologne while performing this lab.

All students should be cautious when working with wildlife. Students allergic to insect and bee stings should be excused from this exercise.

Aunt Flossie and the Bumblebee

Last week Aunt Flossie came to watch the soccer game, and she was chased by a big yellow-and-black bumblebee. Everyone tried not to laugh, but Aunt Flossie did look pretty funny. She was running and screaming, all perfumed and dressed in a bright floral dress, shiny jewelry, and a huge hat with a big purple bow. No one could understand why the bumblebee tormented Aunt Flossie and left everyone else alone. She said that she would not come to another game until you determine why the bee chased her.

Your job is to design an experiment that will determine why the bee was attracted to Aunt Flossie. You may simulate the situation by using objects that contain the same sensory clues that Aunt Flossie wore that day—bright, shiny colors and strong scents.

Materials

• to be determined by each experimental design and approved by the teacher

Ask a Question

1. Use the information in the story above to help you form questions. Make a list of Aunt Flossie's characterists on the day of the soccer game. What was Aunt Flossie wearing? What do you think she looked like to a bumblebee? What scent was she wearing? Which of those characteristics may have affected the bee's behavior? What was it about Aunt Flossie that affected the bee's behavior?

Form a Hypothesis

2. Write a hypothesis about insect behavior based on your observations of Aunt Flossie and the bumblebee at the soccer game. A possible hypothesis is, "Insects are attracted to strong floral scents." Write your own hypothesis.

124

Datasheets for LabBook
Datasheet

CLASSROOM TESTED & APPROVED

Barry Bishop
San Rafael Junior High
Ferron, Utah

Test the Hypothesis

3. Outline a procedure for your experiment. Be sure to follow the steps in the scientific method. Design your procedure to answer specific questions. For example, if you want to know if insects are attracted to different colors, you might want to display cutouts of several colors of paper.

4. Make a list of materials for your experiment. You may want to include colored paper, pictures from magazines, or strong perfumes as bait. You may not use living things as bait in your experiment. Your teacher must approve your experimental design before you begin.

5. Determine a place to conduct your experiment. For example, you may want to place your materials in a box on the ground, or you may want to hang items from a tree branch. **Caution:** Be sure to remain at a safe distance from your experimental setup. Do not touch any insects. Have an adult help you release any insects that are trapped or collected.

6. Develop data tables for recording the results of your trials. For example, a data table similar to the one at right may be used to record the results of testing different colors to see which insects are attracted to them. Design your data tables to fit your investigation.

Analyze the Results

7. Describe your experimental procedure. Did your results support your hypothesis? Explain.

8. Compare your results with those of your classmates. Which hypotheses were supported? What conclusions can you draw from the class results?

Communicate Results

9. Write a letter to Aunt Flossie telling her what you have learned. Tell her what caused the bee attack. Invite her to attend another soccer game, and advise her about what she should or should not wear!

Effects of Color

Color	Number of bees	Number of ants	Number of wasps
Red			
Blue			
Yellow			

DO NOT WRITE IN BOOK

Lab Notes

This lab may need to be done during a certain season in your geographical area. Some students may want to extend their data collection period to several days or weeks.

Answers

7. Students should describe their experimental procedure and include as many steps of the scientific method as possible. All answers will depend on student observations.

8. Answers will vary.

9. Letters will vary, but should demonstrate what the students have learned about insect behavior.

Science Skills Worksheet
"Designing an Experiment"

The Cricket Caper
Teacher's Notes

Time Required

One to two 45-minute class periods

Lab Ratings

EASY ————————→ HARD

TEACHER PREP 🍼🍼🍼
STUDENT SET-UP 🍼🍼
CONCEPT LEVEL 🍼🍼
CLEAN UP 🍼🍼

MATERIALS

The materials listed on the student page are enough for a single student or a small group of students. Instead of 600 mL beakers, you may use the bottom halves of 2 clear plastic 2 L bottles. You will need to prepare these ahead of time. The cut on the bottle should be as even as possible to facilitate taping the open ends together in step 5.

Safety Caution

Remind students to review all safety cautions and icons before beginning this lab activity.

Lab Notes

Explain to the students that they must move slowly so they won't startle the cricket and alter its behavior. The apple must be removed in step 4 before the containers are taped together. The apple would be an unwanted variable in the tests that follow.

If you decide to extend over two class periods, the cricket will be fine over night in the covered 500 mL beaker. The cricket will need a slice of potato or apple for food and moisture.

The Cricket Caper

Insects are a special class of invertebrates with more than 750,000 known species. Insects may be the most successful group of animals on Earth. In this activity, you will observe a cricket's structure and the simple adaptive behaviors that help make it so successful. Remember, you will be handling a living animal that deserves to be treated with care.

Materials

- 2 crickets
- 600 mL beakers (2)
- plastic wrap
- apple
- hand lens (optional)
- masking tape
- aluminum foil
- lamp
- 2 sealable plastic bags
- crushed ice
- hot tap water

Procedure

1. Place a cricket in a clean 600 mL beaker. Quickly cover the beaker with plastic wrap.

2. Without much movement, observe the cricket's structure. Record your observations in your ScienceLog.

3. Place a small piece of apple in the beaker. Set the beaker on a table. Quietly observe the cricket for several minutes. (Any movement may cause the cricket to stop what it is doing.) Record your observations.

4. Remove the plastic wrap and the apple from the beaker, and quickly attach a second beaker. Join the two beakers together at the mouths with masking tape. Handle the beakers carefully. Remember, a living thing is inside.

5. Wrap one of the joined beakers with aluminum foil. Lay the joined beakers on their sides. If the cricket is not visible, gently tap the sides of the beaker until it is exposed.

6. Record the cricket's location. Shine a lamp on the uncovered side of the beaker. Record the cricket's location after 5 minutes.

7. Without disturbing the cricket, move the aluminum foil to the other beaker. Repeat step 6 to see if you get the same result.

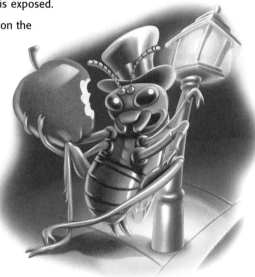

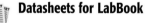
Datasheets for LabBook

CLASSROOM TESTED & APPROVED

Alonda Droege
Pioneer Middle School
Steilacom, Washington

8. Fill one sealable plastic bag halfway with crushed ice and seal it. Fill the other bag with hot tap water and seal it. Lay the bags side by side. Remove the foil from the joined beakers.

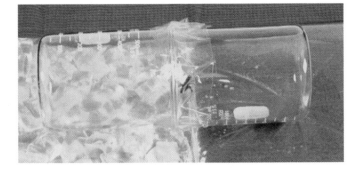

9. Gently rock the beakers until the cricket is in the center. Place the beakers on the plastic bags as shown. Observe the cricket's behavior for 5 minutes. Record your observations.

10. Set the beakers on one end for several minutes to allow them to return to room temperature. Repeat step 9 and 10 three times. (Why is it necessary to allow the beakers to return to room temperature each time?)

11. Set the beakers on end. Carefully remove the masking tape and separate the beakers. Quickly replace the plastic wrap on the beaker with the cricket.

12. Make a data table similar to the one shown. Observe the cricket's movement every 15 seconds for 3 minutes. Record data in the One Cricket column of the table using these codes: 0 = no movement, 1 = slight movement, 2 = rapid movement.

13. Place a second cricket (Cricket B) into the beaker with the first Cricket (Cricket A). Observe both crickets' behavior every 15 seconds. Record data using the codes in step 12.

Analysis

14. Describe the crickets' feeding behavior. Are they lappers, suckers, or chewers?

15. Do crickets prefer light or darkness? Explain.

16. From your observations, what can you infer about a cricket's temperature preferences?

17. Based on your observations of Cricket A and Cricket B, what general statements can you make about the social behavior of crickets?

	One Cricket	Two Crickets	
		A	B
15 s			
30 s			
45 s			
60 s			
75 s			
90 s			
105 s			
120 s			
135 s			
150 s			
165 s			
180 s			

DO NOT WRITE IN BOOK

127

Answers

All answers will depend on the students' observations. The following answers are expected observations.

14. Crickets are chewers.

15. Crickets generally prefer darkness.

16. Crickets will prefer the warm location.

17. If well-fed, crickets will generally tolerate each other very well. However, they will fight and even eat each other if they are not fed well.

A Prince of a Frog
Teacher's Notes

Time Required

One 45-minute class period

Lab Ratings

EASY ————————→ HARD

TEACHER PREP   🧪🧪🧪
STUDENT SET-UP   🧪
CONCEPT LEVEL   🧪🧪
CLEAN UP   🧪

Safety Caution

Remind students to review all safety cautions and icons before beginning this lab activity.

You will need to provide protective gloves for the students. Students' hands may make the frog vulnerable to infection. Also, frogs are known to carry salmonella. Students should wash their hands thoroughly with soap and warm water after handling the frog.

Kerry A. Johnson
Isbell Middle School
Santa Paula, California

A Prince of a Frog

Imagine that you are a scientist interested in amphibians. You have heard in the news about amphibians disappearing all over the world. What a great loss it will be to the environment if all amphibians become extinct! Your job is to learn as much as possible about how frogs normally behave so that you can act as a resource for other scientists who are studying the problem.

In this activity, you will observe a normal frog in a dry container and in water.

Procedure

1. In your ScienceLog, make a table similar to the one below to note all of your observations of the frog in this investigation.

Materials

- live frog in a dry container
- live crickets
- 600 mL beaker
- container half-filled with dechlorinated water
- large rock (optional)
- protective gloves

Observations of a Live Frog	
Characteristic	**Observation**
Breathing	
Eyes	
Legs	
Response to food	
Skin texture	
Swimming behavior	
Skin coloration	

DO NOT WRITE IN BOOK

2. Observe a live frog in a dry container. Draw the frog in your ScienceLog. Label the eyes, nostrils, front legs, and hind legs.

3. Watch the frog's movements as it breathes air with its lungs. Write a description of the frog's breathing in your ScienceLog.

4. Look closely at the frog's eyes, and note their location. Examine the upper and lower eyelids as well as the transparent third eyelid. Which of these three eyelids actually moves over the eye?

5. Study the frog's legs. Note in your data table the difference between the front and hind legs.

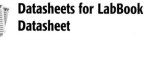

Datasheets for LabBook
Datasheet

Science Skills Worksheet
"Science Drawing"

6. Place a live insect, such as a cricket, in the container. Observe and record how the frog reacts.

7. Carefully pick up the frog, and examine its skin. How does it feel?
   Caution: Remember that a frog is a living thing and deserves to be handled gently and with respect.

8. Place a 600 mL beaker in the container. Place the frog in the beaker. Cover the beaker with your hand, and carry it to a container of dechlorinated water. Tilt the beaker and gently submerge it in the water until the frog swims out of the beaker.

9. Watch the frog float and swim in the water. How does the frog use its legs to swim? Notice the position of the frog's head.

10. As the frog swims, bend down and look up into the water so that you can see the underside of the frog. Then look down on the frog from above. Compare the color on the top and the underneath sides of the frog. Record your observations in your data table.

Analysis

11. From the position of the frog's eyes, what can you infer about the frog's field of vision? How might the position of the frog's eyes benefit the frog while it is swimming?

12. How can a frog "breathe" while it is swimming in water?

13. How are the hind legs of a frog adapted for life on land and in water?

14. What differences did you notice in coloration on the frog's top side and its underneath side? What advantage might these color differences provide?

15. How does the frog eat? What senses are involved in helping the frog catch its prey?

Going Further

Observe another type of amphibian, such as a salamander. How do the adaptations of other types of amphibians compare with those of the frog you observed in this investigation?

129

Answers

11.–15. Have students speculate about the form and function of the frog's structure. Discuss the camouflage coloration of a frog. Ask how the skin of a frog differs from that of a reptile, and how the two different forms have two different functions. Discuss how the frog's skin must stay wet in order for gas exchange to occur. Have students refer to pages 68–72 for more information about frog physiology.

Going Further

Answers will vary, but students should notice several similar adaptations among amphibians.

Preparation Notes

Frogs collected in the wild are best for this activity because they are easily released. Frogs from pet stores must NOT be released into the wild.

If you can divide the class into groups with several observations going on at the same time, you can use a smaller container for each frog. Containers can be a large glass mixing bowl or something similar. Students may bring containers from home as well. Tree frogs are common in pet stores. They are fun to observe, especially if you can find some small crickets to feed them so that students can observe their feeding behavior.

You may substitute another amphibian, such as water doggies, an immature stage of salamanders. Water doggies are especially interesting if they can be kept in the classroom so students can observe their development into salamanders.

Frogs and water doggies may be obtained in pet stores, in the wild, and in bait shops.

Lab Notes

Several years ago, some students who were out collecting frogs for an activity similar to this lab found severe birth defects and mutations among the frogs they found. A good way to introduce this activity may be to find a news clipping from this event or information about frog deformities taken from the Internet. You may also review the material presented in the first chapter of this book.

Concept Mapping: A Way to Bring Ideas Together

What Is a Concept Map?

Have you ever tried to tell someone about a book or a chapter you've just read and found that you can remember only a few isolated words and ideas? Or maybe you've memorized facts for a test and then weeks later discovered you're not even sure what topics those facts covered.

In both cases, you may have understood the ideas or concepts by themselves but not in relation to one another. If you could somehow link the ideas together, you would probably understand them better and remember them longer. This is something a concept map can help you do. A concept map is a way to see how ideas or concepts fit together. It can help you see the "big picture."

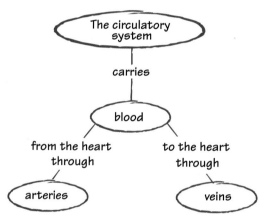

How to Make a Concept Map

❶ Make a list of the main ideas or concepts.

It might help to write each concept on its own slip of paper. This will make it easier to rearrange the concepts as many times as necessary to make sense of how the concepts are connected. After you've made a few concept maps this way, you can go directly from writing your list to actually making the map.

❷ Arrange the concepts in order from the most general to the most specific.

Put the most general concept at the top and circle it. Ask yourself, "How does this concept relate to the remaining concepts?" As you see the relationships, arrange the concepts in order from general to specific.

❸ Connect the related concepts with lines.

❹ On each line, write an action word or short phrase that shows how the concepts are related.

Look at the concept maps on this page, and then see if you can make one for the following terms:

plants, water, photosynthesis, carbon dioxide, sun's energy

One possible answer is provided at right, but don't look at it until you try the concept map yourself.

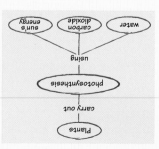

SI Measurement

The International System of Units, or SI, is the standard system of measurement used by many scientists. Using the same standards of measurement makes it easier for scientists to communicate with one another.

SI works by combining prefixes and base units. Each base unit can be used with different prefixes to define smaller and larger quantities. The table below lists common SI prefixes.

Appendix

SI Prefixes			
Prefix	Abbreviation	Factor	Example
kilo-	k	1,000	kilogram, 1 kg = 1,000 g
hecto-	h	100	hectoliter, 1 hL = 100 L
deka-	da	10	dekameter, 1 dam = 10 m
		1	meter, liter
deci-	d	0.1	decigram, 1 dg = 0.1 g
centi-	c	0.01	centimeter, 1 cm = 0.01 m
milli-	m	0.001	milliliter, 1 mL = 0.001 L
micro-	μ	0.000 001	micrometer, 1 μm = 0.000 001 m

SI Conversion Table		
SI units	From SI to English	From English to SI
Length		
kilometer (km) = 1,000 m	1 km = 0.621 mi	1 mi = 1.609 km
meter (m) = 100 cm	1 m = 3.281 ft	1 ft = 0.305 m
centimeter (cm) = 0.01 m	1 cm = 0.394 in.	1 in. = 2.540 cm
millimeter (mm) = 0.001 m	1 mm = 0.039 in.	
micrometer (μm) = 0.000 001 m		
nanometer (nm) = 0.000 000 001 m		
Area		
square kilometer (km^2) = 100 hectares	1 km^2 = 0.386 mi^2	1 mi^2 = 2.590 km^2
hectare (ha) = 10,000 m^2	1 ha = 2.471 acres	1 acre = 0.405 ha
square meter (m^2) = 10,000 cm^2	1 m^2 = 10.765 ft^2	1 ft^2 = 0.093 m^2
square centimeter (cm^2) = 100 mm^2	1 cm^2 = 0.155 in.^{2}	1 in.^{2} = 6.452 cm^2
Volume		
liter (L) = 1,000 mL = 1 dm^3	1 L = 1.057 fl qt	1 fl qt = 0.946 L
milliliter (mL) = 0.001 L = 1 cm^3	1 mL = 0.034 fl oz	1 fl oz = 29.575 mL
microliter (μL) = 0.000 001 L		
Mass		
kilogram (kg) = 1,000 g	1 kg = 2.205 lb	1 lb = 0.454 kg
gram (g) = 1,000 mg	1 g = 0.035 oz	1 oz = 28.349 g
milligram (mg) = 0.001 g		
microgram (μg) = 0.000 001 g		

Temperature Scales

Temperature can be expressed using three different scales: Fahrenheit, Celsius, and Kelvin. The SI unit for temperature is the kelvin (K).

Although 0 K is much colder than 0°C, a change of 1 K is equal to a change of 1°C.

Three Temperature Scales

	Fahrenheit	Celsius	Kelvin
Water boils	212°	100°	373
Body temperature	98.6°	37°	310
Room temperature	68°	20°	293
Water freezes	32°	0°	273

Temperature Conversions Table

To convert	Use this equation:	Example
Celsius to Fahrenheit °C ⟶ °F	$°F = \left(\dfrac{9}{5} \times °C\right) + 32$	Convert 45°C to °F. $°F = \left(\dfrac{9}{5} \times 45°C\right) + 32 = 113°F$
Fahrenheit to Celsius °F ⟶ °C	$°C = \dfrac{5}{9} \times (°F - 32)$	Convert 68°F to °C. $°C = \dfrac{5}{9} \times (68°F - 32) = 20°C$
Celsius to Kelvin °C ⟶ K	$K = °C + 273$	Convert 45°C to K. $K = 45°C + 273 = 318\ K$
Kelvin to Celsius K ⟶ °C	$°C = K - 273$	Convert 32 K to °C. $°C = 32\ K - 273 = -241°C$

Measuring Skills

Using a Graduated Cylinder

When using a graduated cylinder to measure volume, keep the following procedures in mind:

1 Make sure the cylinder is on a flat, level surface.

2 Move your head so that your eye is level with the surface of the liquid.

3 Read the mark closest to the liquid level. On glass graduated cylinders, read the mark closest to the center of the curve in the liquid's surface.

Using a Meterstick or Metric Ruler

When using a meterstick or metric ruler to measure length, keep the following procedures in mind:

1 Place the ruler firmly against the object you are measuring.

2 Align one edge of the object exactly with the zero end of the ruler.

3 Look at the other edge of the object to see which of the marks on the ruler is closest to that edge. **Note:** Each small slash between the centimeters represents a millimeter, which is one-tenth of a centimeter.

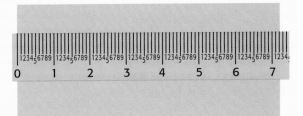

Using a Triple-Beam Balance

When using a triple-beam balance to measure mass, keep the following procedures in mind:

1 Make sure the balance is on a level surface.

2 Place all of the countermasses at zero. Adjust the balancing knob until the pointer rests at zero.

3 Place the object you wish to measure on the pan. **Caution:** Do not place hot objects or chemicals directly on the balance pan.

4 Move the largest countermass along the beam to the right until it is at the last notch that does not tip the balance. Follow the same procedure with the next-largest countermass. Then move the smallest countermass until the pointer rests at zero.

5 Add the readings from the three beams together to determine the mass of the object.

6 When determining the mass of crystals or powders, use a piece of filter paper. First find the mass of the paper. Then add the crystals or powder to the paper and re-measure. The actual mass of the crystals or powder is the total mass minus the mass of the paper. When finding the mass of liquids, first find the mass of the empty container. Then find the mass of the liquid and container together. The mass of the liquid is the total mass minus the mass of the container.

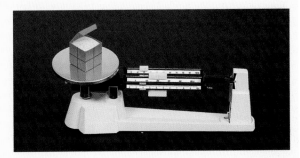

Scientific Method

The series of steps that scientists use to answer questions and solve problems is often called the **scientific method.** The scientific method is not a rigid procedure. Scientists may use all of the steps or just some of the steps of the scientific method. They may even repeat some of the steps. The goal of the scientific method is to come up with reliable answers and solutions.

Six Steps of the Scientific Method

1 **Ask a Question** Good questions come from careful **observations.** You make observations by using your senses to gather information. Sometimes you may use instruments, such as microscopes and telescopes, to extend the range of your senses. As you observe the natural world, you will discover that you have many more questions than answers. These questions drive the scientific method.

Questions beginning with *what, why, how,* and *when* are very important in focusing an investigation, and they often lead to a hypothesis. (You will learn what a hypothesis is in the next step.) Here is an example of a question that could lead to further investigation.

Question: How does acid rain affect plant growth?

2 **Form a Hypothesis** After you come up with a question, you need to turn the question into a **hypothesis.** A hypothesis is a clear statement of what you expect the answer to your question to be. Your hypothesis will represent your best "educated guess" based on your observations and what you already know. A good hypothesis is testable. If observations and information cannot be gathered or if an experiment cannot be designed to test your hypothesis, it is untestable, and the investigation can go no further.

Here is a hypothesis that could be formed from the question, "How does acid rain affect plant growth?"

Hypothesis: Acid rain causes plants to grow more slowly.

Notice that the hypothesis provides some specifics that lead to methods of testing. The hypothesis can also lead to predictions. A **prediction** is what you think will be the outcome of your experiment or data collection. Predictions are usually stated in an "if . . . then" format. For example, **if** meat is kept at room temperature, **then** it will spoil faster than meat kept in the refrigerator. More than one prediction can be made for a single hypothesis. Here is a sample prediction for the hypothesis that acid rain causes plants to grow more slowly.

Prediction: If a plant is watered with only acid rain (which has a pH of 4), then the plant will grow at half its normal rate.

3 **Test the Hypothesis** After you have formed a hypothesis and made a prediction, you should test your hypothesis. There are different ways to do this. Perhaps the most familiar way is to conduct a **controlled experiment.** A controlled experiment tests only one factor at a time. A controlled experiment has a **control group** and one or more **experimental groups.** All the factors for the control and experimental groups are the same except for one factor, which is called the **variable.** By changing only one factor, you can see the results of just that one change.

Sometimes, the nature of an investigation makes a controlled experiment impossible. For example, dinosaurs have been extinct for millions of years, and the Earth's core is surrounded by thousands of meters of rock. It would be difficult, if not impossible, to conduct controlled experiments on such things. Under such circumstances, a hypothesis may be tested by making detailed observations. Taking measurements is one way of making observations.

Test the Hypothesis

4 **Analyze the Results** After you have completed your experiments, made your observations, and collected your data, you must analyze all the information you have gathered. Tables and graphs are often used in this step to organize the data.

Analyze the Results

5 **Draw Conclusions** Based on the analysis of your data, you should conclude whether or not your results support your hypothesis. If your hypothesis is supported, you (or others) might want to repeat the observations or experiments to verify your results. If your hypothesis is not supported by the data, you may have to check your procedure for errors. You may even have to reject your hypothesis and make a new one. If you cannot draw a conclusion from your results, you may have to try the investigation again or carry out further observations or experiments.

Draw Conclusions

Do they support your hypothesis?

No

Yes

6 **Communicate Results** After any scientific investigation, you should report your results. By doing a written or oral report, you let others know what you have learned. They may want to repeat your investigation to see if they get the same results. Your report may even lead to another question, which in turn may lead to another investigation.

Communicate Results

Scientific Method in Action

The scientific method is not a "straight line" of steps. It contains loops in which several steps may be repeated over and over again, while others may not be necessary. For example, sometimes scientists will find that testing one hypothesis raises new questions and new hypotheses to be tested. And sometimes, testing the hypothesis leads directly to a conclusion. Furthermore, the steps in the scientific method are not always used in the same order. Follow the steps in the diagram below, and see how many different directions the scientific method can take you.

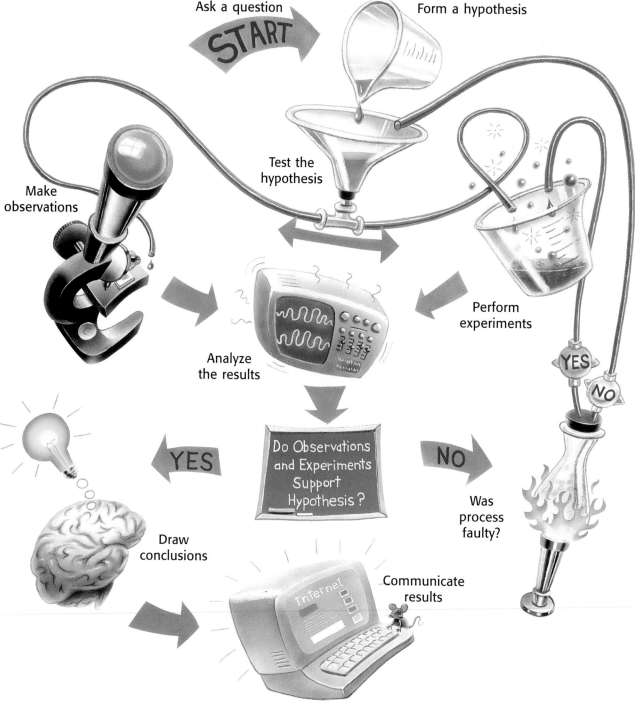

Ask a question

START

Form a hypothesis

Make observations

Test the hypothesis

Perform experiments

Analyze the results

YES

NO

YES

Do Observations and Experiments Support Hypothesis?

NO

Draw conclusions

Was process faulty?

Communicate results

Making Charts and Graphs

Circle Graphs

A circle graph, or pie chart, shows how each group of data relates to all of the data. Each part of the circle represents a category of the data. The entire circle represents all of the data. For example, a biologist studying a hardwood forest in Wisconsin found that there were five different types of trees. The data table at right summarizes the biologist's findings.

Wisconsin Hardwood Trees	
Type of tree	**Number found**
Oak	600
Maple	750
Beech	300
Birch	1,200
Hickory	150
Total	3,000

How to Make a Circle Graph

1 In order to make a circle graph of this data, first find the percentage of each type of tree. To do this, divide the number of individual trees by the total number of trees and multiply by 100.

$$\frac{600 \text{ oak}}{3,000 \text{ trees}} \times 100 = 20\%$$

$$\frac{750 \text{ maple}}{3,000 \text{ trees}} \times 100 = 25\%$$

$$\frac{300 \text{ beech}}{3,000 \text{ trees}} \times 100 = 10\%$$

$$\frac{1,200 \text{ birch}}{3,000 \text{ trees}} \times 100 = 40\%$$

$$\frac{150 \text{ hickory}}{3,000 \text{ trees}} \times 100 = 5\%$$

2 Now determine the size of the pie shapes that make up the chart. Do this by multiplying each percentage by 360°. Remember that a circle contains 360°.

$20\% \times 360° = 72°$ $25\% \times 360° = 90°$
$10\% \times 360° = 36°$ $40\% \times 360° = 144°$
$5\% \times 360° = 18°$

3 Then check that the sum of the percentages is 100 and the sum of the degrees is 360.

$20\% + 25\% + 10\% + 40\% + 5\% = 100\%$
$72° + 90° + 36° + 144° + 18° = 360°$

4 Use a compass to draw a circle and mark its center.

5 Then use a protractor to draw angles of 72°, 90°, 36°, 144°, and 18° in the circle.

6 Finally, label each part of the graph, and choose an appropriate title.

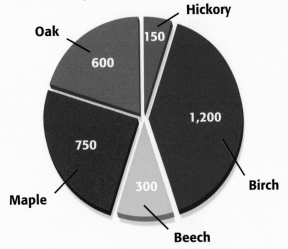

A Community of Wisconsin Hardwood Trees

Line Graphs

Line graphs are most often used to demonstrate continuous change. For example, Mr. Smith's science class analyzed the population records for their hometown, Appleton, between 1900 and 2000. Examine the data at left.

Because the year and the population change, they are the *variables*. The population is determined by, or dependent on, the year. Therefore, the population is called the **dependent variable**, and the year is called the **independent variable**. Each set of data is called a **data pair.** To prepare a line graph, data pairs must first be organized in a table like the one at left.

Population of Appleton, 1900–2000	
Year	Population
1900	1,800
1920	2,500
1940	3,200
1960	3,900
1980	4,600
2000	5,300

How to Make a Line Graph

1 Place the independent variable along the horizontal (x) axis. Place the dependent variable along the vertical (y) axis.

2 Label the x-axis "Year" and the y-axis "Population." Look at your largest and smallest values for the population. Determine a scale for the y-axis that will provide enough space to show these values. You must use the same scale for the entire length of the axis. Find an appropriate scale for the x-axis too.

3 Choose reasonable starting points for each axis.

4 Plot the data pairs as accurately as possible.

5 Choose a title that accurately represents the data.

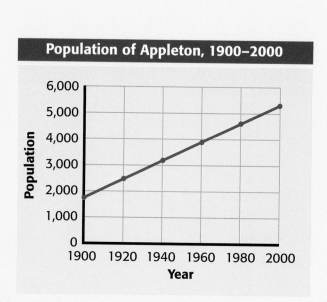

How to Determine Slope

Slope is the ratio of the change in the y-axis to the change in the x-axis, or "rise over run."

1 Choose two points on the line graph. For example, the population of Appleton in 2000 was 5,300 people. Therefore, you can define point *a* as (2000, 5,300). In 1900, the population was 1,800 people. Define point *b* as (1900, 1,800).

2 Find the change in the y-axis.
(y at point *a*) − (y at point *b*)
5,300 people − 1,800 people = 3,500 people

3 Find the change in the x-axis.
(x at point *a*) − (x at point *b*)
2000 − 1900 = 100 years

4 Calculate the slope of the graph by dividing the change in y by the change in x.

$$slope = \frac{change\ in\ y}{change\ in\ x}$$

$$slope = \frac{3,500\ people}{100\ years}$$

$$slope = 35\ people\ per\ year$$

In this example, the population in Appleton increased by a fixed amount each year. The graph of this data is a straight line. Therefore, the relationship is **linear.** When the graph of a set of data is not a straight line, the relationship is **nonlinear.**

Using Algebra to Determine Slope

The equation in step 4 may also be arranged to be:

$$y = kx$$

where y represents the change in the y-axis, k represents the slope, and x represents the change in the x-axis.

$$slope = \frac{change\ in\ y}{change\ in\ x}$$

$$k = \frac{y}{x}$$

$$k \times x = \frac{y \times x}{x}$$

$$kx = y$$

Bar Graphs

Bar graphs are used to demonstrate change that is not continuous. These graphs can be used to indicate trends when the data are taken over a long period of time. A meteorologist gathered the precipitation records at right for Hartford, Connecticut, for April 1–15, 1996, and used a bar graph to represent the data.

Precipitation in Hartford, Connecticut April 1–15, 1996

Date	Precipitation (cm)	Date	Precipitation (cm)
April 1	0.5	April 9	0.25
April 2	1.25	April 10	0.0
April 3	0.0	April 11	1.0
April 4	0.0	April 12	0.0
April 5	0.0	April 13	0.25
April 6	0.0	April 14	0.0
April 7	0.0	April 15	6.50
April 8	1.75		

How to Make a Bar Graph

1 Use an appropriate scale and a reasonable starting point for each axis.

2 Label the axes, and plot the data.

3 Choose a title that accurately represents the data.

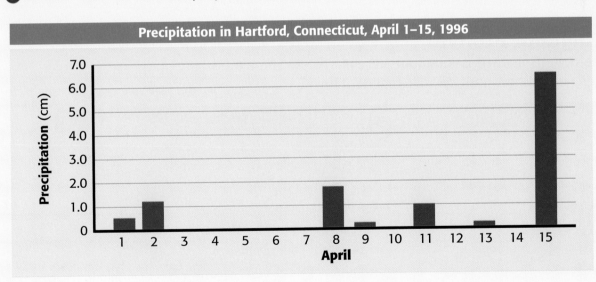

The Six Kingdoms

Kingdom Archaebacteria

The organisms in this kingdom are single-celled prokaryotes.

Archaebacteria		
Group	**Examples**	**Characteristics**
Methanogens	*Methanococcus*	found in soil, swamps, the digestive tract of mammals; produce methane gas; can't live in oxygen
Thermophiles	*Sulpholobus*	found in extremely hot environments; require sulphur, can't live in oxygen
Halophiles	*Halococcus*	found in environments with very high salt content, such as the Dead Sea; nearly all can live in oxygen

Kingdom Eubacteria

There are more than 4,000 named species in this kingdom of single-celled prokaryotes.

Eubacteria		
Group	**Examples**	**Characteristics**
Bacilli	*Escherichia coli*	rod-shaped; free-living, symbiotic, or parasitic; some can fix nitrogen; some cause disease
Cocci	*Streptococcus*	spherical-shaped, disease-causing; can form spores to resist unfavorable environments
Spirilla	*Treponema*	spiral-shaped; responsible for several serious illnesses, such as syphilis and Lyme disease

Kingdom Protista

The organisms in this kingdom are eukaryotes. There are single-celled and multicellular representatives.

Protists		
Group	**Examples**	**Characteristics**
Sacodines	*Amoeba*	radiolarians; single-celled consumers
Ciliates	*Paramecium*	single-celled consumers
Flagellates	*Trypanosoma*	single-celled parasites
Sporozoans	*Plasmodium*	single-celled parasites
Euglenas	*Euglena*	single-celled; photosynthesize
Diatoms	*Pinnularia*	most are single-celled; photosynthesize
Dinoflagellates	*Gymnodinium*	single-celled; some photosynthesize
Algae	*Volvox*, coral algae	4 phyla; single- or many-celled; photosynthesize
Slime molds	*Physarum*	single- or many-celled; consumers or decomposers
Water molds	powdery mildew	single- or many-celled, parasites or decomposers

Kingdom Fungi

There are single-celled and multicellular eukaryotes in this kingdom. There are four major groups of fungi.

Fungi		
Group	**Examples**	**Characteristics**
Threadlike fungi	bread mold	spherical; decomposers
Sac fungi	yeast, morels	saclike; parasites and decomposers
Club fungi	mushrooms, rusts, smuts	club-shaped; parasites and decomposers
Lichens	British soldier	symbiotic with algae

Kingdom Plantae

The organisms in this kingdom are multicellular eukaryotes. They have specialized organ systems for different life processes. They are classified in divisions instead of phyla.

Plants		
Group	**Examples**	**Characteristics**
Bryophytes	mosses, liverworts	reproduce by spores
Club mosses	*Lycopodium,* ground pine	reproduce by spores
Horsetails	rushes	reproduce by spores
Ferns	spleenworts, sensitive fern	reproduce by spores
Conifers	pines, spruces, firs	reproduce by seeds; cones
Cycads	*Zamia*	reproduce by seeds
Gnetophytes	*Welwitschia*	reproduce by seeds
Ginkgoes	*Ginkgo*	reproduce by seeds
Angiosperms	all flowering plants	reproduce by seeds; flowers

Kingdom Animalia

This kingdom contains multicellular eukaryotes. They have specialized tissues and complex organ systems.

Animals		
Group	**Examples**	**Characteristics**
Sponges	glass sponges	no symmetry or segmentation; aquatic
Cnidarians	jellyfish, coral	radial symmetry; aquatic
Flatworms	planaria, tapeworms, flukes	bilateral symmetry; organ systems
Roundworms	*Trichina,* hookworms	bilateral symmetry; organ systems
Annelids	earthworms, leeches	bilateral symmetry; organ systems
Mollusks	snails, octopuses	bilateral symmetry; organ systems
Echinoderms	sea stars, sand dollars	radial symmetry; organ systems
Arthropods	insects, spiders, lobsters	bilateral symmetry; organ systems
Chordates	fish, amphibians, reptiles, birds, mammals	bilateral symmetry; complex organ systems

Using the Microscope

Parts of the Compound Light Microscope

- The **ocular lens** magnifies the image 10×.

- The **low-power objective** magnifies the image 10×.

- The **high-power objective** magnifies the image either 40× or 43×.

- The **revolving nosepiece** holds the objectives and can be turned to change from one magnification to the other.

- The **body tube** maintains the correct distance between the ocular lens and objectives.

- The **coarse-adjustment knob** moves the body tube up and down to allow focusing of the image.

- The **fine-adjustment knob** moves the body tube slightly to bring the image into sharper focus.

- The **stage** supports a slide.

- **Stage clips** hold the slide in place for viewing.

- The **diaphragm** controls the amount of light coming through the stage.

- The light source provides a **light** for viewing the slide.

- The **arm** supports the body tube.

- The **base** supports the microscope.

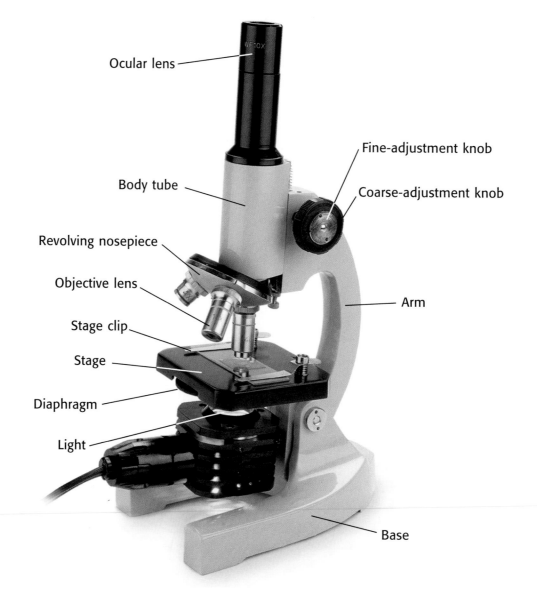

Ocular lens

Fine-adjustment knob

Body tube

Coarse-adjustment knob

Revolving nosepiece

Objective lens

Arm

Stage clip

Stage

Diaphragm

Light

Base

Proper Use of the Compound Light Microscope

1 Carry the microscope to your lab table using both hands. Place one hand beneath the base, and use the other hand to hold the arm of the microscope. Hold the microscope close to your body while moving it to your lab table.

2 Place the microscope on the lab table at least 5 cm from the edge of the table.

3 Check to see what type of light source is used by your microscope. If the microscope has a lamp, plug it in, making sure that the cord is out of the way. If the microscope has a mirror, adjust it to reflect light through the hole in the stage.
Caution: If your microscope has a mirror, do not use direct sunlight as a light source. Direct sunlight can damage your eyes.

4 Always begin work with the low-power objective in line with the body tube. Adjust the revolving nosepiece.

5 Place a prepared slide over the hole in the stage. Secure the slide with the stage clips.

6 Look through the ocular lens. Move the diaphragm to adjust the amount of light coming through the stage.

7 Look at the stage from eye level. Slowly turn the coarse adjustment to lower the objective until it almost touches the slide. Do not allow the objective to touch the slide.

8 Look through the ocular lens. Turn the coarse adjustment to raise the low-power objective until the image is in focus. Always focus by raising the objective away from the slide. *Never focus the objective downward.* Use the fine adjustment to sharpen the focus. Keep both eyes open while viewing a slide.

9 Make sure that the image is exactly in the center of your field of vision. Then switch to the high-power objective. Focus the image, using only the fine adjustment. *Never use the coarse adjustment at high power.*

10 When you are finished using the microscope, remove the slide. Clean the ocular lens and objective lenses with lens paper. Return the microscope to its storage area. Remember, you should use both hands to carry the microscope.

Making a Wet Mount

1 Use lens paper to clean a glass slide and a coverslip.

2 Place the specimen you wish to observe in the center of the slide.

3 Using a medicine dropper, place one drop of water on the specimen.

4 Hold the coverslip at the edge of the water and at a 45° angle to the slide. Make sure that the water runs along the edge of the coverslip.

5 Lower the coverslip slowly to avoid trapping air bubbles.

6 Water might evaporate from the slide as you work. Add more water to keep the specimen fresh. Place the tip of the medicine dropper next to the edge of the coverslip. Add a drop of water. (You can also use this method to add stain or solutions to a wet mount.) Remove excess water from the slide by using the corner of a paper towel as a blotter. Do not lift the coverslip to add or remove water.

Glossary

A

abdomen the body part of an animal that usually contains the gut and other digestive organs (41)

altricial chick (al TRISH uhl) a chick that hatches weak, naked, and helpless (94)

amniotic egg (AM nee AH tik) an egg containing amniotic fluid to protect the developing embryo; usually surrounded by a hard shell (88)

amphibian a type of vertebrate ectotherm that usually begins life in the water with gills and later develops lungs (68)

antennae feelers on an arthropod's head that respond to touch, taste, or smell (42)

Archaebacteria (AHR kee bak TIR ee uh) a classification kingdom containing bacteria that thrive in extreme environments (140)

asymmetrical without symmetry (28)

B

bilateral symmetry a body plan in which two halves of an organism's body are mirror images of each other (28)

biological clock an internal control of natural cycles (12)

brain the mass of nerve tissue that is the main organ of the nervous system (29)

brooding when a bird sits on its eggs until they hatch (93)

C

camouflage the coloration and/or texture that enables an animal to blend in with its environment (9)

carnivore a consumer that eats animals (107)

cartilage a flexible tissue that gives support and protection but is not rigid like bone (61, 65)

cell wall a structure that surrounds the cell membrane of some cells and provides strength and support to the cell membrane (5)

cephalothorax (SEF uh loh THOR aks) the body part of arachnids that consists of both a head and a thorax and that usually has four pairs of legs attached (43)

circadian rhythm a natural, daily cycle (12)

closed circulatory system a circulatory system in which a heart circulates blood through a network of vessels that forms a closed loop (38)

coelom (SEE luhm) a cavity in the body of some animals where the gut and organs are located (29)

communication a transfer of a signal from one animal to another that results in some type of response (14)

compound eye an eye that is made of many identical, light-sensitive cells that work together (42)

compound light microscope a microscope that consists of a tube with lenses, a stage, and a light source (142)

consumer an organism that eats producers or other organisms for energy (7)

contour feather a feather made of a stiff, central shaft with many side branches called barbs (89)

controlled experiment an experiment that tests only one factor at a time (135)

D

denticles small, sharp, toothlike structures on the skin of cartilaginous fishes (66)

diaphragm (DIE uh FRAM) the sheet of muscle underneath the lungs of mammals that helps draw air into the lungs (101)

down feather a fluffy, insulating feather that lies next to a bird's body (89)

E

ectotherm an animal whose body temperature fluctuates with the environment's temperature (62)

embryo an organism in the earliest stage of development (6)

endoskeleton an internal skeleton (47)

endotherm an animal that maintains a constant body temperature despite temperature changes in its environment (62)

estivation a period of reduced activity that some animals experience in the summer (11)

Eubacteria (YOO bak TIR ee uh) a classification kingdom containing mostly free-living bacteria found in many varied environments (140)

exoskeleton an external skeleton made of protein and chitin; found on arthropods (42)

external fertilization the fertilization of eggs by sperm that occurs outside the body of the female (64)

F

fins fanlike structures that help fish move, turn, stop, and balance (64)

Fungi a kingdom of complex organisms that obtain food by breaking down other substances in their surroundings and absorbing the nutrients (141)

G

ganglia groups of nerve cells (29)

gestation period (jeh STAY shuhn) the time during which an embryo develops within the mother (104)

gills organs that remove oxygen from the water and carbon dioxide from the blood (64)

gut the pouch where food is digested in animals (29)

H

head the body part of animals where the brain is located (41)

hibernation a period of inactivity that some animals experience in winter that allows them to survive on stored body fat (11)

host an organism on which a parasite lives (34)

hypothesis a possible explanation or answer to a question (134)

I

innate behavior a behavior that is influenced by genes and does not depend on learning (10)

internal fertilization the fertilization of an egg by sperm that occurs inside the body of a female (64)

invertebrate an animal without a backbone (5, 28)

L

landmark a fixed object used to determine location during navigation (13)

lateral line system a row or rows of tiny sense organs along the sides of a fish's body (64)

learned behavior a behavior that has been learned from experience or observation (10)

lift an upward force on an object caused by differences in pressure above and below the object; lift opposes the downward pull of gravity (92)

lung a saclike organ that takes oxygen from the air and delivers it to the blood (68)

M

mammary glands glands that secrete a nutritious fluid called milk (99)

mandible a jaw found on some arthropods (43)

marsupial a mammal that gives birth to live, partially developed young that continue to develop inside the mother's pouch or skin fold (103)

medusa a body form of some cnidarians; resembles a mushroom with tentacles (32)

metamorphosis the process in which an insect or other animal changes form as it develops from an embryo or larva to an adult (45, 70)

migrate to travel from one place to another in response to the seasons or environmental conditions (11)

monotreme a mammal that lays eggs (102)

multicellular made of many cells (5)

O

open circulatory system a circulatory system consisting of a heart that pumps blood through spaces called sinuses (38)

organ a combination of two or more tissues that work together to perform a specific function in the body (6)

P

parasite an organism that feeds on another living creature, usually without killing it (34)

pheromone (FER uh MON) a chemical produced by animals for communication (15)

placenta a special organ of exchange that provides a developing fetus with nutrients and oxygen (104)

placental mammal a mammal that nourishes its unborn offspring with a placenta inside the uterus and gives birth to well-developed young (104)

polyp a body form of some cnidarians; resembles a vase (32)

precocial chick (pree KOH shuhl) a chick that leaves the nest immediately after hatching and is fully active (94)

predator an organism that eats other organisms (8)

preening the activity in which a bird uses its beak to spread oil on its feathers (89)

prey an organism that is eaten by another organism (8)

primate a type of mammal that includes humans, apes, and monkeys; typically distinguished by opposable thumbs and binocular vision (111)

Protista a kingdom of eukaryotic single-celled or simple, multicellular organisms; kingdom Protista contains all eukaryotes that are not plants, animals, or fungi (140)

R

radial symmetry a body plan in which the parts of the body are arranged in a circle around a central point (28)

S

scales bony structures that cover the skin of bony fishes (66)

scientific method a series of steps that scientists use to answer questions and solve problems (134)

segment one of many identical or almost identical repeating body parts (39)

sexual reproduction reproduction in which two sex cells join to form a zygote; sexual reproduction produces offspring that share characteristics of both parents (6)

social behavior the interaction between animals of the same species (14)

swim bladder a balloonlike organ that is filled with oxygen and other gases; gives bony fish their buoyancy (66)

T

tadpole the aquatic larvae of an amphibian (70)

territory an area occupied by one animal or a group of animals from which other members of the species are excluded (14)

therapsid (thuh RAP sid) a prehistoric reptile ancestor of mammals (73, 98)

thorax the central body part of an arthropod or other animal; where the heart and lungs are located (41)

tissue a group of similar cells that work together to perform a specific job in the body (6)

V

variable a factor in a controlled experiment that changes (135)

vertebrae (VUHR tuh BRAY) segments of bone or cartilage that interlock to form a backbone (61)

vertebrate an animal with a skull and a backbone; includes mammals, birds, reptiles, amphibians, and fish (4, 60)

W

water vascular system a system of water pumps and canals found in all echinoderms that allows them to move, eat, and breathe (48)

Index

Credits

Abbreviations used: (t) top, (c) center, (b) bottom, (l) left, (r) right, (bkgd) background

ILLUSTRATIONS

All illustrations, unless otherwise noted below by Holt, Rinehart and Winston.

Scope and Sequence: T11, Paul DiMare, T13, Dan Stuckenschneider/Uhl Studios, Inc.

Chapter One Page 5 (chart), Sidney Jablonski; 5 (ant, beetle, bug, fish, mollusk, sponge, starfish, worm), Barbara Hoopes-Ambler; 5 (jellyfish), Sarah Woodward/Morgan-Cain & Associates; 5 (spider, fly), Steve Roberts; 5 (butterfly), Bridgette James; 5 (elephant), Michael Woods/Morgan-Cain & Associates; 6 (bl), Kip Carter; 10 (cl), Keith Locke/Suzanne Craig Represents Inc.; 12 (tr), Gary Locke/Suzanne Craig Represents Inc.; 12 (bl), Tony Morse/Ivy Glick; 16 (b), John White/The Neis Group; 20 (br), John White/The Neis Group; 23 (bl), Sidney Jablonski.

Chapter Two Page 29 (tl), Barbara Hoopes-Ambler; 29 (tc), Sarah Woodward/Morgan-Cain & Associates; 29 (tr), Alexander & Turner; 29 (cr,br), Alexander & Turner; 31, Alexander & Turner; 32, John White/The Neis Group; 33, Morgan-Cain & Associates; 34, Alexander & Turner; 37 (tr), Alexander & Turner; 41, Felipe Passalacqua; 43 (c), John White/The Neis Group; 43 (cr), Will Nelson/Sweet Reps; 45, Steve Roberts; 46, Bridgette James; 48 (tl), Alexander & Turner ; 48 (b), Alexander & Turner ; 55 (cr), Barbara Hoopes-Ambler.

Chapter Three Page 61 (t), Alexander & Turner ; 64 (cl), Will Nelson/Sweet Reps; 66 (br), Kip Carter; 66 (b), Barbara Hoopes-Ambler; 68 (br), Peg Gerrity; 70 (c), Will Nelson/Sweet Reps; 73 (c), Barbara Hoopes-Ambler; 75 (c), Kip Carter; 82 (bl), Will Nelson/Sweet Reps; 83 (bl), Marty Roper/Planet Rep; 83 (tr), Rob Schuster/Hankins and Tegenborg; 84 (bc), Ron Kimball; 85 (bc), Ka Botz.

Chapter Four Page 89 (feather), Will Nelson/Sweet Reps; 89 (bird), Will Nelson/Sweet Reps; 89 (closeup), Kip Carter; 89 (digestive system), Kip Carter; 90 (c), Will Nelson/Sweet Reps; 91, Will Nelson/Sweet Reps; 92 (c), Will Nelson/Sweet Reps; 97 (br), Kip Carter; 98 (bl), Howard Freidman; 112 (cr), Will Nelson/Sweet Reps; 115 (c), Yuan Lee; 117 (tr), Sidney Jablonski.

LabBook Page 124 (br), Keith Locke/Suzanne Craig Represents Inc.; 125 (tr), John White/The Neis Group; 126 (br) Marty Roper/Planet Rep.

Appendix Page 132 (t), Terry Guyer; 136 (b).

PHOTOGRAPHY

Cover and Title page: John Cancalosi/Peter Arnold, Inc.

Table of Contents v(tr), Zig Leszczynski/Animals Animals; v(cr), Lee Foster/FPG International; v(b), Peter Van Steen/HRW Photo; vi(tl), C. K. Lorenz/Photo Researchers, Inc.; vi(tcl), Gail Shumway/FPG International; vi(bcl), SuperStock; vi(bl), Leroy Simon/Visuals Unlimited; vii(tr), Frans Lanting/Minden Pictures; vii(cr), George D. Lepp/Stone; vii(br), Scott Daniel Peterson/Liaison.

Scope and Sequence: T8(l), Lee F. Snyder/Photo Researchers, Inc.; T8(r), Stephen Dalton/Photo Researchers, Inc.; T10, E. R. Degginger/Color-Pic, Inc., T12(l), Rob Matheson/The Stock Market

Master Materials List: T26(bl, br), Image ©2001 PhotoDisc

Feature Borders: Unless otherwise noted below, all images copyright ©2001 PhotoDisc/HRW. "Across the Sciences" 84, 118, all images by HRW; "Eye on the Environment", 24, clouds and sea in bkgd, HRW; bkgd grass, red eyed frog, Corbis Images; hawks, pelican, Animals Animals/Earth Scenes; rat, Visuals Unlimited/John Grelach; endangered flower, Dan Suzio/Photo Researchers, Inc.; "Weird Science", 25, 56, 57, 85, 119, mite, David Burder/Stone; atom balls, J/B Woolsey Associates; walking stick, turtle, EclectiCollection.

Table of Contents: v(br), Uniphoto; vi(tl), Leonard Lessin/Photo Researchers, Inc.; vii(bl), Visuals Unlimited/R. Calentine; vii(tr), Robert Brons/BPS/Stone; viii(tr), Frans Lanting/Minden Pictures; viii(br), Biophoto Associates/Photo Researchers, Inc.; ix Centre National de Prehistoire, Perigueux, France; x(tl), G. Randall/FPG Int'l; x(bl), Fran Heyl Associates; xi(bl), SuperStock; xi(br), Phil Degginger; xii(bl), Richard R. Hansen/Photo Researchers, Inc.; xiii(tl), Daniel Schaefer/HRW Photo; xiii(br), Visuals Unlimited/James Beverigde; xiii(bl), Brian Parker/Tom Stack; xiii(tr), Carl Roessler/FPG Int'l; xiv(cr), Edwin & Peggy Bauer/Bruce Coleman; xiv(tl), Tui De Roy/Minden Pictures; xv(tl), Stuart Westmorland/Stone; xvii(tc), Dr. Dennis Kunkel/Phototake, Inc.; xvii(br), Image Bank; xviii(bl), Lennart Nilsson/Albert Bonniers Forlag AB, A CHILD IS BORN

Chapter One: p. 2-3 Bruce Coleman, Ltd./Natural Selection; 3 HRW Photo; James L. Amos/Peter Arnold; 4(b), David B. Fleetham/FPG Int'l; 6(tl), David M. Phillips/Photo Researchers, Inc.; 6(c), Visuals Unlimited/Fred Hossler; 7(tl), Gerard Lacz/Peter Arnold; 7(cr), Manoj Shah/Stone; 7(tr), Stephen Dalton/ Photo Researchers, Inc.; 7(br), Stephen Dalton/Photo Researchers, Inc.; 8 Tim Davis/Stone; 9(tr), J.H. Robinson/Photo Researchers, Inc.; 9(bl), W. Peckover/ Academy of Natural Sciences Philadelphia/VIREO; 9(br), Visuals Unlimited/Leroy Simon; 10(bl), Visuals Unlimited/A.J. Copley; 11(tr), George D. Lepp/Stone; 11(bl), Michio Hoshino/Minden Pictures; 13(t), FPG Int'l; 14(cl), Fernandez & Peck/Adventure Photo & Film; 14(bl), Peter Weimann/ Animals Animals; 15(tr), Lee F. Snyder/Photo Researchers, Inc.; 15(br), Johnny Johnson/Animals Animals; 16(tl), Ron Kimball; 17(tr), Planet Earth Pictures; 17(cr), Richard R. Hansen/Photo Researchers, Inc.; 20(c), Keren Su/Stone; 20(tr), Stephen Dalton/Photo Researchers, Inc.; 21 Lee F. Snyder/Photo Researchers, Inc.; 22 Visuals Unlimited/Leroy Simon; 24 John Elk/Stone; 25 Wayne Lawler/AUSCAPE

Chapter Two: p. 26-27 W. Gregory Brown/Animals Animals; 27 HRW Photo; 28(tr), SuperStock; 28(cl), Carl Roessler/FPG Int'l; 28(c), J Carmichael/ Image Bank; 28(bl), David B. Fleetham/Tom Stack; 30(cl), Jeffrey L. Rotman/ Peter Arnold, Inc.; 30(br), Dr. E.R. Degginger; 30(bl), Keith Philpott/Image Bank; 31(br), Nigel Cattlin/Holt Studios International/Photo Researchers, Inc.; 32(bl), Randy Morse/Tom Stack & Associates; 32(cl), Biophoto Associates/ Science Source/Photo Researchers, Inc.; 32(tl), Lee Foster/FPG Int'l; 34(tl), Visuals Unlimited/T. E. Adams; 34(b), CNRI/Science Photo Library/Photo Researchers, Inc.; 35(tr), Visuals Unlimited/R. Calentine; 35(c), Visuals Unlimited/A. M. Siegelman; 36(cl), SuperStock; 36(cr), Dr. E.R. Degginger, FPSA; 36(c), Stephen Frink/Corbis; 36(tr), Holt Studios Int./Photo Researchers, Inc.; 37 Visuals Unlimited/David M. Phillips; 38 David Fleetham/FPG Int'l; 39(br), Daniel Schaefer/HRW Photo; 39(tr), Milton Rand/Tom Stack & Associates; 40(cl), St. Bartholomew's Hospital/Science Photo Library/Photo Researchers, Inc.; 40(tl), Mary Beth Angelo/Photo Researchers, Inc.; 41(tr), SuperStock; 41(cl), Will Crocker/Image Bank; 41(bl), Sergio Purcell/FOCA; 42(tl), CNRI/ Science Photo Library/Photo Researchers, Inc.; 42(cl), Visuals Unlimited/A. Kerstitch; 42(bl), Dr. E.R. Degginger, FPSA; 43 David Scharf/Peter Arnold; 44(tl), Visuals Unlimited/R. Calentine; 44(cr), SuperStock; 44(bc), Uniphoto; 44(cl), Stephen Dalton/NHPA; 44(br), Gail Shumway/FPG Int'l; 45(cr), Joe McDonald; 47(cl), Darryl Torckler/Stone; 47(blb), Visuals Unlimited/Cabisco; 47(blt), Paul McCormick/Image Bank; 47(tr), Robert Dunne/Photo Researchers, Inc.; 47(cr), Chesher/Photo Researchers, Inc.; 49(cr), Visuals Unlimited/Marty Snyderman; 49(tr), Andrew J. Martinez/Photo Researchers, Inc.; 49(bl), Visuals Unlimited/Daniel W. Gotshall; 51 Victoria Smith/HRW Photo; 52 Keith Philpott/Image Bank; 53(cl), Uniphoto; 53(tc), SuperStock; 54 Ken Philpott/Image Bank; 56(c), Visuals Unlimited/ Diane R. Nelson; 57(br), Mark Norman/Archfull

Chapter Three: p. 58-59 J. Schauer/Max Planck Institute; 59 Visuals Unlimited; 59 HRW Photo; 60(c), Louis Psihoyos/Matrix; 60(bc), Norbert Wu/Peter Arnold; 60(bl), Randy Morse/Tom Stack; 61 Grant Heilman; 62 Uniphoto; 63(bl), Doug Perrine/DRK Photo; 63(tr), Brian Parker/Tom Stack; 63(cl), Animals Animals; 63(br), Visuals Unlimited/Ken Lucas; 63(c), Bruce Coleman; 65(tr), Hans Reinhard/Bruce Coleman; 65(c), Index Stock; 65(b), Martin Barraud/Stone; 66(tl), Visuals Unlimited/Science Visuals Unlimited; 66(cl), Navaswan/FPG Int'l; 67(tr), Bruce Coleman; 67(cl), Steinhart Aquarium/Tom McHugh/Photo Researchers, Inc.; 68(cl), Michael Fogden/DRK Photo; 68(bl), Visuals Unlimited/Nathan W. Cohen; 69(tr), David M. Dennis/Tom Stack & Associates; 69(br), C.K. Lorenz/Photo Researchers, Inc.; 70 Michael and Patricia Fogden; 71(tr), M.P.L. Fogden/ Bruce Coleman; 71(br), Zig Leszczynski/Animals Animals; 71(cr), Stephen Dalotn/NHPA; 72(tl), Leonard Lee Rue/Photo Researchers, Inc.; 72(tr), Breck P. Kent; 72(cl), Telegraph Color Library/FPG Int'l; 73 Visuals Unlimited/ Rob & Ann Simpson; 74(tc), Gail Shumway/FPG Int'l; 74(tl), Gail Shumway/FPG Int'l; 74(bc), Stanley Breeden/DRK Photo; 74(br), Visuals Unlimited/Joe McDonald; 76(tl), Bruce Coleman; 76(c), Mike Severns/ Stone; 76(bl), Kevin Schafer/Peter Arnold; 76(br), Wayne Lynch/DRK Photo; 77(t), Wolfgang Kaehler; 77(cr), Michael Fogden/DRK Photo; 80 Uniphoto; 81(cl), Michael Fogden/DRK Photos; 81(tr), Brian Parker/Tom Stack & Assoc.; 82 Steven David Miller/Animals Animals Earth Scenes

Chapter Four: p. 86-87 Nigle J. Dennis/Photo Researchers, Inc.; 87 HRW Photo; 88(cl), Anthony Mercieca/Photo Researchers, Inc.; 88(tr), Stan Osolinski/FPG Int'l; 88(c), Gail Shumway/FPG Int'l; 88(b - inset), Runk/Schoenberger/ Grant Heilman; 88(bl), Douglas Faulkner/Photo Researchers, Inc.; 92(b), Ben Osborne/Stone; 93(b), D. Cavagnaro/DRK Photo; 93(tr), Frans Lanting/Minden Pictures; 93(cr), Joe McDonald/DRK Photo; 94(tr), Thomas McAvoy/Time Life Syndication; 94(br), Hal H. Harrison/Grant Heilman; 95(bc), Gavriel Jecan/ Stone; 95(cr), APL/J. Carnemolla/Westlight; 95(bl), Kevin Schafer/Stone; 96(cl), Tui De Roy/Minden Pictures; 96(cr), Wayne Lankinen/Bruce Coleman; 96(tr), S. Nielsen/DRK Photo; 96(bl), Greg Vaughn/Stone; 96(br), Fritz Polking/Bruce Coleman; 97(tl), Stephen J. Krasemann/DRK Photo; 97(cr), Visuals Unlimited/S. Maslowski; 97(tr), Frans Lanting/Minden Pictures; 98(cl), Gerard Lacz/Animals Animals; 98(cr), Tim Davis/Photo Researchers, Inc.; 98(c), Nigel Dennis/Photo Researchers, Inc.; 99(cl), Hans Reinhard/Bruce Coleman; 100(tl), David E. Myers/Stone; 100(cl), Tom Tietz/Stone; 100(bl), Konrad Wothe/WestLight; 101 Kathy Bushue/Stone; 102(cl), Edwin & Peggy Bauer/ Bruce Coleman; 102(bl), Dave Watts/Tom Stack; 103(tr), Jean-Paul Ferrero/AUSCAPE; 103(cl), Hans Reinhard/Bruce Coleman; 103(bc), Art Wolfe/Stone; 104(bl), Wayne Lynch/DRK Photo; 104(br), Visuals Unlimited/ John D. Cunningham; 105(tr), Gail Shumway/FPG Int'l; 105(tl), D. R. Kuhn/Bruce Coleman; 105(br), Lynda Richardson/Peter Arnold; 105(bl), Frans Lanting/ Minden Pictures; 106(tr), David Cavagnaro/Peter Arnold; 106(tl), John Cancalosi; 106(c), S. C. Bisserot/Bruce Coleman; 106(b), EyeWire, Inc.; 107(cr), Uniphoto; 107(tr), Gail Shumway/FPG Int'l; 107(bl), Arthur C. Smith III/Grant Heilman; 107(cl), Joe McDonald/Bruce Coleman; 108(tr), Scott Daniel Peterson/Liaison; 108(cl), Gail Shumway/FPG Int'l; 108(b), Roberto Arakaki/International Stock; 109 Art Wolfe/Stone; 110(c), Francois Gohier; 110(tr), Flip Nicklin/Minden Pictures; 110(b), Tom & Therisa Stack; 111(l), J. & P. Wegner/Animals Animals; 111(tr), Inga Spence/Tom Stack; 114(c), Frans Lanting/Minden Pictures; 115 Gerard Lacz/Animals Animals; 116 S. C. Bisserot/ Bruce Coleman; 118(b), Will & Deni McIntyre/Stone; 118(c), Tom & Pat Leeson/ Photo Researchers, Inc.; 119(br), Raymond A. Mendez/Animals Animals

Labook: "LabBook Header": "L", Corbis Images, "a", Letraset-Phototone, "b" and "B", HRW, "o" and "k", Images Copyright ©2001 PhotoDisc, Inc.; 50-51 Victoria Smith/HRW Photo; 121(cl), Michelle Bridwell/HRW Photo; 121(br), Image ©2001 PhotoDisc, Inc./HRW Photo; 122(bl), Stephanie Morris/HRW Photo; 122(cl), Victoria Smith/HRW Photo; 123(tr), Jana Birchum/HRW Photo; 128 Rod Planck/Photo Researchers, Inc.

Appendix: 142 CENCO

Sam Dudgeon/HRW Photos: all Systems of the Body background photos. p. viii-1, 18, 19, 113, 120, 121(bc), 122(br, tr), 123(tl), 127, 133(br)

Peter Van Steen/HRW Photos: p. 4(cl), 79, 99(br), 123(b), 129, 133(tr)

John Langford/HRW Photos: p. 121(tr)

Self-Check Answers

Chapter 1—Animals and Behavior

Page 6: Like other vertebrates, humans have a skull and a backbone.

Chapter 2—Invertebrates

Page 33: Because medusas swim through the water by contracting their bodies, they must have a nervous system that can control these actions. Polyps move very little, so they don't need as complex a nervous system.

Page 43: Segmented worms belong to the phylum Annelida. Centipedes are arthropods. Centipedes have jointed legs, antennae, and mandibles. Segmented worms have none of these characteristics.

Chapter 3—Fishes, Amphibians, and Reptiles

Page 69: Amphibians use their skin to absorb oxygen from the air. Their skin is thin, moist, and full of blood vessels, just like a lung.

Page 75: 1. Thick, dry skin and amniotic eggs help reptiles live on dry land. 2. The hard shell prevents fertilization, so the egg must be fertilized before the shell is added.

Chapter 4—Birds and Mammals

Page 90: 1. Down feathers are not stiff and smooth and could not give structure to the wings. They are adapted to keep the bird warm. 2. Birds need tremendous amounts of food for fuel because it takes a lot of energy to fly.

Page 104: Monotremes are mammals that lay eggs. Marsupials bear live young but carry them in pouches or skin folds before they are able to live independently. Placentals develop inside the mother's body and are nourished through a placenta before birth.

Page 109: 1. Bats bear live young, have fur, and do not have feathers. 2. Rodents and lagomorphs both are small mammals with long sensitive whiskers and gnawing teeth. Unlike rodents, lagomorphs have two sets of incisors and a short tail.